MATTHEW JAMES EVERINGHAM

A Convict of the First Fleet

Ian J White

Matthew James Everingham – A Convict Of The First Fleet

ISBN 979-8-88831-935-2

Published by the Author, in association with Ingram Spark, Melbourne.

First published October 2022

© 2022. Ian J. White

All rights reserved

No part of this book may be reproduced or transmitted in any form or by any means, graphic, electronic, or mechanical, including photocopying, without written permission from the publisher.

Review

In *Matthew James Everingham*, author Ian White recounts the life of his First Fleet convict ancestor in a way that is eminently readable, entertaining and enlightening. As I read of Matthew's arrest and incarceration in London at fifteen and his eventual transportation to the new colony at Sydney Cove, I found myself engaging more and more with this young, pioneer settler and hoping he would do well in his new land. Through clever use of largely fictional dialogue, Ian White manages to bring Matthew's life and times alive in a way that makes us feel we are present, looking on, as he marries Elizabeth Rymes and raises a large family, all the while battling many daunting challenges and setbacks. As a result, it is difficult not to feel disappointed, along with them, when all their hard work comes to nothing or when tragedy strikes. Ian White writes in a gentle, respectful, yet realistic way about his ancestors and I commend him for this, along with his obvious determination to be as meticulous as possible in all the historical detail included in this book. I also commend him for the utmost respect conveyed for the original inhabits of our land and for his sensitive depiction of them throughout.

Jo-Anne Berthelsen, writer and speaker
www.jo-anneberthelsen.com

The Everingham Convict Trilogy

Matthew James Everingham – A Convict of the First Fleet

Though the third book written in the trilogy, this book reaches much further back into antiquity and, in chronological terms, the first of the three. While perhaps preferable, it is not necessary to read the books in chronological order

Elizabeth Rymes – A Remarkable Life

Chronologically, the second book in the trilogy, although it was the first of the three to be written.

The Woodbury Line – An Australian Convict Family

Chronologically the third book in the trilogy, tracing Matthew and Elizabeth's descendants through their eldest daughter, Sarah, aka Sally.

Details of all books can be found at
www.themustardseed.net.au/books

DEDICATION

For my precious little great-nephew, Theo Clifton, far too young to know that Matthew James Everingham was his seven-times-great-grandfather but through this book he will learn of it, one day.

Ian White

This book speaks, in part, about white settlement and the colonisation of Australia and affirms the dispossession of the original indigenous inhabitants.

The author acknowledges the unique status of Australia's First Peoples as the original peoples of this land and recognises their cultures, histories, ongoing relationships and obligations to the land.

About The Author

Ian has lived in parts of South-East Asia and in every mainland Australian state and territory.

For almost fifty years, Ian has worked in the foreign language industry, first serving twelve years in military intelligence, followed by twenty-five years teaching languages in Australian secondary schools and now, in semi-retirement, managing a small online foreign language translation agency.

Ian now lives in the beautiful Hunter Valley in New South Wales, not all that far distant from the areas in which Matthew and Elizabeth Everingham toiled and raised their family of 10 children. Ian now fills his days managing the online translation agency, gardening, reading and writing for his own pleasure.

Ian has authored more than twenty textbooks used in Australian secondary schools for the teaching of a foreign language, and three books in the Christian non-fiction genre. He is also the author of *Elizabeth Rymes – A Remarkable Life* and *The Woodbury Line – An Australian Convict Family*, two books which together with *Matthew James Everingham – A Convict Of The First Fleet* form a trilogy of books about the Everingham dynasty in Australia.

Details of Ian's books can be found at www.themustardseed.net.au and readers can also contact Ian through that site.

Acknowledgements

Once again I find myself humbled when I think of the many who have played a part in getting this book to print.

Perhaps the first person who should be thanked is a lady I never had the opportunity to meet – the late Ms Valerie Ross, whose exhaustive research and writing has made Matthew Everingham the most researched and documented convict ever to be transported to these shores. Her three books *Cornstalks*, *Matthew Everingham – A First Fleeter And His Times* and *A Hawkesbury Story* must be the starting point for any person researching the Everingham family and I acknowledge the influence that Ms Ross' wonderful and comprehensive work has had on my own writing.

I am grateful to family and friends who inspired and encouraged me during the writing of this book. I find that friends who have read my earlier works are such a wonderful source of encouragement. They always exhort me to hopefully greater things each time I set my mind to a new project.

Sarah Brightson is a longstanding friend and a colleague from my teaching days, and I thank Sarah for the assistance given to me in representing Elizabeth Everingham's dialogue in a readable form. Elizabeth, as we know, was illiterate, and getting her words into a realistic representation of her speech with mixed tenses, double negatives, split infinitives, incorrect conjugation, dropped consonants, dropped vowels etc. was a large part of Elizabeth's character development in this book and in the two other books in the trilogy. We laughed a lot, especially when I began writing other sections of the narrative in the same style. Thank you, Sarah, for what has been an important and very enjoyable part of the process.

I thank my good friend Danny Tedeshi of *Inlingua Text* for the design of the covers on this book. In my other role as manager of a small online translation agency I have worked with Danny for many years and I know of his exceptional talents in the field of typesetting and graphic design. His work in designing the covers of this book has been exceptional, as always. Thank you Danny.

During my research for the writing of this book, I sought assistance from the Hawkesbury Central Library in the Deerubbin Centre in Windsor, The Maitland City Library and the Mitchell Library Collection at the State Library of New South Wales. The staff at those facilities were amazingly helpful and generous with their time and I greatly appreciate their assistance.

It must be said that when I set my mind to writing the first book which would become part of this trilogy, *Elizabeth Rymes – A Remarkable Life*, I had little understanding of what white colonisation of this land had meant for the indigenous peoples – the forced dispossession of their land, desecration of their sacred sites, denial of access to their food sources and the genocidal intent of many settlers, not to mention the myriad infectious diseases which were brought to these shores by the white colonialists and which killed so many of the indigenous people. When I had completed the first book in the trilogy I felt I had gained some limited understanding of the matter. It was, however, during the writing of the second book, *The Woodbury Line*, and even more so during the writing of this book, that indigenous people have helped me come to a deeper understanding and appreciation of the issues and I thank them, not as individuals but as the respected First Nations peoples of this land. Coming to that understanding has, I believe, made me a better person and even if there be no other benefit to flow from the writing of these books, that alone has made it a most worthwhile project.

Finally, but far from least, I thank my editor Jo-Anne Berthelsen for her meticulous work and for her guidance which helped me avoid many careless errors. Jo-Anne has edited all three books in the Everingham Convict Trilogy. Each time, before approaching her with the draft of a new book, I prayed she would be able to find time in her busy schedule to work with me on the manuscripts, for there is no other editor I would prefer to work with. If there should be any literary acclaim attached to the three books in this trilogy, much of that is due to Jo-Anne's painstaking work. Thank you, Jo-Anne.

Ian J White
2022

AUTHOR'S NOTES

This is the third book written in the trilogy about my convict ancestors – the other two in the series being *Elizabeth Rymes – A Remarkable Life* and *The Woodbury Line – An Australian Convict Family*. This book reaches much further back into antiquity than the other two books and could be read as a prequel to the other two, though it is not necessary to do so.

In both previous works I have attempted to place the family members and other characters within the known facts of their lives and to supplement those facts by asking myself, "What would they have been thinking?" and "What would they have said?" As I freely acknowledged in both those earlier books, that strategy led to a combination of fact, social and political history and fiction, because their conversations, of course, were not recorded for us.

The same approach has been used in this book but perhaps to a greater extent, primarily because it reaches further back into an earlier age where known facts are less easily discovered. That may lead some readers to consider this work, particularly the early chapters, to be a work of fiction, but I prefer to use the term "supposition" rather than fiction, for there is certainly an underlying basis of fact in the narrative. The supposition is used to fill in the gaps between the facts and, of course, the further we go back in history, the more gaps we encounter.

Suppose, for example, you were a guest in the Great Hall of Laxton Castle in the early 13th century. Knowing what we do know of the family's role in history over the ensuing centuries, yet knowing also that there are gaps in our knowledge, what do you *suppose* you might have heard as you sat there eavesdropping? I hope and believe that what you would have heard in that situation is not far removed from what I have described, whilst still acknowledging that my telling of the story does, indeed, resort to supposition. Similar interactions and situations are treated in the same way throughout this work. The reader is encouraged, however, to remember that Matthew Everingham and his family did exist, as did other persons named in this narrative, and that, whilst I make no claim to being an historian and do not claim this book to be an historical record, there is a fundamental basis of fact in the telling of their story.

Some readers may disagree with my portrayal of Matthew Everingham's parentage. Others, particularly indigenous readers, may take issue with my depiction of the Everingham family's relationship with the First Peoples of this country. They may be right. Let me say here that, if anything I have written has offended indigenous people, then that has certainly not been my intent and I unreservedly apologise for any such offence unwittingly given, including by omission. For an understanding of the basis of my views on these issues, I would direct readers to the 'Author's Closing Comments' on pages 303-309.

Ian J White
2022

1

"And who, pray tell, is this Robert Everingham?" demanded the feisty Lady Isabel de Birkin of her father, Sir John de Birkin.

The year was 1225 and the two were standing in the Great Hall of Laxton Castle, a motte-and-bailey castle that had first been built soon after the Norman Conquest, one and a half centuries earlier. Following the Norman Conquest, England's new king, William the Conqueror (or William I), initiated a system of land grants to the powerful knights and noblemen who had fought alongside him, intending that they and their descendants should remain loyal and could be called upon for future service to their Liege Lord if necessary.

Geoffrey Alselin, an Anglo-Norman, had been given properties, including Laxton in Nottinghamshire, which had previously been an estate of the Saxons of England. Thus, Geoffrey Alselin was the first owner of Laxton after it was taken from the Saxons in 1066. Alselin and his descendants were also given hereditary rights as Keepers of the Royal Forests of Nottinghamshire and Derbyshire. In Laxton, Geoffrey Alselin commenced the long task of building a motte-and-bailey castle. Construction would be completed by Alselin's son-in-law, Robert de Caux and, in the early twelfth century Laxton, including the castle, was owned by Robert de Caux. It was an era when feudal lords cared only for what they could get and hold, by whatever means, and had little thought for the rights of their fellow countrymen.

Robert de Caux had inherited the rights as Keeper of the Royal Forests of Nottingham and administered those lands on behalf of the Sheriff of Nottingham, often with brutality and heartlessness in his dealings with the peasant population.

Adam de Birkin (1135-1185), son of Peter de Birkin and Emma de Birkin née Lascelles, had been born in Birkyn, Yorkshire, and in 1175 had married Matilda de Caux, more commonly known as Maud de Caux. Maud had been born in 1153, in Lessington, later to be known as Laxton, and was the one child and heir of Robert de Caux and his wife Sibyl de Caux née Basset. Thus, with the marriage of Adam de Birkin and Matilda (Maud) de Caux, hereditary rights to Laxton Castle, and rights as Keeper of the Royal Forests, passed to the de Birkin family. After his marriage to Matilda de Caux, Adam de Birkin would live only another ten years, but long enough to father an heir to Laxton Castle – his son John de Birkin.

Sir John de Birkin's children were Thomas de Birkin and Isabel de Birkin – the same Isabel who now stood arguing with him in the Great Hall. Thomas de Birkin, Isabel's brother and heir to Laxton Castle, died during his father's lifetime leaving Isabel as heir apparent and ensuring that the motte-and-bailey castle would remain in the family's hereditary control – if she married.

Motte-and-bailey castles were a medieval style of defensive stronghold constructed from timber and earth works. The fortification consisted of a large and steep mound of earthworks, raised up to forty metres in height and up to one hundred metres in diameter, flattened on top to provide foundation for the building of a wooden defensive tower. The huge mound itself was known as the *motte*, an old French word meaning mound or hillock, and the defensive tower built thereon was known as the keep.

The keep overlooked an enclosed courtyard, called the *bailey*, at the base of the motte, where the noblemen and other residents of the castle lived. The keep was connected to the bailey via the steep scarp of the motte, most commonly by a flying bridge but sometimes by steps cut into the motte, allowing residents in the bailey to retreat into the fortified tower if threatened. The entire complex was surrounded by raised walls of earth topped with wooden fences. On some castles a surrounding moat was added.

By the beginning of the 13th century, however, more effective strategies for laying siege to castles, together with the constant need to replace wooden battlements, saw the emergence of grand stone castles, many of which would still be found in Britain and across Europe more than eight hundred years later, with towers, drawbridges, stone battlements with arrow slits, all surrounded by a deep moat.

Thus, when Isabel de Birkin stood in confrontation with her father in the Great Hall of Laxton Castle in the year 1225, Laxton Castle was already obsolete as a defensive stronghold and was beginning to fall into a state of disrepair.

Fig. 1. Illustration of a typical motte-and-bailey castle

"Are you going to tell me?" Isabel de Birkin demanded of her father. "Who is this Robert Everingham, and why in God's name should I marry him?"

"I'll answer the second part of your question first," her father replied. "You *will* marry him because I command it so."

There was little Isabel could say in response to that. Truculent by nature she might be, as well as capable of being shrewish and aggressive towards any husband if the need should arise – and it probably would. Yet in matters of choosing a marriage partner, women of the noble class had no choice but to submit to the demands of their fathers. Seething with inner rage, she nonetheless waited in silence for her father to continue.

"You're twenty-three years of age," he said to her, "and the doors to the keep are not being knocked down by suitors. In and of yourself, you are of little value to a nobleman seeking a wife. If it weren't for your hereditary entitlements, I wouldn't be able to give you away!"

Isabel released a long sigh, her anger still burning within her. She was not an unattractive woman – not at all. She stood tall and lithe, with long auburn hair, green eyes, and high cheekbones. She was never seen in public unless dressed in the manner demanded of her privileged position and, given the right circumstances, she could be engaging and alluring, even flirtatious if it suited her. But her age was her Achilles' heel, and she knew her father was right. Noblemen sought out young wives, teenage women most of the time, and, if her father did not marry her off soon, she might die a lonely old woman.

"So, tell me about Robert Everingham," she asked, her voice still combative.

"Robert Everingham," her father began, "is part of the noble family of Everingham in York."

"God in Heaven!" Isabel exploded. "You'd marry me to a Yorkshireman?"

"Hold your blasphemous tongue, you irreverent shrew," her father roared at her as he made the sign of the cross over his heart, as if to ward off imminent attacks on his soul, be it by God or by the evil one. "In the name of the Father and of the Son and of the Holy Spirit. Amen," he mumbled, as he completed his affected, pious act.

Isabel tossed her head, her hair falling over her shoulder, not in a sensuous display – although she was certainly capable of that if the occasion demanded it. Instead, her action stemmed partly from defiance and partly from contempt of her father's hypocrisy, for she knew him to be a man of perfidious Christian beliefs, despite the pious façade of adherence he presented to outsiders.

Sir John waited a few moments for his anger to subside before continuing.

"You forget yourself, girl," he scolded her, more quietly. "My father, and your own grandfather, Adam FitzPeter, Lord of Birkyn, was a Yorkshireman. He came from the village of Birkyn, not twenty miles from York. Where do you think we got the name de Birkin from?"

He closed his eyes and shook his head in disdain at his daughter's lack of knowledge.

"Do you have nothing in that head of yours other than empty space? You, yourself, have Yorkshire blood!"

"Thomas of York de Everingham," Sir John continued, "married a young Yorkshire woman named Ragenhilda de Cordonville – did you hear me say *young*, girl? Not twenty-three!

Their son is Robert Everingham, thirty-five years of age. I hear tell the family is hopeful that he will soon become Sir Robert de Everingham. No doubt a marriage to the heiress of Laxton Castle would enhance those prospects."

"It's difficult to see how," Isabel countered, waving her arms around to indicate the so-called Great Hall. "This castle is falling to pieces!"

"Aye, it's of an age, and that be the truth of it," Sir John said. "And not just here in the bailey. The keep needs a lot of work too. I'm not sure we'd hold off a serious siege. But we still have our holdings in Laxton village. Provided you marry Robert Everingham, and provided he accepts the conditions of marriage, we'll make those assets part of the dowry, but contingent upon my death. So, they will become your inheritance when I die – please God, that will not be for some time."

"Clearly Mr Robert Everingham from York doesn't really need to marry into our family to get a title. Seems he'll get one anyway. So, what does he want?"

"He wants a wife, you stupid girl!" Sir John screamed at his daughter. "He wants heirs!"

"And what of the dowry? If your holdings in Laxton village will not be part of it until after your death, what, pray tell, will be the dowry at the time of marriage?"

Sir John looked around for a while before answering.

"The castle, of course," he said. "Laxton Castle."

"Anything else?" Isabel asked.

Her father nodded.

"The Keepership. He'll be given the Keepership of the Royal Forests. If he manages that wisely, it will be lucrative for him and for your family."

Isabel de Birkin may have been slow-witted in the opinion of her father, but she knew about the important things of life. She knew about dowries. She knew that, within families of lower socio-economic standing, a dowry was often considered a price that the bride's family would pay to secure a husband who would provide for a daughter. It was commonly called a "bride-price", though in reality it should have been called a "husband-price".

Not so, however, within noble families. In medieval England, a dowry was the only way that assets could be transferred to a daughter. The dowry might include immovable property such as land, buildings, even castles, and more portable property such as jewellery, furnishings and livestock. The dowry that a wife brought with her was typically sequestered from the property of her husband and other male members in the family, including sons. It was considered the wife's property and, though it was accessible and useable by the husband, it could not be disposed of without the wife's consent. And should the husband pre-decease his wife, which was the most common occurrence, the dowry would revert to the legal ownership of his widow, as indeed it would if the husband divorced or abandoned his wife. It was an effective and quite a secure way of passing inheritances to a daughter. Even the Keepership would become the inheritance of the future Everingham descendants. Sir John's plan was shrewd, though his counsellors had told him it put his very life at risk. Yes, he would be able to transfer the entirety of his estate to his daughter but holding some of it back until after his death, the counsellors warned, would leave his life very much in the balance and in the hands of his new son-in-law, should said son-in-law become impatient.

In the year 1225, Robert Everingham married Lady Isabel de Birkin in the church of St. Michael the Archangel in Laxton and, the following year, by virtue of that marriage, became Robert de Everingham. His wife, Lady Isabel de Everingham née Birkin, thereafter, was known as "The Lady of Laxton".

Sir John de Birkin died at Laxton Castle in 1227. Despite his death having occurred only two years after the marriage of his daughter Isabel de Birkin to Robert Everingham, and notwithstanding the warnings of his counsellors, his death appeared to have been by natural causes. On his death, as he had planned, all remaining holdings of the de Birkin family passed to the dowry of his daughter, Isabel, and would in due time be inherited by her descendants.

Robert de Everingham (I) (formerly Mr Robert Everingham) died on 1st June 1246 in Southwell, Nottinghamshire, and his wife, Isabel de Everingham née Birkin, The Lady of Laxton, died on 13th July 1252 in Laxton, Nottinghamshire. The hereditary line of descent, however, had been secured for the Everingham family. Adam de Everingham, son of Robert and Isabel de Everingham, and therefore heir to the Everingham estate and title, had been born in Laxton in 1231.

The Everingham descendants held Laxton Castle until the early 15th century, though they did not always live there. And throughout those centuries, the first-born son of an Everingham family was in most instances named either Robert de Everingham or Adam de Everingham, so that even members of the family themselves often lost track of who was who. "Which Robert de Everingham or which Adam de Everingham are you talking about?" they would ask.

Adam de Everingham (I), son of Robert and Isabel de Everingham, married Isabel Ros and produced the next heir of the Everingham family, Robert de Everingham (II), born in Lincolnshire on 9th February 1256.

In 1271, Sir Robert de Everingham (II) married Alice de la Hyde who, at the time of their marriage was eleven years of age. His heir would be Adam de Everingham, born in 1281. Sir Robert de Everingham (II) gained his knighthood because he was one of the knights of Edward I, but one should not automatically think that a knight was one riding off to battle on a strong steed, with lance and suit of armour. Some knights were appointed to posts which demanded a combination of military and administrative skills, while others were appointed to posts as diplomats, councillors, judges and sheriffs. Given that Sir Robert de Everingham (II) was the hereditary Chief Keeper of the Royal Forests, it seems likely that he was given his title in that capacity.

The Keepership of the Royal Forests was stripped from the Everingham family upon the death of Robert de Everingham (II) in 1287 because his heir, Adam de Everingham, was only six years of age at the death of his father. For three generations, from 1225 – 1287 the head of the house of Everingham had held Keepership of the Royal Forests in Nottinghamshire, including Sherwood Forest. Whether any of them, in the execution of their duties, ever encountered a band of merry men led by one Robin of Laxton, is not known.

Adam de Everingham (II), the great grandson of Robert Everingham and Isabel Everingham née Birkin fought for King Edward I in the wars in Scotland in 1303 and, three years later, was made Knight of the Bath, together with Prince Edward and other persons of rank, when he attended the prince during yet another expedition into Scotland.

In 1309, in the 2nd year of the rule of Edward II, Adam de Everingham (II) was summoned to parliament as a Baron,[1] thereby commencing the hereditary position as Baron de Everingham. Upon his death in 1341, the title of Baron de Everingham passed to his heir, Baron Adam de Everingham (III). This Adam, however, was to be the last Baron de Everingham.

The Barony of Everingham fell into abeyance upon the death of Baron Adam de Everingham (III) in 1388 because he lacked a male heir. Sir William de Everingham of Skinningrove was the only son of the second and last Baron, Adam de Everingham (III) (1307 – 1388). Sir William fathered his first daughter Joan in 1363, his second daughter Katherine in 1366, and his only son William in 1368. On the 16th August 1369, Sir William de Everingham died in the lifetime of his father Adam (III), and therefore did not inherit the title of Baron. Sir William's infant son of two years of age died in 1370, again in the lifetime of Adam (III), his grandfather, and therefore he too did not inherit the title. On 8th February 1388, Baron Adam de Everingham (III) (1307 – 1388) died, leaving his granddaughters Joan and Katherine as his only heirs. With no male heir the Barony fell into abeyance. Stone effigies of Baron Adam de Everingham (II) and his wife lie to this day in Laxton Church.

1. Extinct Peerages, Burke's Peerage Ltd., London, 1883, p. 193.

The Barony de Everingham

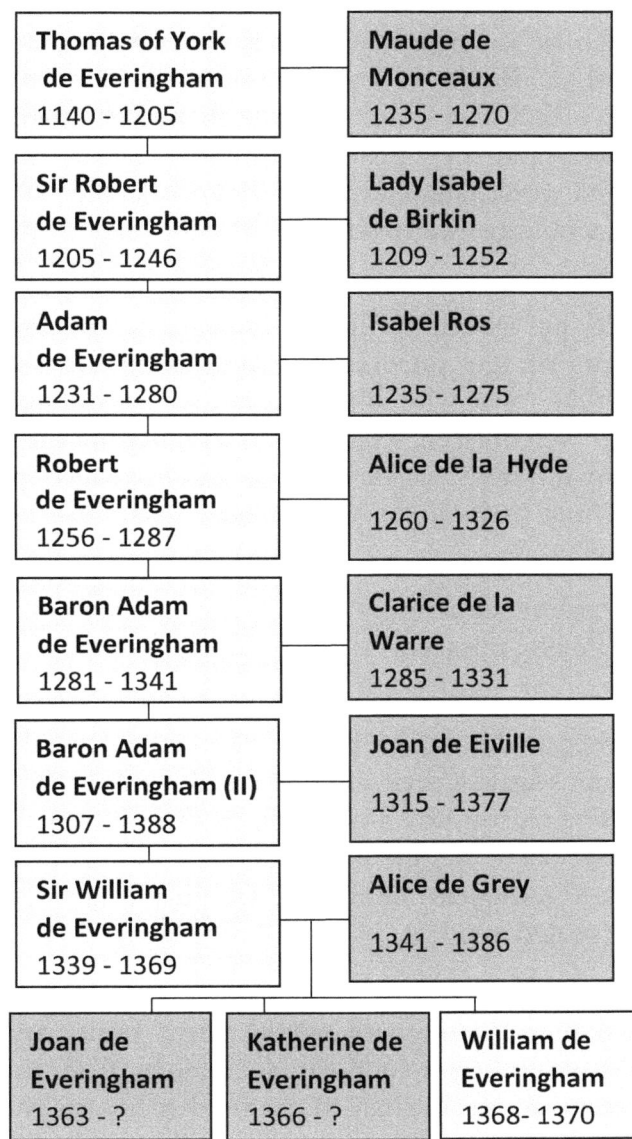

2

It may safely be assumed that when Robert Everingham wed Isabel de Birkin in Laxton Castle in 1225, the couple gave little thought to the possibility that some five centuries and forty generations later, one of their descendants would stand before a judge charged with fraud and would be transported to the other side of the world.

Yet, there he stood, Matthew James Everingham, fifteen years of age, prisoner in the dock of the Old Bailey. Unlike most who appeared before his honour, the lad was well dressed, well-spoken and, despite three weeks remand in Newgate Prison, had managed to some extent to maintain his grooming.

"A proper dandy, aint y'?" fellow prisoners in Newgate had mocked him. "Why 'asn't y' daddy come t' git 'is little boy released?"

Such sentiments were reasonable, for a family of wealth and influence could, indeed, have intervened to have the minor charges against their son dismissed. And yet, they had not. The reason was a mystery, and would remain so, for just where Matthew James Everingham fitted into the de Everingham family and who his father was, was not revealed in court.

Later, extensive research into the precise parentage of Matthew James Everingham would prove futile[1] and give rise to a number of suppositions, ranging from the claim that he was an orphan to claims that he was the son of Earl Robert de Everingham.[2]

It is known that Matthew was born in 1769[3] but that was an era when official documentation was sadly lacking, for it was not until 1837 that the registration of births became mandatory in England. Certainly, many of Matthew's Australian descendants believe Matthew was born to the noble family de Everingham[4] but then they would say that, wouldn't they?

Notwithstanding the fact that there are gaps in our knowledge of Matthew's parentage, given that he had clearly received a good education it, seems reasonable to suppose that the well-spoken young man standing in the dock of the Old Bailey on 7th July 1784 was not an orphan, but none other than the son of Earl Robert de Everingham and Lady Alice de Everingham.

Mr Justice Rose pulled his spectacles down to the end of his nose to look over their thick tortoiseshell frames, squinting his eyes at the accused standing in the dock before him. The boy was not the youngest offender to come before him, but the judge concluded he could not have been more than fifteen years of age, perhaps less.

What's this young fellow doing here? he thought to himself. *He hasn't even been charged with theft – just the lesser charge of fraud and deception.*

Yet, the judge had no choice but to proceed with the case, and so he turned to look at the Clerk, standing to his left.

"Read the indictment," he said.

"Matthew James Everingham," read the Clerk in a commanding voice, "indicted for that he being a profligate person, on the 17th of June last, did falsely pretend to Owen Owens, servant to Samuel Shepherd, Esquire in the Middle Temple, that he was sent to Mr Shepherd from Mr Clermont's for Burn's Justice and Compton's Practice, meaning certain books, by which he obtained the same books, value ten shillings, the property of the said Samuel Shepherd, whereas he was not sent with that message."

Matthew had worked as a messenger and apprentice copy boy to William Clermont, Esq, an attorney at law of the Middle Temple, during which time he had lived in Clermont's chambers in Elm Street, in the Temple. Unfortunately, because of lack of work, Clermont fell on hard times and had to dismiss Matthew who had then taken a room in a cheap lodging house off Chancery Lane, hoping to find work as a copy boy or messenger for one of the many attorneys in the Temple and surrounds. Work, however, had been hard, nay impossible, to find and, when Matthew fell behind on his rent, he forged a plan, totally out of character for him. He would go to the chambers of Attorney Samuel Shepherd in Pump Court, saying he had been sent by Clermont, as he often had been, to borrow some books which he would then be able to sell, and thus pay the rent.

It was a minor charge and, as the indictment was read, the judge questioned in his own mind the motives of Samuel Shepherd in prosecuting the boy. In 18th century England, there were no public prosecutors and victims of crimes had themselves to find witnesses, probably pay them, and bring the prosecution case before the court. Furthermore, even on the handing down of a guilty verdict, the aggrieved victims were generally unable to recover costs.

Samuel Shepherd is an attorney, Judge Rose thought. *He knows this and yet he brings a charge, knowing he can gain nought other than possibly the ten shillings value of the books, and that from a boy with no capacity to pay. It must simply be a matter of principle for him.*

The judge released a long sigh and turned again to the Clerk of the Court.

"First witness," he said.

"The Court calls Owen Owens," the Clerk announced, whereupon a young man of similar age to Matthew was escorted to the witness box, casting an apologetic glance at Matthew as he passed by him. Over the past year Matthew and Owens, a young man from Cardiff in Wales, had come to know each other quite well because of the frequent dealings between the chambers of William Claremont and those of Samuel Shepherd. After Owens had been sworn by the Clerk of the Court to give evidence truthfully, the judge addressed the young witness.

"Please state your name and station for the court," he said.

"I am Owen Owens. I am a servant to Mr Samuel Shepherd."

"And do you have evidence to present in this case?"

The young man took a deep breath and cast another apologetic look at Matthew in the dock before proceeding.

"I was servant to Mr Shepherd on the 17th of June last. The prisoner came to me on the 17th of June in the morning, about ten or eleven. He came with Mr Clermont's compliments to Mr Shepherd, and said he would be obliged to him, if he would lend him Burn's Justice or Compton's Practice. I gave him the two books and asked him whether he lived with Mr Clermont or not. He said he did."

"Were Mr Shepherd and Mr Clermont acquainted?" asked the judge.

"Yes, they were," Owens replied. "They are."

Owen Owens was dismissed from the witness box and the court called William Clermont who was duly sworn before being addressed by the judge.

"You are William Clermont, attorney at law in the Middle Temple, are you not?" the judge asked.

"I am, My Lord."

"And are you acquainted with the accused?"

"I am, My Lord. The prisoner at the bar was my servant, but not on the 17th of June. I had dismissed him some three weeks earlier than that date."

"And why did you dismiss him? Was it because of any dishonesty?"

"No, My Lord, it was not. I had to dismiss him because there had been little work."

"Did you send him anywhere on the 17th of June?"

"I did not, My Lord. I did not send him anywhere."

The judge sighed as he dismissed William Clermont from the witness stand. *There's little point in calling further witnesses,* he thought. *The boy's guilt is already proven.* Yet, Shepherd had one more witness to be called.

"The Court calls Richard Bannister," the Clerk announced in a loud and commanding voice, whereupon an elderly man, perhaps of seventy years, using a walking cane, was escorted to the witness box and sworn to tell the truth to the Court.

"Please state your name and station for the court," the judge asked.

"Pardon?" said Bannister, cupping his hand behind his right ear. "I am hard of hearing."

"Please tell us your name and your occupation," the judge asked with raised voice.

"Oh, I am Richard Bannister. I am a bookseller in Bellyard, Temple-bar."

"And what evidence do you have that is pertinent to this case?" the judge asked, keeping his voice raised.

"The prisoner came to me about the middle of June," Bannister said. "I did not take any particular notice then of the time. He brought to me to sell two books, including Compton's Practice, and I gave him five shillings for it. If it had been the latest edition of the book, it would have been worth more, but not being the latest edition, five shillings was the full value of it."

"What does the latest edition sell for, if new?"

"Sixteen shillings, My Lord. I asked him whose books they were, and he told me that they belonged to his master, Mr William Clermont of Elm Court. He asked me but three shillings, but I said, 'My lad I can give you five shillings each for them, but you must produce me some authority, or I shall detain the books.' He said he himself lived in Elm Court, Temple, with Mr Clermont, upon which he went away and later returned, bringing me a letter, on the authority of which I bought them. I thought it might be some distressed member of the law who needed money. I could not tell."

The judge looked at the letter that had been submitted in evidence, a letter clearly written by a young hand but attempting to incorporate the legal style and missives that had been learned from his master.

Surely, this doddery old fool should have recognised this as a letter written by the boy himself, the judge thought. Frowning, His Lordship read the letter to himself for a second time, before asking the Clerk to present it to the jury.

Finally, the judge turned his attention back to accused, standing in the dock.

"Prisoner in the dock, do you wish to say anything in your defence?"

"My Lord," Matthew replied, his voice breaking, "I was in great distress."

The judge groaned inwardly as the last vestige of hope for the young man before him dissipated. This boy, he knew, was going down. The defence of "I was in great distress" was often heard in the court and it was never grounds for acquittal. It meant that the accused had been in a very difficult situation, without sufficient money to pay for rent, food or other necessities. It was a reason, not an excuse.

The judge banged his gavel.

"Gentlemen of the jury," he said, "Please retire to consider your verdict."

The jurymen, for of course they were all men, huddled together in a corner of the courtroom to mumble amongst themselves. Watching them, the judge felt sympathy for this young man standing before him.

How could it have come to this? he thought to himself. *Surely this boy's family should have come forward and moved to have the charges dismissed before it got this far.*

The jurymen were resuming their seats.

"Members of the jury," the judge asked, "have you considered the facts and determined your verdict?"

The jury foreman rose to his feet.

"We have, M' Lord," he said.

"And is your verdict unanimous, or by what numbers do you judge?"

"We are unanimous, M' Lord."

"In the charge of committing fraud and deceit against the prisoner in the dock, how do you find?"

"Guilty, M' Lord," the jury foreman replied.

The judge banged his gavel but seemed to hold his breath for several moments before speaking.

"Matthew James Everingham, inasmuch as you have been found by your peers to be guilty of the charge against you, this court hereby sentences you to seven years imprisonment and transportation to a place of banishment beyond the seas, to His Majesty King George the Third's colony in America."

He banged the gavel and, again, paused for some moments before speaking.

"Take the prisoner down," he said.

Samuel Shepherd slumped in his seat as His Lordship left the bench and retired to his chambers behind the Court. Shepherd was distraught at the severity of the sentence handed down and regretful that he had prosecuted one so young.

What have I done? he thought to himself as the Court emptied, Matthew's case having been the last scheduled for the day's business. He sat there for some time, consumed by his own thoughts until he finally determined that his only course of action was to make a personal appeal for the judge to mitigate the severity of the sentence.

Two days later, at noon on Friday 9th July 1784, Shepherd found himself seated in the antechamber of Judge Lionel Rose, waiting for the judge to leave the bench, for he had been promised a short audience with the judge during the lunch break.

"His Lordship will see you now, Mr Shepherd," said the judge's young assistant, himself no older than Matthew Everingham.

"Thank you for seeing me, Lionel," Shepherd said as he entered the room, dispensing with titles because the two were well acquainted. "I've asked to see you because…"

"I know why you're here, Samuel," the judge said, cutting him off. "It's young Everingham."

"It is," Shepherd said as he sat down facing the judge across his desk. He sat there for some moments resting his chin on his hands which were clasped together with interwoven fingers, almost as if in prayer.

"It's a death sentence, Lionel," he finally said as he looked up at the judge. "The lad will not survive seven years of incarceration."

"Then, why did you prosecute him, Samuel? I could never understand your motivation in doing that."

"The lad needed to be taught a lesson," Shepherd responded. "I thought he'd likely be sent to a workhouse, perhaps for a few months, where he could work while reflecting on his own stupidity and thus be dissuaded from committing further and more serious crimes. That's what he needs. But seven years imprisonment … and transportation…" His speech tapered off as anguish and self-reproach overcame him.

The judge pushed a jug of water and a glass across the table towards him.

"Samuel," he said, "had the boy appeared before me two weeks earlier than he did, that is exactly how I would have sentenced him, perhaps even to only two months in a house of correction. Things change, Samuel."

"How so?"

"Crime is on the rise, Samuel. Central London has become a cesspool of prostitution, theft, assault and fraud. The King, through his privy council, has instructed, nay *commanded* judges of the court to impose heavier sentences as a deterrent to those who might otherwise be lured into such crimes."

Shepherd took a sip of his water.

"But Matthew Everingham is not of that ilk," he said. "He's a young boy who made a stupid mistake. He's no felon. Indeed, I'm sure he's been well raised in a good family."

"What do you know of his family?" Judge Rose asked.

"I know nothing myself," Shepherd admitted, "but Clermont tells me there's a noble family de Everingham of York. He thinks Matthew is from that family."

"Then, it's a great pity they did not see fit to come and give a character reference to the court. It would have helped," the judge responded.

"It seems to me it's the more heinous crimes such as murder, assault and rape that should be given harsher penalties," Shepherd said then. "We rarely see a death sentence handed down these days."

"True enough that is," Judge Rose agreed. "I myself am loath to hand down a death sentence. I think or hope that, as a society, we might be starting to move past that, although, that having been said, I think you'll see an increase in the number of death sentences in coming months. The pressure of a sovereign is difficult to resist – and dangerous."

Samuel Shepherd considered the judge's words.

He's really quite enlightened for our times, he thought. *It seems he struggles to be fair where possible, even being opposed to death sentences.*

"So," Shepherd asked, "in the case of young Everingham, there's nothing you can do?"

The judge spread his hands in a gesture of helplessness.

"My hands are tied, Samuel. What options do I have, other than to sentence offenders to the minimum term of seven years?"

"And the transportation?"

Judge Rose shrugged.

"It might not happen, anyway," he said. "The colony in North America has become unavailable because of those damn colonists and their war of independence. If this country is going to continue shipping felons to banishment beyond the seas, another place will need to be found. Your Matthew Everingham could well serve his seven years in this country."

Shepherd nodded, as he rose to leave.

"If he lives that long," he said.

After his trial in the Old Bailey, Matthew was returned to his cell in Newgate Prison where he would languish for the next three months, listed on the prison inventory as a "prisoner upon orders awaiting transportation". He was, at least, appreciative that the prison warder had returned him to the same cell he had occupied pre-trial, for he had established something of a rapport with the five other prisoners sharing the cell. Amongst them was Noah Wright, a carriage maker and wheelwright of about fifty years of age who had been convicted of stealing two blankets from a boarding house. Noah had recognised the vulnerability of a boy of Matthew's age incarcerated with men, most of whom were much older, and almost all of whom were perverted, depraved and predatory.

"Stick by me, Matthew," Noah had said to him. "I'll watch your back, lad."

When Noah said he would watch Matthew's back, he meant it quite literally, for many were the men in Newgate who, having been long separated from female companionship, sought gratification by violating fellow prisoners, especially young men. Matthew had already been raped and beaten several times and, despite Noah's best efforts to protect him, it would continue to occur periodically. For that reason, Matthew spent most of his time in his cell, venturing out only for meals and then only when necessary, frequently skipping meals. He hated the men who had raped and beaten him, of course, and it also embittered him against his family who had abandoned him to such treatment.

In mid-September 1784, Mathew, together with more than a hundred other male prisoners in Newgate, were taken from their cells, chained together, and loaded onto wagons which then set off heading east, following the south bank of the River Thames.

"I think this is it, Matthew," Noah said. "Looks to me like we're being transported."

"Where to?" Matthew asked.

"I imagine we'll find out soon enough, lad," Noah replied. "Now that prisoners are no longer being sent to America, all they say is 'a place of banishment beyond the seas'. God alone know what that means."

At Barking Reach, near Woolwich, the wagons stopped beside a wharf shrouded in thick fog like the smoke of a recent battle. The wharf itself was formed by large stones held in place by walls of strong stakes. The prisoners, still in chains, were ordered out of the wagons and bustled towards the end of the wharf. As they shuffled along the uneven stones, out of the fog the ghostly silhouette of a large ship appeared, lying only a short distance off the end of the wharf.

The prisoners, in groups of ten, were loaded into longboats in order to transport them out to the ship. Yet, as they approached the ship in the longboats, it became clear they would not be boarding an ocean-going vessel.

"I don't think we're going beyond the seas in that," Matthew said to Noah. "It has no masts or sails. Looks like something your namesake may have built – an ark."

The *Censor*, moored on the Thames off the end of the wharf in Woolwich, was a 731-ton former French frigate, captured by the Royal Navy and which had then been procured by shipowners Duncan Campbell and James Bradley. Moored only a couple of hundred yards from *Censor* was the *Justitia*, an old, retired Indiaman, also devoid of masts and rigging.

In 1776, the British Parliament had passed the "Public Act, 16 George III, c. 43" which would commonly become known as "The Hulks Act". It was described in the legislation as:

> *An Act to authorise, for a limited time, the punishment by hard labour of offenders who, for certain crimes, are or shall become liable to be transported to any of His Majesty's colonies and plantations.*[5]

The act included provision for the British government to hold such offenders in facilities to be provided to the government under private contract, an initiative designed to relieve the strain on Britain's over-stretched prison system and to provide a place of temporary confinement for prisoners awaiting transportation.

It was Duncan Campbell who put forward the proposition that his fleet of decommissioned sailing ships could be reconfigured as floating prisons – ships permanently moored on the Thames, stripped of their masts, rudders and rigging and thus retaining only their ability to float. Below the top deck, Campbell proposed, the remaining decks would be reconfigured with prison cells of iron bars where the prisoners would be held in chains and sent ashore each day in guarded work-gangs to perform their hard labour. It was a proposal which the British government viewed as a convenient solution to the problem of London's overcrowded and bursting prisons.

The first use of a prison hulk was the *Tayloe*, privately owned by Campbell who, in July 1776, was named "Overseer of Convicts on the Thames" and awarded a contract for the housing of transportees and for arranging the effective use of their labour whilst awaiting transportation. The *Tayloe* soon became overcrowded and Campbell and his business partner, James Bradley, quickly introduced numerous other hulks onto the Thames.

By 1784, when Matthew and Noah were imprisoned on the *Censor*, hulks owned by Campbell and by other contractors were moored at various places along the Thames, including at Woolwich, Deptford, and Wapping, on the River Lea at Gosport, as well as at the Royal Navy Dockyard at Sheerness and the harbours of Plymouth, Portsmouth and even Cork.

When the prisoners came on board, they were issued with their prison garb – grey shirt, grey trousers and grey jacket, all printed with black broad arrows. Below deck, the prisoners were housed in cage-like cells of iron bars, eight men to a cell. Living space was limited, with barely enough space for eight hammocks, each being six feet long and two feet wide. Men who committed infractions were flogged, then chained in leg irons on the floor, denying them, for a time, access to the hammocks. The prisoners were given food twice a day, with little nutrition and in such inadequate amounts that many were frequently unable to perform the arduous work assigned to the work-gangs.

Prisoners were not segregated according to age or the seriousness of their crimes. Old and young, those who had committed serious crimes and those who, like Matthew, had committed very minor crimes were indiscriminately pushed into cells with one another. Matthew and Noah found themselves sharing a cell with six other prisoners, two of whom were rapists of around forty years of age who had escaped execution when their death sentences were commuted to life imprisonment with transportation. Their other cellmates were one blind forger who was about seventy years of age, one other young man of about Matthew's age who had been convicted of minor theft, one man of about thirty years of age convicted of purposely damaging the king's property, one in his fifties convicted of barratry which was the common designation for frequently stirring up quarrels by spreading false rumours and/or prosecuting malicious lawsuits, and one man of indeterminate age who was a cripple and quite mad. None of the prisoners knew the nature of the crime for which the madman had been convicted.

Six days a week, the prisoners were taken onshore in guarded work-gangs to engage in exhausting and backbreaking work, building more stone wharfs or clearing the shores of the Thames of mud, gravel, stones and river reeds. The work, from the perspective of the authorities, was dual purpose for it was not merely improving the navigability of the Thames, but at the same time providing a public moral spectacle for all who saw the prisoners at work. Fall foul of the law and you too could end up in a work-gang like this!

The hulks sat in the stagnant waters of the Thames, surrounded by all manner of floating garbage and flotsam, including human excrement, whilst, on board, rats scavenged amongst the filth. The cramped, unsanitary conditions and the inadequate nutrition provided to prisoners combined to create conditions akin to a petri-dish wherein diseases like smallpox, typhus, dysentery, scurvy and cholera became endemic. Upwards of forty percent of prisoners held in the hulks died before they could be transported to their place of banishment.

That, perhaps, was by design for, with the American colony having become unavailable as a place of banishment, the authorities were still endeavouring to settle on a new destination for transportation. In the meantime, each death on the hulks was viewed as a convenience, allowing yet another prisoner to be transferred from London's prisons to a hulk. The madman sharing Matthew's cell died within three months of coming aboard *Censor*, to be replaced by a man of around fifty years of age who had been convicted of coining – counterfeiting the king's currency.

Prisoners lived from day to day, losing all track of the passing months and years, and Matthew watched as many of his fellow prisoners died or descended into permanent conditions of clinical depression and even into insanity. He took care of his own personal hygiene, as he had been trained to do, and he encouraged Noah to do likewise. Noah, however, was an older man and the savage work regime had weakened him, making him more susceptible to disease. Some two and a half years after he and Matthew had come aboard *Censor*, the lack of nutrition, particularly the lack of Vitamin C, saw Noah become increasingly weak and frail as scurvy took hold of his body.

It was one night in mid-November 1786, when the prisoners were lying in their hammocks, that Matthew felt a weak tug at his sleeve and turned to find Noah dragging his emaciated body to the edge of his hammock so he could whisper to Matthew.

"I'm not going to make it, lad," he whispered. "I don't have much left in me. But you're young and strong and you know how to look after yourself."

Matthew did not attempt to console Noah with empty platitudes and assurances – they both knew his time had come and that even death might be a welcome escape for him.

"You take care of yourself and keep looking to better times ahead, Matthew," he continued. "Don't allow yourself to become disheartened by these circumstances. This too shall pass."

Noah had become something of a father figure to Matthew and, as he held his hand, Matthew realised Noah wanted to impart some final advice to him.

"You're educated," Noah continued, his ragged breath coming with increasing difficulty. "You can read and write, something none of these other prisoners can do. When you get to wherever they send you, make yourself useful to them. Make a new life for yourself there."

A short time later, Noah fell into a coma and Matthew banged on the bars of the cell.

"Guard! Guard!" he called. "This man needs a doctor."

"Tomorrow!" the guard called back from the other end of the deck.

Noah died that night, and Matthew wept for the man who had been his friend and mentor since the first day of his incarceration. When the morning meal, if it could be called a meal, was brought to the cells, the guard called out to Matthew.

"Does he still need a doctor?"

"No," Matthew said. "He's dead."

For another six months, Matthew continued living in the appalling conditions aboard *Censor* and working in the work-gangs onshore. At times, his spirit was tested, and sometimes he would fall into near depression as he wondered whether he would ever be transported to another place. Yet on such occasions, he would fortify himself by drawing on his inner strength and promising himself that he would live, if for no other reason than to honour his departed friend, Noah.

He was eighteen years of age and had already served almost three years of his seven-year sentence when Noah's words, "This too shall pass" were realised. Together with more than two hundred of the healthiest prisoners from *Censor* and the other hulks, Matthew was chained and loaded onto open wagons for the overland journey to Portsmouth Harbour.

As the wagons pulled away from Woolwich, Matthew looked back at the hulks and reminded himself of Noah's advice – "Wherever they send you, Matthew, make yourself useful to them. Make a new life for yourself there."

That I'll do, he promised himself. *That I'll do.*

1. Valerie Ross, considered an authority on the Everingham dynasty, documents extensive but ultimately unproductive research into the parentage of Matthew James Everingham. Refer to *Matthew Everingham – A First Fleeter and his Times*, Ross, V. Library of Australian History, Sydney, 1980, pp.15-17
2. In all likelihood, just one missing detail would prove the determining factor. Had we the name of his father or of his mother, had we the place of birth or the exact date of birth, had we the name of the school he attended – for he had clearly been given an excellent education – any of these single facts would prove to be the missing link, the missing piece of the jigsaw.
3. Matthew's headstone in Wilberforce cemetery, New South Wales, declares that at the date of his death, 25th December 1817, he was forty-eight years of age which, if correct, would mean he was born in 1769. The register of deaths in St Matthew's Church, Windsor, endorses those dates.
4. Barry Everingham (1939-2018), an Australian born writer, broadcaster and author, claims that Matthew is descended from Robert de Everingham who married Isabel de Birken in 1279 – see *The Great Everingham Dynasty* by Barry Everingham, https://independentaustralia.net/australia/australia-display/the-great-everingham-dynasty,3161, (accessed May 2022).
5. https.discovery.nationalarchives.gov.uk (accessed May 2022).

3

Riding at anchor in Portsmouth harbour were the eleven ships which would comprise the First Fleet. Six of the ships would carry convicts and supplies, whilst the remaining five ships would carry mostly supplies, stores and provisions for the new settlement – sufficient it was thought or hoped, to last for two years – and also small contingents of official passengers and marines.

The British government had finally settled on a new place of banishment for its criminal refuse, choosing Botany Bay which had been visited by Captain James Cook in 1770. After Dutch navigators had charted the northern, western and part of the southern coasts of the great southern continent, this newly found land had become known as New Holland. The region around Botany Bay, Cook had named New South Wales, yet, the British Admiralty continued to refer to the land as New Holland and would continue to do so until a permanent British settlement could be established at Botany Bay.

On 1st September 1786, the British Government had placed the first of a series of advertisements in the *London Morning Herald* for the leasing of the required shipping, with the cost of the outward voyage to New Holland to be paid by the government. On arrival in New Holland, after unloading their cargo and disembarking their passengers, including convicts, the ships would be free to return to England by whatever route their captains may decide and at their own expense. The successful tender was William Richards

Jnr who lived on Queens Row, Walworth, and declared himself in his submission to be a prominent shipbroker. He, indeed, did own some ships and he sub-contracted other ships for the voyage from Calvert and Co. Richards was paid the exorbitant fee of £54,000 for organising the ships of the First Fleet.

Four companies of marines, approximately 250 men, were to accompany the fleet under the command of Major Robert Ross and, on arrival in New Holland, to guard the convicts and maintain law and order. Significant detachments of marines sailed on each of the convict transport ships, with smaller numbers on the supply ships, together with their wives and children.

Official fleet passengers included Captain Arthur Phillip, RN, Governor elect of the Colony of New South Wales; Major Robert Ross, Lieutenant Governor elect and commander of the marines; Captain David Collins, Judge Advocate; Augustus Alt, Surveyor; John White, Principal Surgeon; William Balmain, Assistant Surgeon and Reverend Richard Johnson, Chaplain. All travelled with their wives and children. The precise number of persons sailing on the First Fleet is not known but is believed to be in the vicinity of 1,530 souls, although that would have included approximately 250 sailors who would soon return to England and not remain to establish the colony. Those who would be left on the shores of an unknown country included 696 convicts.

Alexander, weighing in at 448 tons, was the largest of the convict transport ships and would carry two hundred and thirteen male convicts. *Scarborough* (420 tons) would sail with two hundred and eight male convicts, *Charlotte* (339 tons) would carry twenty female convicts, *Prince of Wales* (334 tons), fifty female convicts, *Lady Penrhyn* (331 tons), one hundred and two female convicts and *Friendship* (276 tons) would sail with seventy-seven male convicts and twenty-six female convicts.

Amongst the ships carrying mostly stores and provisions for the new settlement, including livestock, were *HMS Supply* (170 tons), *Fishburn* (378 tons), *Golden Grove* (353 tons) and *Borrowdale* (274 tons).

They would be joined and led by *HMS Sirius* which, at 540 tons, was the largest ship of the fleet. *HMS Sirius* would be the flagship of the fleet and would carry some supplies, as well as approximately 200 people, including seamen, marines, officers and their families. *HMS Sirius* would be captained by Captain John Hunter RN, but would also carry Captain Arthur Phillip RN, Commodore of the fleet and of the entire expedition.

HMS Sirius and *HMS Supply* were the only Royal Navy ships accompanying the fleet. They were under orders to remain in New Holland at least until the arrival of the next fleet, whenever that might be. The other nine transport ships of the fleet, as per contract, would be free to make their own way back to England by whatever route their captains deemed appropriate. Because the return journey would be at the owner's expense, several would sail from Sydney to China to load shipments of tea for the English market.

On 4th March 1787, the first prisoners arrived at Portsmouth harbour by overland wagon from Woolwich – 210 men, including Matthew Everingham. Over the next days and weeks, more prisoners would arrive from the hulks in other parts of England and also women prisoners from Newgate and other prisons.

On arrival at Spithead, all convicts were given soap and ordered to bathe thoroughly, under guard and in many cases under duress, for many of those men had not bathed for years. When the supervising guards were satisfied the men were clean, each prisoner was examined individually by the Surgeon-General of the fleet, before being provided with a new set of prison garb. The procedure was all part of a protocol that had been insisted upon by Captain Arthur Phillip who would lead the fleet and attempt to establish a viable colony in an unknown environment on the other side of the world. Aware that it would be a daunting task, Phillip had insisted that only healthy prisoners be embarked on the fleet at Spithead and he meant to take every precaution to ensure that fit and healthy men disembarked in New Holland.

Phillip had also requested a list of prisoner names, their ages and the nature of the crimes for which they had been sentenced. He intended to segregate the prisoners, putting the worst offenders together, whilst those who were perhaps younger and who had committed lesser crimes would be embarked on different ships. This, he believed, would make guarding of the more hardened criminals easier, whilst at the same time protecting the less troublesome prisoners from the negative influence of others. In the end, the requested list did not eventuate and, as had been the case in the prison hulks, prisoners were mixed indiscriminately.

The quarters in which the convicts would be housed below deck, however, were a vast improvement on the iron-barred cells that Matthew had been accustomed to on the prison hulk. Each man had a bunk of his own in a large area which had first been sanitised by the firing of gunpowder and then whitewashed with lime. Within the convict quarters, prisoners were not chained or ironed and, provided they caused no trouble, they were left very much to their own devices. The thick bulkheads dividing the convict quarters from the area occupied by the marines had small peepholes through which the marines could keep an eye on the prisoners and through which muskets could be fired, should the need arise.

The prisoners' diet was also a significant improvement on the meagre rations with which they had been provided on the hulks and even in Newgate prison, despite the fact that they were not subjected to hard labour or indeed to any labour at all. It seemed to Matthew he was being better cared for than at any other time since his incarceration.

Strange, he thought. *Now they're preparing to send me to the other side of the world, with no guarantee that we'll get there, and yet I'm being cared for better than if I were to remain here in England.*

Matthew was embarked on *Scarborough*, along with two hundred and seven other prisoners, all of whom were allowed on deck on a rotation basis in groups of twenty.

On deck, they were chained and ironed. Yet, in spite of having to be restrained in such a manner, Matthew looked forward to his times on deck. It would be ten weeks before the fleet set sail and those passing weeks would be boring and monotonous at times. Yet, to Matthew, it was much more preferable to the daily grid of the work-gangs he had endured for the past three years. The breaks on deck meant fresh air and what he regarded as interesting periods of watching the loading and the preparations being made for the voyage. Not all of the prisoners were of like mind, however.

Very few, if any of the prisoners had ever been to sea before and remained apprehensive about their chances of surviving the voyage to New Holland which, as far as any of them knew, might just as well be on the other side of the world – and it was!

"Do y' think these small tubs are gonna make it t' New 'olland?" Samuel Mobbs asked his fellow convicts on deck one day.

Mobbs was twenty-three, a building plasterer from Oxfordshire who had been convicted in the Old Bailey almost three years earlier. He had been found guilty of stealing a handkerchief valued at one shilling and sentenced to seven years imprisonment with transportation.

"I don't like the way this ship's rollin', and we ain't even at sea yet," Mobbs continued. "I can't see ships like these makin' it across the ocean."

"These are pretty big ships," said Thomas Hylids who had been a ships' carpenter before his conviction and incarceration, "'nd from what I can see, this is a sound ship. She'll make it."

"Might seem like a big ship 'ere in 'arbour," Mobbs countered, "but the ocean out there's bloody wide. It goes on f'ever."

"What worries me," said William Blunt, who was lucky to have had his death sentence commuted and who had been part of Matthew's work-gang whilst the two were held on the hulk *Censor* at Woolwich, "is 'ow they's gonna find the bloody place. Tellin' is only one man's ever been there, 'nd somehow these sailors 'ave gotta find the same place ag'in."

Others nodded in agreement. "Good point, Will," one responded.

"But they's loading plenty o' supplies," added Jacob Bellett, a twenty-two year old Londoner who had been convicted of stealing a quantity of silk, "'nd them soldiers is bringing their wives 'nd kids on board. Seems they're confident, at least."

Matthew, whilst choosing to remain silent rather than be an active participant in this discussion, thought Bellett was making a good point. The sight of families coming on board buoyed his confidence in surviving the voyage ahead.

The whole harbour today, as on every other day he had been on deck, was a hive of activity, with longboats and barges shuttling all manner of goods and provisions out to the eleven ships that sat close to each other at anchor. Matthew had seen quite a lot of furniture and even a piano belonging to the ship's surgeon loaded onto the ships, together with tents, implements for agricultural endeavour, axes, saws and other building tools, blacksmithing tools, carriage wheels and large barrels, some containing water and others filled with salted meat. Even livestock had been loaded, including horses, cows, swine and chickens.

Wherever New Holland is, Matthew thought, *I think they're intending to get there, and we're going there to stay.*

"Well, oi'll tell y'all one thing," declared Francis Carthy, a thirty-one-year-old Irishman, "soon as we make landfall, oi'll be orff. Oi've had me gutful o' 'ard labour."

"You're planning t' escape?" Mobbs asked.

"Oi am, laddie, f' sure 'nd be certain," Carthy said with conviction. "'nd any of y' dat 'ave any brains 'd do duh same. There's no way I'm gonna work me guts out in New 'olland."

"But we don't know what the place 'll be like," said Mobbs. "If y' take off, y' might git et by savages."

"Oi'll take me chances with duh savages," Carthy declared. "One thing we know, der'll be no prison dere, so the moment me feet hit dry land oi'm gonna scamper."

Matthew sat listening and contemplating the voyage that lay ahead and the unknown destination. He had little if any comprehension of what his new land would be like, yet he considered escape to be an extreme and probably foolhardy option.

Francis Carthy had been born in Ireland in 1756 and, on 14th April 1786, in Bodmin Assizes, he had been tried and found guilty of highway robbery in company, and the theft of a watch valued at twenty shillings. He had been sentenced to death but had escaped the hangman's noose when his sentence was commuted to seven years with transportation. He had been held on the prison hulk *Dunkirk* in Plymouth harbour for a year before being transferred to *Scarborough* for transportation to New Holland.

Carthy was still listed on the victualling lists when the fleet reached Cape of Good Hope but doesn't appear on the list of convicts being unloaded in Sydney Cove. Somehow, it seems, Carthy had managed to make good on his boast to scamper the moment his feet hit dry ground. There were later claims that he had escaped overboard somewhere in the Southern Ocean and had been eaten by a shark, but that story was discounted.

In London, whilst all the loading had been going on at Portsmouth, Arthur Phillip had spent many hours making plans for what he knew would be no small undertaking. To sail to perhaps the most distant point on earth to a place where only one small party of Englishmen had ever been – and that eighteen years earlier – to establish from scratch a successful colony in an unknown land, based on a large contingent of prisoners convicted of all manner of crimes, perhaps in the face of hostility from local natives, and to survive there for upwards of two years until the next fleet would arrive with much needed supplies, must have appeared to many, and at times to Phillip himself, an exercise in folly. On 9th May 1787, Phillip arrived in Portsmouth and the next day went aboard *HMS Sirius* where he issued orders for the fleet to prepare for imminent departure. John Hunter, captain of *HMS Sirius* and later to be the second Governor of the Colony of New South Wales, wrote in his journal that Phillip "issued the signals and other necessary orders to Lieutenant John Shortland, the agent for transports, to be delivered to the masters of the different ships."[1]

Part of those orders were to secure the convicts in their quarters below decks, and so it was that on Saturday 12th May 1787, Matthew Everingham went below deck, after taking his last ever look at English shores.

The next morning, the convicts in their quarters below decks heard the ship's bell being rung – eight bells, in peals of two. Matthew, over the past several weeks, had learned that eight bells sounded the change of shift for the ship's crew, yet this morning the bells came at an unusual time – mid-morning.

Moments later came shouted commands from the bosun, relaying the captain's orders.

"All hands on deck!"

Running feet were heard on the deck above the convicts' heads, and marines peered anxiously through their peep holes, ordered to ensure there was no rebellion from the convicts at this critical moment.

"Weigh anchor!" the bosun called.

Chains rattled and the ship shifted as the anchor was hauled up, with the sailors chanting as they leaned against the long hand bars of the capstan.

"Heave-ho! Heave-ho!"

"We're gettin' underway, lads," one of the convicts called to the others.

"Starboard your helm!" called the bosun.

The ship shuddered as she swung around and came onto the breeze, causing Samuel Mobbs to shout out to the other convicts.

"I told y' this tub wouldn't make it t' New 'olland. Feels like we's gonna sink even b'fore we git outa the harbour."

"Breeze on the starboard quarter!" called the bosun.

Matthew felt the ship move and heard the masts creak as the sails filled with breeze.

"Mind your starboard helm!"

The sound of the water against the hull of *Scarborough* had now changed. Matthew realised the gentle slap of the swell against the ship whilst she was at anchor had been replaced by the sloshing sound of the hull passing through water as the ship got underway. Instead of rocking slightly as each small swell within the harbour slapped the hull, *Scarborough* was now slicing through small swells, rising a little as she did so, then dropping slightly to meet the next swell. *Scarborough* was moving – she was moving slowly, but she was definitely moving.

"Helm a-midships!"

HMS Sirius led the fleet out of Portsmouth harbour and into the English Channel.

"What day is it?" one of the convicts called on *Scarborough*.

"Day after yesterday," came the reply from a fellow convict.

It was left to one of the marines peering through the peep hole to provide a definitive answer.

"It's Sunday," he called, "13th of May 1787."

---

1. Hunter, John (1793), *An Historical Journal of the Transactions at Port Jackson and Norfolk Island*, chapter 1, Project Gutenberg Australia, (retrieved 28 May 2022)

4

In the channel, just off the Mother Bank at the Isle of Wight, the fleet rendezvoused with their Royal Navy escort, the 24-gun man-of-war *HMS Hyaena*, which would accompany the fleet into the north Atlantic.

Having cleared the English Channel off Falmouth the fleet picked up a nor-easterly breeze that would carry them all the way to their first port of call at Teneriffe. The smaller and faster *HMS Supply* was sent ahead to act as pathfinder for the rest of the fleet and became the object of Matthew's attention whenever he was on deck. Standing as close as he was permitted to the forecastle, he would peer ahead, scanning the horizon for *Supply* which he would sometimes be able to see and sometimes not. On *Scarborough*, the ship's bell rang out every hour and, after two hours, Matthew and the other convicts on deck would be taken below, allowing yet another group of their fellow convicts to take their turn on deck.

Some two hundred miles south and west of Cape Cornwall, the southernmost tip of England, their escort *HMS Hyaena* fell back a few miles and fired thirteen guns.

"Dear God in Heaven!" screamed the ever-anxious Samuel Mobbs who was on deck at the time. "They're firing on us! They're not sendin' us t' a new land. They're gonna sink us out 'ere!"

But *Hyaena* had not fired on the fleet. She had merely fired her guns, without shot – a farewell salute as she turned and headed back to Portsmouth.

The fleet enjoyed relatively calm seas with fair winds. Matthew, like the vast majority of the other convicts, Samuel Mobbs perhaps being the exception, found themselves enjoying the voyage, with the summer sunshine of the northern hemisphere making their time on deck very pleasant. On one such afternoon, however, whilst Matthew was sitting and enjoying the sunshine, the marines suddenly became quite belligerent, turned their muskets on the convicts and hustled them below to their quarters. An informer amongst the convicts, it transpired, had told the Commander of the Marines there were a number of men amongst the convicts who were planning to take control of *Scarborough*.

An investigation into the planned insurrection was held and two convicts, Thomas Griffiths and Philip Farrell, were found to be the ringleaders. They were immediately transferred to the flagship, *HMS Sirius*, whilst some other co-conspirators were secured in chains on *Scarborough* and would remain so until arrival in New Holland.

On board *Sirius*, Griffiths and Farrell were each given twenty-four lashes then transferred to *Prince of Wales*. The *Prince of Wales* carried fifty female convicts, but if Griffiths and Farrell had any thoughts of fraternising with the women, these were not to be realised. They too would be restrained in chains and irons until arrival in New Holland.

On 3rd July, some six weeks out from Portsmouth, the fleet caught up with their pathfinder, *HMS Supply,* which had come to anchor in the Spanish port of Santa Cruz on the island of Teneriffe the day before. The fleet would stay there a week, taking on renewed supplies of fresh meat, vegetables, fruit and water. After going ashore to pay his respects to the Governor of Santa Cruz, Arthur Phillip took the opportunity to go on board *Scarborough,* for he remained concerned about the possibility of further insurrection amongst the prisoners there. All convicts on *Scarborough* were assembled under armed guard in the convict quarters below deck, all seated on bunks or on the floor, in readiness for Phillip to address them. Matthew found himself sitting on his bunk near the rear of the assembled convicts as Phillip entered the convict quarters, escorted by yet more armed marines.

Phillip was a man of small and unimpressive stature, but the moment he began to speak, he commanded attention and respect.

"Your destiny is in your own hands," he began. "Recently, two of your number conspired to take control of this ship by force of arms. Where they planned to sail to and how they thought they could sail a ship of this size, beggars belief. They were misguided men and were transferred to my flagship, *HMS Sirius.*"

"Is they still alive, sir?" one of the convicts called.

"Of course," Phillip replied, "though they've been appropriately punished."

He did not inform the convicts that the two would-be mutineers had been transferred to the *Prince of Wales*. That, he thought, was none of their concern.

"Now, I want orderliness and compliance to return to this ship," Phillip continued. "You have been well cared for, well fed and given certain freedoms on deck. But those benefits are part of a two-way transaction. In return, we expect your cooperation and your compliance until we reach New Holland."

Cornelius Teague, forty-six years of age and one of the oldest convicts on board *Scarborough*, rose to his feet to address Phillip. Matthew Everingham, seated at the rear, watched with interest. He knew Teague – Cornball Teague as they called him. Teague had been convicted of stealing ninety gallons of cyder and sentenced to seven years with transportation.

"Beggin' y' pardon, sir," Teague commenced, "ken y' be tellin' us 'ow much longer will be the voyage t' New 'olland?"

Phillip stretched out his arm and flattened his hand, an indication for Teague to resume his seat.

"It's a way," he said. "By my reckoning, another six months, maybe more."

There was a general murmur of astonishment amongst the convicts at the length of the voyage yet to come, but Teague was already on his feet again.

"'nd ken y' be tellin' us, sir, 'ow many more ports o' call will there be b'fore we reach New 'olland?"

"That," said Phillip, "is information I am not at liberty to share with you. What I can tell you is that those who display good behaviour and remain compliant to orders will be rewarded in New Holland with privileged positions, perhaps even with their own grants of land. Troublesome prisoners will not be rewarded and will find life in New Holland much more difficult."

As he left the convict quarters, Phillip spoke to the captain of the marines.

"On the whole, they seem like a reasonable bunch," he said, "yet I notice amongst them a number who appeared surly and intractable. Keep a close eye on them."

The fleet sailed from Santa Cruz with the tide on 10th June 1787 and, after clearing the southernmost point of the island of Teneriffe, Matthew heard the bosun's call, "Helm, sou-by-sou-west!"

A week later, the fleet was approaching the Cape de Verde and Phillip, ever anxious to top up the supplies for the fleet, intended to put into the harbour at Praia. On arrival there, however, he found the pathfinder, *HMS Supply,* laying off the harbour entrance and was advised that entering the harbour would be a risky undertaking.

"Hold your helm!" the bosun called, and the fleet sailed on.

Towards the end of June, as the fleet approached the equator, they encountered squalls and storms. Matthew sheltered on deck and watched, as the sailors set spare sails to capture rainwater. The storms had blown the fleet about a hundred miles off course but, by the first week of July, the weather had cleared, and the more reliable south-east-trade-winds were filling their sails. They crossed the line on 15th July and Phillip ordered a course for Rio de Janeiro.

Matthew was on deck when the call of the lookout atop the main mast was heard – "Land-ho off the starboard bow!" Matthew and the other convicts on deck rushed to the starboard rail and peered expectantly at the horizon until land came into sight. It was the coast of South America near São Mateus and four days later, on 6th August, the fleet entered the harbour of Rio de Janeiro. *HMS Sirius* saluted the Portuguese fort with thirteen guns.

"Don't panic, Mobbs," Matthew said jokingly to Samuel Mobbs. "It's just a celebration. We're not declaring war on them."

The other convicts in the vicinity laughed and one of them called, "We'll look after y', Mobbsy."

53

The fleet spent a month at Rio de Janeiro, taking on supplies and making repairs to the sails and the rigging. Supplies taken on board included fresh meat, fresh vegetables and fruit, fresh water and a large shipment of rum. It was during this time that Lieutenant John Shortland came on board *Scarborough* from the flagship *HMS Sirius*. Shortland and several other officers from *Sirius* had been tasked by Phillip with visiting each of the convict transport ships and preparing lists noting each convict's age, previous occupation and family details – details Phillip believed would be useful when the time came to assign convicts to appropriate tasks in New Holland.

On *Scarborough*, Shortland set up a small desk on the deck in the sunshine, and the convicts were called to him one at a time.

"Name?" Shortland asked Matthew when his turn came.

"Matthew Everingham."

Shortland consulted his full list of convicts.

"It says here, Matthew James Everingham," he said. "Is that correct?"

"That's correct."

"And what kind of work did you do in England, before you were convicted?" Shortland asked.

"I was an apprentice clerk to an attorney in London," Matthew replied.

"In the Temple?"

Matthew nodded.

"So, you're educated? You can read and write?"

"Yes, I can," Matthew replied.

"And numbers? Can you manage numbers?"

"I can work out most things," Matthew said, recalling the words of his friend Noah on the hulk *Censor* – "Make yourself useful to them, Matthew."

"How old are you, Everingham?" Shortland asked.

"I'm eighteen, I think," Matthew said. "I'm not rightly sure because I've lost track of the date."

"It's Friday, 14th August 1787," Shortland informed him.

Matthew nodded.

"Yes, eighteen then."

Shortland was making notes in his ledger and, without looking up, he said, "Tell me about your family, Everingham."

When he got no answer, he looked up and asked again.

"Your family, man. What kind of family are you from?"

"The kind that turns their back on a son when he's in need," Matthew said quietly.

Shortland looked at him for some moments before writing in his ledger: "Seems bitter at being abandoned by his family."

"Thank you, Everingham," he said. "I hope things go well for you in New Holland."

Matthew left Shortland at his desk and wandered over to the port rail of the ship to look at the naked Brazilian natives who surrounded the ship in small canoes, attempting to sell vegetables and fruit to those on board. When they realised the convicts had no money with which to buy their fares, some of the natives threw oranges, figs and guavas to the convicts.

It was also while the fleet was at anchor in Rio de Janeiro that all convicts were assembled on deck in irons and guarded by armed marines, whilst gunpowder was again exploded in the convict quarters. It was the first time the convict quarters had been sanitised since leaving Portsmouth.

The fleet sailed from Rio with the tide on Sunday 4th September and Arthur Phillip ordered a course dead south. He was headed to his next port of call at the Cape of Good Hope on the southernmost tip of the African continent but the fleet would sail south until it picked up the Roaring Forties before turning east. The Roaring

Forties are strong winds that blow from west to east at latitudes below forty degrees south, and Phillip knew these winds would carry the fleet across the South Atlantic in good time. After turning east, at forty degrees south, the fleet then crossed from the east coast of South America to the west coast of the African continent, a distance of around three thousand five hundred miles, in less than six weeks. They came to anchor in False Bay near Cape Town on 14th October 1787.

At the Cape, Phillip was determined to take on as many additional stores as possible. This was to be the fleet's last port of call before arriving in New Holland and the final leg of the voyage would take up to three months. As well as provisions for the next three months, Phillip ordered the ships be loaded with provisions that would be useful in establishing a settlement on foreign shores, including two bulls, seven cows, one stallion, three mares, forty-four sheep, thirty-two pigs, four goats and a very large quantity of poultry of every kind.[1]

Lieutenant Daniel Southwell, midshipman on *HMS Sirius*, wrote to his mother from the Cape describing some of the goods and livestock taken on board.

> *"Were you to take a view of our ship below you would be apt to take it for a livery stable of note ... Among the stock are many of the feathered kind, and also plants of various sorts. These all together will take up much room, and the ship is lumber'd. The people, considering the number, are much crowded, for the cattle are to occupy a deck which till now was theirs..."*[2]

Although the decision to load up the ships at the Cape had been a prudent one, it would have the effect of slowing them down. From the outset, even as she left Portsmouth, *HMS Sirius* had been slow and cumbersome, overloaded with passengers, furniture and all manner of supplies for the new settlement. The extra load added at the Cape would make her even slower and more difficult to manoeuvre, especially in the rough seas of the Southern Ocean that lay ahead.

Phillip plotted a course from the Cape of Good Hope that would see the fleet sail south once again to pick up the Roaring Forties before turning east, with intention to cross the Southern Ocean to the south of the continent of New Holland. The course he had set for the fleet called for them to round the south-east corner of Van Diemen's Land, which they believed was part of the New Holland continent, then sail north following the coast, but at least five miles offshore, until they arrived at Botany Bay.

As the fleet sat at anchor in False Bay, on board *HMS Sirius* a discussion was going on between Arthur Phillip and John Hunter, Captain of *Sirius*.

"The larger ships are delaying the smaller and faster ships, John," Phillip said, looking at the chart of the Southern Ocean spread on the table before them.

"That can't be helped," Hunter replied, "and it's going to get worse from here on, with all the extra provisions we've loaded. *Sirius* is going to sail like a pig with this load."

The two men contemplated the chart, sipping on their glasses of rum, before Phillip made a momentous decision.

"I'm going to split the fleet, John," he said.

Hunter looked at him in disbelief.

"I'll transfer to *Supply* and take the smaller and faster ships. I'll take *Scarborough*, *Alexander* and *Friendship*. You'll follow with *Sirius* and the rest of the fleet."

"I don't see the point of that," Hunter replied. "The Southern Ocean can be treacherous, so I hear. I think it'd be safer to stick together."

Phillip took another sip of his rum and considered the matter for several moments before making a firm decision.

"No," he said. "You're a very competent captain, John. I have every confidence in you leading the larger ships to New Holland. If I go ahead with the faster ships, I can get there before you and the convicts can start unloading the supplies and perhaps make a start on constructing facilities for the settlement."

The decision had been made, and Phillip turned to leave the chartroom.

"See you in Botany Bay," he said as the two men shook hands.

The vanguard of the fleet, led by *HMS Supply,* sailed from Cape of Good Hope on 12th November and headed south. Then with the Roaring Forties filling their sails, they turned east to head across the Southern Ocean. For more than two weeks, they made good time in relatively good sailing conditions, although, towards the end of that two week period the seas became noticeably rougher. On 1st December the Roaring Forties suddenly turned into weather approximating the Screaming Sixties, with gale force winds tearing at the sails and the rigging. The ships were battered by waves in excess of twenty feet, sometimes thirty feet. *Supply, Scarborough, Alexander* and *Friendship* set only storm sails and attempted to fight the ocean – there was nothing else to be done. Each oncoming wave struck the ships like a solid and impenetrable wall of water, washing over them and threatening to take them down. Even the crews feared for their lives and those on deck lost sight of the other ships amidst the huge waves and the constant spray of water, making a coming together with another ship a real possibility as they were hit by each oncoming wave.

No convicts were on deck, for the ships had been battened down with all bar crew confined to quarters below deck. Few if any of the convicts had ever been to sea before this voyage and, as the ships battered against the worst conditions of the entire voyage, almost all joined Samuel Mobbs in fearing for their lives. With the ship being battered so mercilessly, Matthew's bunk and several others broke away from their secure positions on the convict deck and were thrown back and forth across a floor awash with urine and vomit.

Matthew held tight to his bunk as it was thrown about, believing *Scarborough* could not survive this storm and that the next wave would finally break the ship, flood into the convict quarters and take them all to a watery grave.

Only Thomas Hylids, the former ships' carpenter, gave voice to any encouragement.

"She'll hold, boys," he called. "If she were going to break, she'd have done so by now."

Finally, on 1st January 1788, as the ships rounded the southernmost point of Van Diemen's Land and limped up the east coast of what they believed to be part of the New Holland continent, the storm abated. The ships were protected from the westerly winds by the land mass of Van Diemen's Land on their windward side. Some days later, the ship's crew were surprised to find themselves crossing the rough seas of what would later be named Bass Strait, separating Van Diemen's Land from the continent, although they still believed that the two were joined at some point further west.

The ships were off a headland on the New Holland continent, later to be named Cape Howe when, on 7th January 1788, Matthew Everingham passed the mid-point of his seven year sentence. He had served three and a half years, a fact of which he was totally oblivious because he had again lost track of the date.

Two weeks later, on the morning of 19th January, *Supply*, *Scarborough*, *Alexander* and *Friendship* sailed into Botany Bay and came to anchor less than a mile off the golden crescent of an attractive, sandy beach. Arthur Phillip stood on the quarter deck of *Supply* scanning the land through his telescope. Beyond the beach, he saw thickly wooded hills giving rise to several wispy columns of smoke telling of other lives for whom this land was not a place of banishment, but home.

Then, as he swept the telescope to the northern end of the beach, he observed a large group of men, perhaps fifty in number. The men were black and naked and stood brandishing spears and other bent sticks threateningly towards the ships. Through the telescope Phillip could tell the black men were shouting but, of course, he could not hear them and would not have been able to understand their language even if he had heard them. The message they were sending, however, was patently obvious.

"You are not welcome here!"
"This is our land! Go away!"

Standing on the deck of *Scarborough*, Matthew Everingham was also looking at those black men, though of course he could not see them as clearly as Phillip. Nonetheless, it was evident to him too that the black men were displeased with their arrival. That evening, Matthew sat below deck with some of his fellow convicts, chatting about their arrival in a new land.

"The natives don't seem so happy to see us," he said. "Could be we'll have trouble with them. How much trouble, I suppose, depends on how many of them there are."

"Savages," one of the men in the group said. "They're not natives, they're bloody savages. Did y' see they wasn't even wearin' no clothes. A few musket shots in the gut'll put 'em in their place."

It was Charlie Peat who had spoken. Charlie occupied the bunk next to Matthew's and Matthew distrusted and disliked him intensely.

Charles Peat was a man with a chequered past. First convicted of highway robbery in the Old Bailey in 1781, he was sentenced to death,[3] but his sentence was commuted, on condition of service in the Royal Navy. Two days later, he joined *HMS Prince Edward* as an ordinary seaman, but later deserted. In April 1783, he was arrested and convicted of having broken the condition of His Majesty's pardon and was sentenced to seven years with transportation.[4] He was then transferred to a hulk, as a prisoner awaiting transportation. In 1784 he again appeared in the Old Bailey, this time indicted for "feloniously returning from transportation, and being found at large in this kingdom without any lawful cause before the expiration of the term of seven years."[5] It seems he had somehow escaped from the hulk. Given his repeated appearances before the courts, Peat had escaped this indictment with a remarkably lenient sentence – seven years with transportation to New Holland.

Matthew eyed Peat purposely but said nothing. Peat, he decided, could certainly be trouble when they got ashore – a man best avoided.

As Matthew sat chatting with others in the convict quarters on *Scarborough*, the native men were sitting around their campfire, discussing the new arrivals. They remembered their fathers telling them of a large ship seemingly carried below large billowing white clouds and bringing white skinned foreigners who had visited their shores almost twenty years earlier. Those men had come ashore, left a strange piece of red, white and blue fabric of some kind blowing in the wind atop a tall pole and then, after a short sojourn, had left.

"Our fathers drove them off," said the man who appeared to be the leader of their tribe. "We'll do the same. No foreigners will be allowed to invade our land."

Yet, this time it would be different. This time, no amount of shouting and threatening with spears would work. This time, the men in their tall ships carried below the white billowing clouds were no interlopers. This time, they had come to stay.

1. Chisholm, Alec H. (ed.), *The Australian Encyclopaedia*, Vol. 4, p. 72, "First Fleet", Halstead Press, Sydney, 1963.
2. Horton, Allan (1967). *Southwell, Daniel (1764–1797)*. Australian Dictionary of Biography, National Centre of Biography, Australian National University.
3. *Old Bailey Proceedings Online* (www.oldbaileyonline.org, version 8.0, 01 June 2022), December 1781 (s17811205-1).
4. *Old Bailey Proceedings Online* (www.oldbaileyonline.org, version 8.0, 01 June 2022), July 1784, trial of CHARLES PEAT (t17840707-6).
5. https://peopleaustralia.anu.edu.au/biography/peat-charles-30840 (accessed June 2022)

5

On 21st January 1788, just two days after his arrival, Phillip was surprised to see the rest of the fleet led by *HMS Sirius* laying off the entrance to Botany Bay. They had sailed behind the low pressure front that had so battered the ships led by Phillip on *HMS Supply* and, with fair winds and calmer seas, they had actually made better time than Phillip and the vanguard of the fleet.

"Have you been ashore?" John Hunter asked as he and Phillip sat drinking tea in *Supply's* chart room.

"I have," Phillip replied, shaking his head and conveying a general sense of disappointment. "I went ashore yesterday – took a large contingent of marines because the natives seemed hostile. Some of the natives had their faces and bodies painted with some type of white paint or pigment, perhaps designed to make them appear more aggressive. As for the land, it's not good, John."

Phillip did not mention that he had also taken ashore a small number of convicts, nor did he mention, because he didn't know, that when the landing party had returned to the ships, they had done so with one less convict. Francis Carthy had made good on his promise to escape the moment his feet hit dry land. He was never seen or heard of again.

Hunter sipped his tea and waited for Phillip to continue.

"We found no fresh water, John. Cook, in his journal says there is a freshwater stream, and there must be for, of course, the natives would need it, but we couldn't find it. The area is a marshland and the dry soil, where it can be found, is little more than sand. What possessed Cook to declare it a suitable place for the establishment of a colony is beyond me."

"The impression I got from Cook's journals," Hunter replied, "is that he was more interested in the discoveries of Joseph Banks who was on board."

"Yes, *Sir* Joseph Banks now," said Phillip emphasising the word "Sir". "He's done very well for himself and apparently he's done great botanical work but I don't think that warrants Cook naming this place Botany Bay. You'd think the first place discovered in a new land might be named after the king – George's Bay, perhaps, but no, he called it Botany Bay."

The two men sat in silence for some time, each reflecting on their own disparaging thoughts of Captain James Cook.

"Well, we can't stay here," Phillip eventually said. "Tomorrow I'll take a longboat and a couple of cutters along the coast and look for a more suitable location."

"North or south?" Hunter asked.

Phillip walked over to the chart table, Hunter following, and the two studied the chart for several minutes.

"North, I think, John," Phillip finally said. "We've seen the coast south of here, albeit from a distance. I think we'll search north."

Then, almost as an afterthought he summoned the ship's First Mate.

"Mate!" he called. "Our copy of Captain Cook's journals, if you please."

He thumbed through the journals and, finding the place he sought, he read from it.

> *At noon we were by observation in the Latitude of 33degrees-50minutes about 2 or 3 miles from the land and abreast of a Bay or Harbour wherein there appeared to be safe anchorage which I called Port Jackson.*[1]

He bent over the chart table and pointed to a location on the chart about twenty miles north of Botany Bay.

"This is the place Cook named Port Jackson," he said. "Not that any place Cook makes note of inspires confidence. I mean, the man didn't even enter it to take a look, but I think that's where I'll start."

The next morning, 22nd January 1788, standing on the deck of Scarborough, Matthew Everingham and Thomas Hylids observed a longboat and two cutters loaded with marines making their way out of the bay towards the open ocean. Matthew liked Thomas and the two had become close friends during the voyage.

"Where do you reckon they're off to, Tom?" Matthew asked.

"Well, they're not abandoning us, that's f' sure," his friend replied. "They're not gonna get far in those small boats."

"I think that was Commodore Phillip in the longboat," Matthew said. "You remember when he came on *Scarborough* during the voyage? I'm pretty sure it was him."

The longboat and the cutters made their way north, staying as close to shore as they could without risking the disaster of being smashed against the rocky coast. They passed heavily wooded headlands, several crescent shaped beaches of golden sand and places where the ocean waves crashed against cliffs as they had done for millions of years. Beyond one very long crescent beach, the edge of the continent became a continuous line of sandstone cliffs which, eventually, gave way to a broad inlet with yet more sandstone cliffs on the northern side of the inlet.

"This is the place," Phillip declared. "The place Cook called Port Jackson. Let's take a look."

Passing through the harbour entrance in those small boats was a treacherous undertaking, though Phillip knew the bigger ships would handle it with ease. Both the north head and the south head were formed of high sandstone cliffs guarding an entrance the width of which Phillip estimated to be less than two miles. The party fought their way through rough seas that threatened to capsize their small boats between the two headlands only to be confronted by a third headland dead ahead. Phillip named it Middle Head.

At Middle Head the ocean divided into a north channel and a south channel. The south channel being wider, Phillip decided to take that course and almost immediately the waters became calm and easily navigated.

The longboat and the cutters pulled into a small beach just inside the southern headland and set up camp there for the night. The party slept on the beach and Phillip named it Camp Cove.

The next morning, Phillip was keen to make an early start and was delighted to find the turquoise waters of the harbour widening as he went. On both the north and the south shores of the harbour, heavily wooded hills came down to the water's edge, in places broken by small sandy beaches. The boats passed a small island, not much more than a rocky outcrop, and there they found a cove which Phillip believed would be deep enough to accommodate the ships of the fleet. And, best of all, flowing into that cove was a broad stream. Phillip ordered the boats to be run up onto the beach, then stepped ashore.

As he and the marines stepped ashore, he noticed a small group of native men, naked and carrying spears, standing where the sandy beach met the wooded hills. They did not appear hostile, but they were not especially welcoming either. When Phillip and some marines approached them, they quickly disappeared into the bushland.

Phillip was fixated on the stream, his primary purpose in coming ashore being to find out whether it was fresh water. He approached the stream, knelt in the sand and scooped up a handful of water which he put to his mouth. Then he smiled – the water was cool and fresh.

Phillip had seen enough. He returned to the longboat and ordered the boats to return to Botany Bay. They stopped again at Camp Cove and after spending the night there they made their way out through the heads of the harbour and then headed south, towards Botany Bay, arriving late on the afternoon of 24th January 1788. Arriving at Botany Bay, Phillip ordered the longboat to put him aboard *HMS Supply*, and to fetch Captain John Hunter from *HMS Sirius*.

"Well?" asked John Hunter when he joined Phillip in the chart room of *Supply*. "Did you find a suitable location?"

Phillip was beaming.

"John," he said, "Cook discovered the finest harbour in the world, and he didn't even take time to explore it."

"Is it big enough for the fleet?" Hunter asked.

"Big enough for a thousand ships, John."

"And fresh water?"

"The freshest and purest water I ever tasted," Phillip declared. "A good stream, probably fed by freshwater springs, I imagine. There's also a river flowing into the western extremity of the harbour. We tested it and found it was salt water, but further upstream the water will be fresh. And I imagine the waters of the harbour will be teeming with fish."

"So, we are moving to Port Jackson?"

"We are, indeed, John," Phillip confirmed. "But you'll tarry a while here at Botany Bay with *Sirius* and with your part of the fleet. There are two French ships standing offshore but the weather is building and I doubt they'll attempt to enter the bay for a day or two. If they put in here, you'll remind them that Cook claimed this land for the British king in 1770, and that we have established a settlement in Port Jackson."

Hunter raised an eyebrow.

"Is there a settlement in Port Jackson?" he asked.

"There will be by the time you speak to them, John," Phillip replied, with a smile. "In any event, the legal basis for British claim to this territory dates back to 1770 when Cook laid claim to the land in the name of the British king."

"So, am I to turn the French away" asked Hunter, "refuse them anchorage here?"

"John, whenever did you become so inhospitable?" Phillip asked, in jest. "The French are our neighbours, not our enemies, at least not right now though they often are. No, they should be afforded every assistance within your powers, and are to be informed that they are welcome visitors in British territory. After that has been established you can bring *Sirius* and the rest of the fleet to Port Jackson. I'll take *Supply*, *Scarborough*, *Alexander* and *Friendship* tomorrow morning. I expect I'll see you in Port Jackson within a few days."

That night, Arthur Phillip wrote in his journal.

> *We had the satisfaction of finding the finest harbour in the world, in which a thousand sail of the line may ride in the most perfect security.*[2]

Eat your heart out, Cook, he thought to himself as he put down his quill then, remembering that James Cook had been killed by natives in Hawaii in February 1779, he added, a little more respectfully, *Rest in Peace*. He closed the lid on his inkpot, wiped the ink from his hands and reached for a well-earned glass of rum.

Standing by the rail on *Scarborough*'s deck as she made her way out of Botany Bay, headed for Port Jackson on 26th January 1788, Matthew Everingham watched as two ships flying the French flag passed by off the starboard bow, headed in the opposite direction – into Botany Bay.

"Looks like we beat the French here by a couple of days," he commented to those around him.

The two French ships were *La Boussole* and *La'Astrolabe*, under the command of Jean-François La Pérouse and they carried a total of 225 French crew, officers and scientists. The French government, in 1783, acting under instructions from King Louis XVI himself, had resolved to send an expedition into the Pacific to complete what they viewed as the unfinished work of Captain James Cook. They had been ordered to explore the passages in the Bering Sea, which remained a mystery to European naval forces. On arrival at Botany Bay, they established a base camp on the northern shore of the bay and, after John Hunter had delivered Arthur Phillip's message to La Pérouse, they maintained cordial relations until Hunter and the ships under his command left Botany Bay, headed for Port Jackson, on 28th January. The two French ships stayed in Botany Bay for six weeks and were observed sailing past the heads and the entrance to Port Jackson on 10th March 1788, headed north. They were never seen nor heard from again. When the disappearance of La Pérouse and his ships became known in France, the French government despatched another expedition to find them, but they searched in vain.

On the morning of Saturday, 26th January 1788, the part of the First Fleet commanded by Phillip on *HMS Supply* sailed into Port Jackson. *Scarborough* was the second ship into the harbour, followed by *Alexander* and *Friendship*.

Matthew Everingham was no explorer, nor a sailor, but he recognised a beautiful sight of nature when he saw it, and as he stood by the rail on the deck of *Scarborough* with his friend Thomas Hylids he knew he had never seen such an inspiring seascape. The two spoke very little as they took in their first real vista of the land that would be their home for the rest of their lives. The turquoise water glittered as the sunshine reflected off the small wavelets while seagulls swirled and screeched overhead. Gentle waves lapped at the shore – in places on sandy beaches and yet at other times on rocky headlands where the wooded hills came right down to the water's edge. On the ocean side of one small bay, a colony of large fur seals sat on rocks sunning themselves in the warm January sunshine.

Matthew glanced ahead at *Supply*, the Red Ensign flag, the "Red Duster" as some called it, flying on her stern and the harbour extending before her seemingly without end. Beyond both the north shore and the south shore of the harbour heavily wooded hills set a background of a blueish-grey hue and, here and there, those thin columns of smoke from what Matthew knew were the fires of native camps.

As *Scarborough* sliced through the water she passed by a small crescent beach and Matthew's attention was drawn to several one-man canoes, just off the beach. The canoes were made of bark and in each canoe sat a native man. The natives had seemingly been fishing with spears, not with line and hook, but they had stopped fishing to gaze in awe and disbelief as the huge ships passed by, almost like enormous pelicans gliding over the water beneath large white wings. Matthew waved to them, but they did not wave back, not in anger nor as in a gesture of a friendly welcome – they just sat in their canoes and watched the tall ships pass by, sometimes pointing to the ships as though their friends in the other canoes may somehow have missed them. Matthew tried waving to them again but still the natives did not wave back. He watched them until *Scarborough* had passed them by, and he could see them no longer.

An hour and a half into the harbour, the bosun, standing on the quarter deck began relaying the captain's orders.

"Man the topsail," he shouted.

Matthew watched as the sailors on *Scarborough* climbed the rigging and spread out high above, along the ship's yards.

"Clear away the topsail sheets. Clew up!"

The sails were coming down as the bosun called again.

"Settle away the topsail halyards!"

"Square away"

The deck of *Scarborough* had become a hive of industry with sailors rushing to their assigned tasks in a well drilled manner – never getting in each other's way.

"Let go the anchor!" called the bosun.

Sailors hammered out the chock-pins that held the capstan in place and the chains rattled as the large anchor fell to the bottom.

Thomas Hylids looked at Matthew and spoke the words that signified the end of an eight-and-a-half-month voyage.

"Mate," he said, "I reckon this is it. I reckon this is home for us now."

Mid-afternoon the convicts were again assembled in their quarters below deck and an officer of the marines came to address them.

"Some of you'll be going ashore tomorrow morning," he told them. "Don't think about running away because there's nowhere to run to, but you need to know what to expect when you get on shore."

The convicts waited in silence for him to continue.

"You'll erect tents for your own accommodation and for the accommodation of the women convicts who will arrive with the rest of the fleet. The women's tents will be separated from yours and guarded by marines to keep you from …" he paused, searching for the right word before continuing, "molesting them."

Some of the convicts laughed in derision at his words, already planning to become well acquainted with the women convicts.

"The Governor and other official passengers will stay on board *Supply* but will move to tents within a week or so. You will be put to work, firstly unloading stores and livestock from the other ships, then felling trees and making a clearing on the shore. Your main task over coming weeks and months will be to build stores for the supplies and houses for the officials and the marines. Eventually you will build huts for yourselves and move out of the tents. We're fortunate that here in the southern hemisphere it's summer, so life in the tents should be quite pleasant."

Matthew was, perhaps, one of the few convicts who had made mental note of the subtle difference – houses for the officials, huts for the convicts. No mention had been made regarding the building of a prison.

Having spent his allocated two hours on deck as the ships had entered the harbour that morning, Matthew found himself below deck after the marine officer had left, yet he was anxious to get back on deck. Charlie Peat agreed to let Matthew take his place on deck in the afternoon session.

"We're not movin' anyway," Peat said. "There'll be nothin' t' see 'ere that we're not gonna git thoroughly sick of from now on."

Peat was wrong, for the afternoon session would include the most historic moment in the history of the new colony. Matthew emerged onto deck to find that a bare flagpole had been erected on the shore, apparently brought from England for this purpose and, as he watched, five longboats cast off from *HMS Supply* and were rowed towards the shore. Standing in the bow of the leading longboat was the Commodore of the Fleet, Arthur Phillip in full regalia. He made an imposing sight dressed in his formal, black Royal Navy coat over his white waistcoat. The coat was adorned with gold buttons, gold embroidered buttonholes, gold braiding around the raised collar and gold, tasselled epaulettes on his shoulders. He wore his Captain's two pointed hat, again trimmed with gold braiding and his sword was slung from a gold sash at his waist. Matthew had never seen an officer of the Crown so elaborately dressed.

Phillip's longboat was pulled up onto the sandy beach enabling him to step ashore without getting wet, though the other longboats were tethered as soon as their keels hit the sand.

Matthew watched the landing party approach the flagpole and arrange themselves before it with twenty marines lined up in two ranks to the side of the flagpole. A group of about twenty natives stood some distance off, watching the strange ceremony unfolding on their shores.

"Peat is missing out on a moment of history here," Matthew said to the convict standing alongside him at the rail of *Scarborough*, "not that he's the type of man to care about history, I suppose."

"Peat's a brute," the other convict replied. "He cares only about himself. I hope I don't have to share a tent with him when we finally get ashore."

As the convicts watched from the deck of *Scarborough*, the British flag was raised to the top of the flagpole and all officers on shore saluted the flag. It then appeared to Matthew that Arthur Phillip was making a speech though, from *Scarborough*, he could not make out what was being said. Had he been able to hear Phillip's speech he would have heard Phillip declaring the foundation of the Colony of New South Wales.

"This land," Phillip said, "was first sighted by Captain James Cook, Royal Navy, in 1770, and claimed in the name of His Majesty King George the Third. Cook called this land New South Wales and it forms part of the continent of New Holland, the extent of which remains unknown. Today, the twenty-sixth day of January in the year of our Lord 1788, I, Arthur Phillip, declare the foundation of the Colony of New South Wales and as Governor of the Colony I name this settlement Sydney Cove. God save the King!"

All the officials gathered around the flagpole raised their hats to arm's length three times as they gave three hearty cheers to the king – cheers that were clearly heard from the deck of *Scarborough*, and the marines then fired their muskets into the air sending the watching natives scampering back into the woods.

The invasion had begun.

The official ceremony over, the landing party spent a short time onshore looking at the surrounding site with Phillip waving his arms around in what Matthew thought was probably an indication of the area to be cleared for the new settlement. After a half hour, most of the landing party boarded the longboats and were returned to *Supply*, leaving behind a small contingent of marines to guard the flagpole – it wouldn't do to have the natives steal the king's flag.

The new colony had been established and Matthew Everingham had been witness to it, albeit from a distance. Had Matthew heard the naming of the settlement as Sydney Cove, he may well have wondered at the significance of the name. Arthur Phillip had named Sydney Cove after an English politician, Thomas Townshend, the British Home Secretary, and the 1st Viscount Sydney, for it was Townshend who had developed the plan to establish a penal settlement at Botany Bay.

1. Edwards, P. (ed) *Journals of Captain Cook*, Penguin Classics, London, 1999, p.130
2. Britannica, The Editors of Encyclopaedia. *Port Jackson.* Encyclopedia Britannica, https://www.britannica.com/place/Port-Jackson. (Accessed 1 June 2022).

6

It took ten days for all convicts to be brought ashore. At first, they had to pitch their tents in the small sandy space between the shore and the trees. Then they set about felling the trees to create a clearing for the settlement. Livestock was brought ashore and tethered, for there were no fences, and some convicts were assigned to constantly walk the livestock to drink from the stream. Whilst most were engaged in felling the trees, two teams of convicts were tasked with building two large stores so the load of provisions brought from England and procured at the Cape could be unloaded. Even when the stores were finished, the unloading process would take several weeks. Arthur Phillip was frustrated with the slowness of getting the provisions ashore because he was under instructions from the Home Office to complete the task as quickly as possible and release the transport ships which remained under contract until they could sail from Port Jackson. To the Home Office, time was money.

On 6th May 1788, *Charlotte*, *Lady Penrhyn* and *Scarborough* left Port Jackson and set sail for Canton, China, where they would load tea for the English market.

Matthew had mixed feelings as he stood on the shore, watching *Scarborough* swing onto the breeze and sail towards the heads of Port Jackson. The ship had been his home for more than eight months and, although she held a few memories of harsh experiences, all-in-all that time had been relatively enjoyable – certainly more enjoyable than his incarceration in Newgate prison and on the hulk at Woolwich. He experienced a certain feeling of loss as he thought about what he considered to be "his" ship sailing away and leaving him on a foreign shore. It was as if *Scarborough* was his last link with England and, although she would make a number of other voyages to Sydney Cove, Matthew would never see her again.

.It was not until mid-July that *Borrowdale*, *Alexander*, *Friendship* and *Prince of Wales* would set sail and return to England via Cape Horn. With *Prince of Wales*, Arthur Phillip despatched a message to the Home Office declaring that further supplies were urgently needed, if the colony was to survive. Failing that, he said, a second fleet might arrive and find only graves.

Matthew Everingham stood on the shore at Sydney Cove in the early morning and watched *Prince of Wales*, the last transport to leave.

We're really on our own now, he thought to himself, as he prepared to leave for his assigned place of labour. He had worked for six months as part of a gang digging trenches alongside the stream, in an attempt to trap and save rainwater runoff. The stream itself seemed to rise in marshy ground about a mile inland from the point where it flowed into the harbour at Sydney Cove. From its source, the stream dropped about thirty feet through a series of small, picturesque waterfalls, before reaching the harbour's edge. Later, the trenches alongside the stream would become storage tanks, giving rise to the stream being named Tank Stream.

By the end of July 1788, Surveyor General John White was attempting to bring some measure of order to the layout of the settlement, and the stream neatly divided the settlement into two sections. The eastern side of the stream was allocated for official residences and for government and administrative functionaries, whilst the convicts lived on the western side of the stream. Two rudimentary roads, nothing more than dirt tracks, had been pushed northwards from the shore, one on the east of the stream named Pitt Street, in honour of the English Prime Minister, William Pitt the Younger, and one to the west of the stream named George Street, in honour of the king. Near the point where the stream had its origins, a side street off Pitt Street was appropriately named Spring Street.

"Everingham! Matthew Everingham!" a voice called.

Knee-deep in water, Matthew looked up from where he was digging a trench by the edge of the stream to see an officer of the marines standing on the other side of the stream calling him.

"I'm Everingham," he said, raising his hand and climbing out of the trench.

"You told the registrar on the voyage out here that you can read and write. Is that the truth?" the officer asked.

Matthew nodded. "It is."

"You're to come with me. You've been reassigned."

Matthew waded across the stream and followed the officer to a small stone building with a shingled roof on the eastern side of the stream.

"What's that sign say?" the officer asked, pointing to a small hand-painted sign alongside the door.

"It says 'Commissary of Labour'," Matthew replied, causing the officer to chuckle.

"I guess you really can read," he said. "You're to wait here."

Matthew sat dozing in the winter sunshine – the days were cool, yet with a hint of warm spring weather to come. Then he woke with a start and jumped to his feet when he heard his name called.

"Everingham?" the man asked.

"Yes, sir."

"I am Zachariah Clarke, the Assistant Commissary of Labour. From now on you'll be working with me, assisting me in the allocation of convict assignments and overseeing their work."

Matthew considered his changed circumstances. On the one hand, being an assistant to an assistant would certainly be easier than standing in the stream and digging trenches. At the same time, he wondered whether the other convicts might resent him being in an administrative role over them. Yet he had no option – he would have to try to manage as best he could. As it turned out, he spent much of his time in the Labour Office, often transcribing Clarke's badly written notes into a ledger that listed all the convicts, their trades if, they had one, and the place of their current work assignment. Periodically, he would be sent to visit those worksites, to ensure those allocated to work projects were there and getting on with the tasks. On occasions, Clarke would instruct him to refer insolent or indolent convicts to the captain of the marines for disciplinary action. This was an aspect of his work he disliked immensely and he attempted to do it at arms-length, to mask his involvement from his fellow convicts.

In August, as the days were becoming longer and beginning to warm, Zachariah Clarke took Matthew outside and pointed to a high rocky headland about five hundred yards west of the settlement at Sydney Cove.

"That's called Dawes Point," he said. "There's a Mr Dawes living up there, something of an odd-ball I gather. I've received a request from him, a bit cryptic, but something about a hole in his roof."

"He has a hole in his roof?" Matthew asked.

"From what I understand, he *wants* a hole in his roof. You'd best go and talk to him, find out what it's all about."

The well-worn path to Dawes' Point led from the western extremity of the convicts' encampment through low-lying sandy ground with clumps of blue-grey saltbush. Where the path began to rise, small trees became dominant, their trunks and branches twisted as if in agony and their small leaves, hard won from the harsh environment, giving off the same scent as the larger trees that had been felled – eucalyptus. Matthew reached out to tear a small piece of white bark from one of the trees and studied it as he walked, thinking it seemed almost like paper. As he climbed higher, the land and the trees gave way to a large, flat rock – and a breathtaking sight that caused him to gasp in astonishment. The rock was a natural viewing platform over the settlement of Sydney Cove and the grand, sparkling vista of the harbour, with *HMS Sirius* at anchor below him like a small ship in a panoramic painting by a master artist. Matthew knew he should be getting on to his objective at the top of Dawes' Point, yet his feet were rooted to the rock and his eyes transfixed by the magnificence of the harbour spread before him. He sat on the rock for half an hour taking in every small feature of the harbour and realising how blessed he was, for very few white men, he knew, had seen this priceless view. Finally, he tore himself away and continued climbing through yet more of the spindly paperbark trees, until he came to a small stone house with a shingled roof, atop the gnarled headland.

"Mr Dawes!" he called.

Immediately an unshaven man emerged from the house, wearing a grey flannel shirt, grey trousers and braces.

"Mr Dawes?" Matthew asked.

"Lieutenant Dawes to the likes of you!" Dawes snapped.

"I'm sorry, sir. Not seeing you in uniform I didn't recognise you as an officer. I'm here to talk to you about the work you require on your roof."

Without a word, Dawes turned back into the house, motioning for Matthew to follow. They sat at a small table and Dawes took out a few sheets of paper and a pencil.

"I'm the settlement's resident astronomer," he said, without asking Matthew's name. "Do you know what an astronomer is?"

"Yes, of course, sir," Matthew replied, immediately regretting the words "of course". "You study the stars."

Dawes nodded. "Yes, and the planets. It's why I choose to live on this remote headland, though I must say I rather enjoy it up here by myself."

"The view is magnificent, sir," Matthew said.

"The view? What view?"

"Why, the view of the harbour, of course," Matthew replied, and again thinking, *I must get out of the habit of saying "of course" with this man.*

"The harbour?" Dawes asked. "I suppose so. I haven't noticed it."

Matthew could not believe what he was hearing but managed to keep his thoughts to himself.

"So, the roof, sir?"

Dawes unfolded a piece of paper and spread it on the table. He had sketched an elaborate, domed observatory, with a vertical incision on one side, almost from top to bottom.

"And it needs to move *of course*," he said pointedly.

"Move, sir?" Matthew asked.

"Rotate, man. Rotate!" Dawes responded, his voice rising and his fingers tracing circles in the air under Matthew's nose. "How else am I expected to track the stars across the evening sky?"

"Oh, I see, sir. Of course," Matthew said, this time deliberately adding the offensive words. "I'll see to it, Lieutenant. I'll send a carpenter to work on it for you." And with that, he picked up the sketch and retreated, glad to be getting away from the idiosyncratic Lieutenant Dawes.

"I think I know just the man for the job," Matthew said, as he and Zachariah Clarke stood looking over Dawes' sketch. "Thomas Hylids is by all accounts a good carpenter. I knew him on *Scarborough*."

"Hmm," Clarke said, consulting his register. "No, you can't have Hylids, I'm afraid. The governor has ordered the construction of two packet boats so the river flowing into the western end of the harbour can be explored. Hylids is a ships' carpenter, so he's leading a team working on that task. Construction of the packets is a priority – certainly a greater priority than a hole in a roof."

"I think it'll be a complex job, sir," Matthew retorted, still hoping his friend Thomas Hylids could be released for the job. "It's to be an observatory, not just a hole in the roof."

"No, you can't have Hylids. That's definite," Zachariah Clarke said firmly.

"Well, we have other carpenters, don't we?" Matthew said, conceding defeat on this issue.

"I'm sure we do," Zachariah Clarke replied, running his finger down the list of names on his convict register.

"Yes, here we are. Lucas. Nathaniel Lucas. He was on *Scarborough* with you. You remember him?

"I think so," Matthew replied, "though I didn't know he was a carpenter. Thick set man with ginger hair and a ginger beard?"

"I've no idea what he looks like, but he's a carpenter," Clarke replied. "He's working on house construction at the moment. I'll send for him."

Nathaniel Lucas had been convicted at the Old Bailey of having stolen clothing from his neighbour in Red

Lion Street, Holborn, London, and sentenced to seven years imprisonment with transportation. He introduced himself as Nat and, when Matthew explained what was needed, and why, Lucas looked at him sceptically.

"Takes all kinds, I suppose," he said.

"But it can be done?" Matthew asked.

"Oh, yes, it can be done," Lucas said, after studying Dawes' sketch. "Almost anything can be done. Mind you, it won't be a nice round dome like that," he said, pointing at the sketch. "It'll likely be more angular. After all, it's not St Paul's."

"But it'll rotate?" Matthew asked.

"It'll rotate," Lucas assured him. "Your Mr Dawes will be able to follow his stars."

"I suggest you don't call him Mr Dawes," Matthew said. "He insists on being called Lieutenant."

Lucas rolled his eyes sideways and looked quizzically at Matthew.

"He's a bit of an odd-ball," Matthew said, using the words of Zachariah Clarke. "People who know him would say he's, what's the word… socially inept."

"I don't need him to be sociable," Lucas said, "as long as he stays out of my way while I'm building his bloody observatory. I'll keep you informed on progress."

And, with that, he picked up the sketch and walked off.

Matthew continued his duties as assistant to the Assistant Commissary of Labour, updating the register of convicts within the settlement, assigning them to different works projects and visiting the various work sites. Frequently, the convict labourers raised complaints with him, some frivolous, yet some also worthy of attention, and even some which led to better work outcomes. Many of the complaints were about food, for supplies were short and the colony was existing on half-rations. The Governor decreed that everyone, whether convicts, soldiers or officials, including himself, would be provided with the same rations until such time as the situation improved. Furthermore, the governor's decree stated, any person found attempting to steal food from the colony stores during this time of shortage would be shot.

It was not only food that was in short supply. The supply of building materials had slowed too – stone took time to be quarried and transferred to building sites, especially by hungry men, and the hardwood of the eucalyptus trees was difficult, to work with, taking a toll on saws, axes, and other tools.

"I don't know how we're going to attach shingles to the roof of the new hospital building," Clarke lamented. "The chief builder on the project doesn't want to resort to a bark roof, but we've no nails."

The new hospital building was almost complete. Made of wood, it was almost ninety feet long and thirty feet wide, with a dispensary, a hospital ward for troops and officials and another for convicts. The timber roof frame was in place, but the builders were asking for nails to fix the sheoak shingles.

"I'm going to discuss the problem with a friend of mine," Matthew said. "He may have a solution."

"Pegs," said Thomas Hylids, as soon as Matthew explained the problem to him. "Sharpened pegs made from the local hardwood. It's plenty hard enough to fix sheoak shingles to the roof frame."

When Matthew put the suggestion to Clarke, he ensured that Hylids got the credit for the suggestion.

"Yes, Hylids," Clarke said. "The boat builder. I remember your saying he was a friend of yours. A very helpful suggestion."

"I'm thinking we could have the pegs cut by a team of women convicts." Matthew suggested.

Clarke promptly agreed to this suggestion and, before long, the new hospital had a fine roof.

Three weeks after he had commenced work on Lieutenant Dawes' observatory, Nat Lucas reported to Matthew that the job was complete.

"Any problems?" Matthew asked.

"Not really," Lucas replied. "I used two layers of canvas welded together over the frame with a layer of shipbuilding pitch between them. Hardest part was getting the pitch. Ask for pitch around here and they think you're going to build a canoe and paddle to China."

It was not said in jest. Some convicts believed China was just over the horizon and that escape to that country would be easy.

When Matthew told Clarke the job at Dawes Point had been completed, he was met with a response he would much preferred not to have heard.

"Well, you'd better get yourself up to Dawes Point and make sure the Lieutenant is satisfied with the job."

Matthew's mouth dropped open in dismay.

"Is that really necessary, sir?" he asked.

"Well, you don't think I'm going up there, do you?" Clarke said with a wry smile. "Give him my regards."

This time, on his way to Dawes Point, Matthew stayed an hour on the rock platform, enjoying the panorama of the harbour whilst at the same time deliberately delaying his meeting with the very peculiar Lieutenant.

As he finally approached Dawes' house, he was surprised to see two naked, young native women exiting the house. He passed them only a few yards from the open door and called out, "Lieutenant!"

When he was called into the house, he said nothing about the naked native women who had just exited, but he was uneasy and Dawes could see what he was thinking.

"Get your mind out of the gutter, Everingham," he said. "Those women are helping me with my language studies."

"Oh, I see, sir. Of course."

"And for God's sake, cut out the 'of course' every time you speak to me."

Matthew decided that the safest course of action at that juncture was just to nod.

"Not that I need to explain myself to you or to make any excuses, mind you, but language study is my second passion. Take a look at this lexicon I've been compiling," Dawes said, passing a notebook to Matthew. "You know what a lexicon is, Everingham?"

"Yes, sir," Matthew said, biting his tongue before he could add "of course", though he wanted to. "A lexicon is a list of words with definitions, like a dictionary," he added while taking a seat at the table to better examine the notebook.

Dawes eyed him a little more appreciatively and nodded while Matthew sat down at the table and opened the notebook. On the first page of the notebook, he saw various foreign words in Dawes' neat handwriting.

Gardigal
Wangal
Cammeraygal
Burramattagal
Bidjigal

| *Warrane* | Sydney Cove |
| *Parramatta* | the place of eels |

Mathew looked up at Dawes, waiting for an explanation.

"Those first five words are the names of the tribal groups amongst the natives," he said. "The Gardigal are the people who live around Sydney Cove or at least they did before we arrived. The Wangal live beyond the next cove, to the east. The Cammeraygal live across the water, on the north shore of the harbour. The Burramattagal and the Bidjigal live upstream near the head of the river where we have just established a new sub-settlement. The natives call that place Parramatta. It means 'the place of eels'. I've not been there but apparently the natives catch many eels in the river."

"All those tribal groups end with the suffix *'gal'*," Matthew said.

Dawes raised his eyebrow, surprised at Matthew's intuition and at his use of the word "suffix".

"Yes," he said. "I suspect that the suffix *'gal'* means people or tribe, or perhaps even nation."

If Lieutenant Dawes was slowly beginning to reappraise the intellect of this young convict seated at his table, Matthew was doing the same in respect to Dawes.

"And Warrane?" Matthew said, pointing to the word. "That's what they call Sydney Cove?"

Dawes nodded and waved his hand over the book, indicating that Matthew should turn the page. Matthew did so and found an extensive list of words – foreign words on the left, English words on the right. The notebook was a little untidy where Dawes had crossed out entries, changed the phonetic spelling of the native words or altered the English meanings. In other places, in an attempt to maintain alphabetical listing, he had tried to squeeze new entries in between the lines.

badu	|	water
barawul	|	far away
baruwa	|	close/near
birrong	|	star(s)
dura	|	thirsty or dry
gulah	|	angry

The list continued for many pages. Matthew flipped through to the last page.

walu	|	go/going/gone

Matthew pointed at '*walu*' and looked up at Dawes.

"Verbs aren't conjugated?" he asked.

"Oh, my!" Dawes exclaimed. "Everingham, you are a well-educated young man. No, verbs are not conjugated because the language appears to have no tense. I may be wrong, and there may be errors in the lexicon. It is a work in progress, but that is my thinking at this point in time."

Matthew rose from the table and prepared to leave – he had already been there longer than intended and it was getting late.

"May I make a suggestion, sir?" he asked.

Dawes eyed him silently and nodded.

"If you were to keep the words on a collection of cards, rather than in the notebook, it would be easier to keep things in alphabetical order as new words are added," Matthew said, "and you could make changes or notations as you learned more about the individual words. You could even keep two sets of cards, one arranged alphabetically based on the English words and the other arranged on the alphabetical order of the native words."

"An excellent suggestion, Matthew," Dawes said – the first time he had ever addressed Matthew by his Christian name.

"I've been trying to suggest to Mr Clarke that he do the same with his register of convicts in the settlement. He could make notes on the cards about the convicts' work ethics, about punishments meted out to them, about their emancipation date, and so on," Matthew said. "He too could keep two sets of cards – one based alphabetically on the names of the convicts, the other based on their various trades or skills. But Mr Clarke is resistant to change," he added with a smile, "stuck in his own ways."

"Well, he's going to find his system more difficult when the next fleet arrives with yet more convicts. Perhaps then he'll listen to you, or perhaps he'll just keep a separate register for each fleet."

"Perhaps," Matthew said. "We'll see."

"You come and visit whenever you want, Matthew," Dawes said as he reached out to shake Matthew's hand, also for the first time.

"So?" asked Zachariah Clarke when Matthew arrived back at the Commissary of Labour office, "Any issues with the Lieutenant's observatory?"

"I forgot to ask him," Matthew confessed. Then, seeing the look of astonishment on Clarke's face, he added, "but we had a long discussion. I'm sure he'd have told me if there were any problems. I'll ask him next time I go there."

Late in 1788, Sydney Cove remained a scene dominated by tents, with a random collection of buildings in haphazard positions in a small clearing where most of the trees had been felled, although many stumps remained. Surveyor General John White was continuing to apply some degree of logical planning however, which saw the settlement beginning to take on a more ordered aspect. The convicts, still all living in tents, were domiciled west of the Tank Stream in an area they had named The Rocks. This area formed the rocky western headland of *Warrane*, an area which the Gadigal people knew by the much older name of *Tallawoladah*, where massive outcrops of rugged sandstone were covered with a dry sclerophyll forest of pink-trunked myrtle, blackbutt, red bloodwood and peppermint trees.

East of Tank Stream were the houses, along with some remaining tents, of the civilian administrators and officers of the settlement, with the easternmost part of Sydney Cove having been set aside for the residences of the Governor and Lieutenant-Governor. The foundations for both buildings had been laid in October 1788.

With no supply ships expected from England for two years, successful production of grain and vegetables was essential if the colony was not to starve. In an endeavour to provide the required agricultural produce, the next cove to the east of Sydney Cove had been named Farm Cove where some ten acres had been planted with corn and vegetables. Yet the acreage at Farm Cove produced very little food. The soil there, and everywhere around Sydney Cove, was poor and unsuitable for farming endeavours. Exacerbating the problem was the fact that almost all the convicts had been taken from the streets of London and other British cities and had little or no knowledge of farming techniques.

The situation became so dire that, at the beginning of October 1788, Arthur Phillip despatched *HMS Sirius* to Cape Town, with orders to buy much needed food for the colony. It would be a six month return voyage and, until she arrived back at Sydney Cove, the colonists and the convicts would barely avoid starvation.

Matthew Everingham sat on the rock platform at Dawes Point and watched *Sirius* sail out of the harbour and wondered whether he would still be alive when she returned.

7

With *HMS Sirius* gone, the harbour was empty, except for two packet boats of about ten tons each, and a few longboats. *HMS Supply* had left in late February, soon after the establishment of the Sydney Cove settlement, and few knew where she had gone. Some convicts speculated she had returned to England, some said to China and others thought she had probably been wrecked on the rocky heads at the entrance to the harbour. Wherever she was, she was not at Sydney Cove, and a feeling of abandonment soon settled amongst the convict population. Matthew too was concerned about the settlement having no ships at hand and determined to ask his superior, Zachariah Clarke. If convicts had been despatched anywhere on *Supply*, Clarke would know about it.

"There's a feeling of unease, Mr Clarke," he said. "We're critically short of rations and it'll be months before *Sirius* returns with supplies from the Cape, if she gets back that is."

Clarke nodded and waited, wondering where Matthew was going with this conversation.

"And, with *Sirius* on her mission to the Cape, we've got no ships here at Sydney Cove in case a ship is needed in an emergency, so there's a sense of abandonment. Do you know where *Supply* has gone?"

"Of course," Clarke replied. "I had to assign a contingent of convicts to go with her – about fifty, as I recall. *Supply* has sailed to Norfolk Island."

Matthew looked blankly at Clarke.

"Norfolk Island? Where's that?" he asked.

"It's north-east of here," Clarke said, "about nine hundred miles, maybe a little more."

Matthew was totally bewildered, wondering why the ship had been sent the best part of a thousand miles out into the Pacific Ocean.

"Why on earth has she been sent to Norfolk Island?" he asked.

"My understanding," Clarke said, "is that the governor wants to establish a second penal colony on the island. He's hoping the land there will be suitable for farming. Apparently, Captain Cook wrote in his journal when he discovered the island in 1770 that the land there is quite fertile."

"So, the governor is hoping that farming on Norfolk Island will help provide food for the colony here at Sydney Cove?"

"As I understand it, Matthew."

Matthew shook his head in wonder.

"Seems like a desperate measure," he said. "I wouldn't like to be one of those convicts sent there, with the expectation they grow their own food."

"We're in desperate need of increased food supply, Matthew. I don't need to tell you that. Desperate times call for desperate measures."

In fact, whilst Arthur Phillip was indeed hoping the new colony at Norfolk Island would supply surplus food for the Sydney Cove colony, there was also a strategic imperative in play of which both Mathew Everingham and Zachariah Clarke were totally unaware.

Lieutenant Philip Gidley King was under direct instructions direct from Lord Sydney, the British Home Secretary, acting on behalf of the king, to establish a presence on the island at the earliest possible date. King's written instructions from the Home Office contained the following order:

> *Norfolk Island ... being represented as a spot which may hereafter become useful, you are as soon as circumstances will admit of it, to send a small establishment thither to secure the same to us, and prevent it being occupied by the subjects of any other European power.*[1]

Whilst Arthur Phillip, as Governor of the Colony of New South Wales, had been appointed as the representative of the Crown and held almost absolute power, he acquiesced and gave his approval for Lieutenant King to sail to Norfolk Island with a contingent of convicts, male and female, to establish what was hoped would be a self-sufficient colony on the island. He may have been influenced by the journals of James Cook, wherein Cook had written enthusiastically about the fertility of the island and about flax and giant pines growing there in abundance. Flax would be useful for making fabric, rope and sailcloth, whilst the giant pines, it was hoped, could be used to make replacement masts and spars for ships. He may also have remembered the arrival of the French ships under the command of Jean-François La Pérouse at Botany Bay just days after the arrival of the First Fleet and, not knowing where those ships had gone, believed he should claim Norfolk Island for the British Crown to avoid it becoming a French possession.

As it happened, Cook's assessment of Norfolk Island had been accurate, unlike his assessment of Botany Bay, and a viable, self-sufficient colony was established there. Shipping excess food supplies back to Sydney Cove, however, proved difficult. What Cook had failed to record was that the island was surrounded by rocky cliffs and a treacherous coast, with no safe harbour. Loading and unloading supplies and personnel had to be done by longboats, many of which were wrecked on the reefs in perilous conditions. Over a period of two years, *HMS Supply* would make ten voyages to Norfolk Island and, at Sydney Cove, Thomas Hylids found himself in charge of a team of convicts continually making replacement longboats.

Meanwhile, the packet boats Hylids and others had built were being used to explore the Parramatta River and had found more fertile land upstream than that at Sydney Cove. A small settlement was established there, and convicts were engaged in growing vegetables, wheat and corn. The new settlement was named Rose Hill, but quickly reverted to the Aboriginal name for the area – Parramatta. With no road linking Parramatta to Sydney Cove, however, moving produce back to the hungry settlers at the main settlement remained problematic.

In May 1789, *Sirius* had returned to Port Jackson with supplies from Cape Town, but Arthur Phillip was only too aware that, even these extra supplies, whilst they might save the colony for a time, were not adequate to ensure long term survival. He calculated that, if supplied at the level of full rations, the new provisions would last only four months, so everyone within the colony, bound and free, including the Governor himself, remained on half rations. By January 1790, with no other ships arriving with much needed provisions, Phillip was planning to send *Sirius* on a second supply mission to the Cape, but first he despatched her to Norfolk Island with a further contingent of convicts. The establishment of the Norfolk Island settlement had proven successful for those living there and sending more convicts to the island, Phillip reasoned, would further reduce demand on the ever-dwindling supplies at Sydney Cove.

On 19th March 1790, however, *HMS Sirius* was wrecked on the reef at Slaughter Bay, Norfolk Island, and would never sail again. It was a major catastrophe and left the colonists with only one relatively small ship and insufficient food. Until the arrival of provisions from England, the survival of the colony at Sydney Cove would remain in the balance. In desperation, and with only three months' supplies left, in April 1790, Phillip despatched *HMS Supply* to Batavia in the Dutch East Indies, to purchase more provisions.

Matthew Everingham and Thomas Hylids stood on the small dock which had been built into Sydney Cove and watched *HMS Supply* as her sails filled and she turned towards the heads on her mercy dash to Batavia.

"God's speed," Matthew said as the ship sailed away.

"She's the only ship we've got now," Hylids said, nodding in agreement. "If anything happens to her, we'll be alone here with no way of reaching out to the outside world."

Matthew felt the sea breeze tug at his convict issue clothes which now hung loosely on his light frame and realised he had never been so thin.

Even during those years on Censor, *on the Thames,* he thought, *I was stronger than I am now. The same can be said for Thomas and all of us here – convicts, marine officers and administrators. Many of us are no more than walking scarecrows.*

"There's not a lot of work being done now," Hylids said as they turned and walked back towards the shore. "Men need food if they're to work. Construction's almost ground to a standstill."

As they walked along the dock, Matthew looked at the small settlement in the clearing. He had no idea of the date, but he believed it must be close to two years since they had first landed at Sydney Cove. In that time something attempting to resemble a small English village had been established, although appearances, especially from a distance, were misleading. Neat rows of small houses extended a little over a mile to the north of the point where Arthur Phillip had first raised the British flag. On closer inspection, however, an English observer would have found little similarity to the elusive English village. The houses had walls of timber slabs or, at best, wattle and daub, while roofing was mostly grass thatching or bark. Here and there, some buildings had shingled roofs, but the shingles were made of sheoak timber rather than slate because the settlers had been unable to find slate within the colony. Windows without glass were closed at night with shutters made of boards nailed together, which were taken down during the day to allow air and light into the buildings.

Yet it was not the nature of the buildings which concerned Matthew, or probably any of the other settlers either. The matter consuming the minds of all was the severe shortage of food supplies.

We can live with the rudimentary housing, Matthew thought to himself, *and in time the building practices will improve. But we cannot survive unless new sources of food are found.*

There were signs some of the settlers were attempting to grow vegetable gardens around the houses, but the plants were struggling in the dry and sterile soil. Such was the desperation and concern for survival that Governor Phillip had set aside Saturdays for tending one's own garden or for gathering anything edible from the surrounding bushland.

It makes you wonder how much planning had gone into establishing a settlement on these shores, Matthew thought. *Certainly, the location makes escape difficult, if not impossible, for the convicts, but more thought should have been given to the sustainability of the colony. If* Supply *doesn't return with a load of supplies, or if another fleet with more provisions doesn't arrive soon, we'll be hard pressed to survive.*

Yet when he spoke to his friend Thomas as they stepped off the dock and onto the sand, he shared more positive sentiments.

"We'll get through this, Thomas," he said. "Surely another fleet will soon arrive with provisions for the colony."

"Has Mr Clarke given any indication when that might be?" Hylids asked.

Matthew shook his head.

"He doesn't know. I doubt even the governor knows, but everyone believes it will be soon."

Two days later, at 7am on a Saturday morning, Zachariah Clarke entered the office of the Commissary of Labour and, as usual, found Matthew already at work, copying Clarke's almost illegible notes into the ledger.

"News for you, Matthew," he said. "You've been reassigned."

Matthew looked up from the ledger, quill poised in mid-air above the inkpot, and waited for Clarke to continue.

"You're being sent to Parramatta," Clarke said.

"The place of eels?" Matthew asked, more than a little surprised.

"Eels?" said Clarke, "I don't understand."

"That's what it means," Matthew explained. "Parramatta – it's a native word, means 'the place of eels'. Lieutenant Dawes told me."

"Really? I didn't know," said Clarke, "Anyway, that's where you're being sent."

"And what am I to do in Parramatta?" Matthew asked.

"The same as you've been doing here. You'll be assisting the Superintendent of Labour, Henry Dodd. You'll oversee convict work placements and supervise their work. Perhaps Dodd will let you implement that silly idea you had of using cards. We'll see if it works."

Matthew allowed himself a chuckle.

"It'll work," he said, "but I'm wondering why I'm needed in Parramatta now."

"Ah, well, you'll have some special instructions," Clarke told him.

Matthew waited in silence for Clarke to go on.

"The plan is to send more convicts to Parramatta because farming there is more successful than here, and it will reduce demand on our food supplies. You'll initially be going there with fifty more convicts."

"Initially?"

"Yes," Clarke continued, "they'll arrive in Parramatta on Monday's packet. Their first task will be to build ten huts before they are assigned to work in the fields. Do your best to get those huts built as quickly as possible. As soon as the huts are ready, we'll be sending fifty female convicts. The new huts are needed to try and stop the male convicts from molesting the women. As you know, that's been a problem here."

To say this had been a problem was a gross understatement. The wanton behaviour of both sexes had resulted in widespread revelry and debauchery, from the moment the women convicts had been brought ashore in February 1788. Governor Phillip, outraged by such licentious behaviour, had urged convicts with uncontrollable sexual appetites to marry, and some had done so. The shameless and unchaste behaviour, however, continued to be widespread, and the marines were ordered to "fire with ball" on any man found in the women's camp after dark. That the marines never fired on fellow marines is not an indication that the marines were possessed of a higher level of morality. Even Matthew, himself, it must be said, was not the personification of innocence, for he had been engaged in ongoing trysts with numerous convict women over the past two years. Additionally, on 7th February 1789, a year after coming ashore, he had been charged with "drunkenness and falsehood" and had been severely punished with twenty-five lashes. It seemed he had bartered with sailors to obtain liquor and had then refused to divulge the source of the liquor.

"And now this promiscuous behaviour is to be my problem, in Parramatta?" Matthew asked.

Clarke, sipping his pannikin of tea, chuckled, causing him to cough and splutter as the tea caught in his throat.

"Swings and roundabouts, Matthew," he finally said, when he was able to stop spluttering. "We both know you're no paragon of virtue when it comes to the ladies." He chuckled again before continuing, "At least you'll have more food to sustain your lasciviousness in Parramatta – vegetables, that is. There'll be precious little meat, of course."

Matthew looked at Zachariah Clarke as he considered his new assignment. He swallowed a few times, about to protest at his reassignment, but on each occasion chose not to. He was not looking forward to this change and would much prefer to stay at Sydney Cove, despite the promise of more food in Parramatta. Yet he knew he had no choice in the matter. As a convict, he could be assigned wherever the administration felt he was needed.

"When the next fleet arrives," Clarke continued, "and please God it will be soon, another fifty of the women convicts on board will be sent to Parramatta. They'll be employed at your discretion. Probably most of them will work in the fields but some can be employed as cleaners, cooks, washhouse workers, and the like."

Matthew remained silent, trying to take in the enormity of his new assignment.

"The long-term plan," Clarke continued, "is to build a women's work factory at Parramatta, where many of them will be gainfully employed as a sewing team, producing clothes for convicts, repairing uniforms of the marines, government officials and so forth."

Matthew exhaled a large breath. This was a lot to take in.

"Will I be given written instructions for all this, Mr Clarke?" he asked.

"You will," Clarke nodded, "but you'll be given a lot of discretion in implementing the plan. Sometime in the next year, the Surveyor General will visit Parramatta to choose the site for the work factory. It will be a substantial building, stone, of course, perhaps two stories, and some convicts with building experience will be sent to lead the workforce for its construction."

"It's unlikely I'll be there by the time they start building the factory," Matthew said. "I've only a little over a year to go before my sentence expires."

"Yes, I'm aware of that," Clarke responded. "During your time in Parramatta, the women convicts will still be housed in huts, but probably the sewing team will be established even before the construction of the factory is commenced."

"So, when am I leaving for Parramatta, sir?" Matthew asked.

"Today," Clarke replied. "You're to be on the dock at 10 o'clock and board the packet boat tethered there. The fifty male convicts will follow on Monday."

Two days to get myself established in a new settlement before I'm inundated with a hungry workforce, Matthew thought.

"I wish you luck, Matthew," Clarke said, extending his hand. "You've been an excellent assistant to me here and I'm sure you'll succeed at Parramatta. If you need anything, send a message to me via the packet. I can't guarantee I'll be able to provide what you need, but I'll do my best to support you."

1. *Historical Records of Australia* (HRA), Series I. Vol. 1, p.13
   State Library of New South Wales, Sydney

8

The *Rose Hill* packet, the first river ferry to have been built, sailed on a strong breeze coming off the harbour and passed to the north of Goat Island. Looking around at the wide expanse of the waterway, Matthew considered it to be an arm of the harbour rather than a river.

Perhaps it'll narrow into a river as we go further, he thought. An hour later, the packet passed to the north of a much larger island.

"What's that place called?" Matthew asked, pointing it out to the captain of the packet.

"Depends who y' talk to," the captain answered. "The gov'nor calls it Cockatoo Island. The savages call it *Wareamah*."[1]

"*Wa-ream-ah?*" Matthew asked as he attempted to write a phonetic transcription of the native word in his small notebook.

"Yeah, somethin' like that."

Matthew had become interested in the native language, inspired by the linguistic efforts of the anomalous Lieutenant Dawes. Unlike Dawes, he was not working on a complete lexicon of the language but had restricted himself to recording native place names. If he ever got to meet Dawes again, Matthew thought, perhaps Dawes would find some value in the list he was compiling.

Passing *Wareamah*, the water lost its turquoise colour and seemed to be more brackish. The waterway became something more akin to a river, wending its way westward – a serpentine channel through ever-narrowing bends flanked by hills where the eucalypts grew right down to the water's edge and, in other places, by mudflats, saltmarsh and mangroves.

The winding turns of the river slowed the progress of the *Rose Hill* as she laboured upstream on her way to Parramatta. The sail filled with breeze at times and, at other times, flapped lifelessly against the mast when the fickle wind fell away. The convicts manning the oars cursed each time the breeze fell, thus causing them to exert themselves further to keep the boat moving. They appeared in no hurry and made only a token effort on the oars, waiting and hoping for the breeze to pick up again. The oars dipped deeper and pulled stronger for only a few strokes, each time the officer of the marines called on them to make greater effort.

With the river narrowing further, they passed through an area where the late afternoon sunshine reflected off the still water with a silvery sheen and where the passing of the packet caused only small ripples. Sitting atop boxes on the deck in this quiet section of the river Matthew found himself in a contemplative mood, as he reflected on the changed circumstances of his life. The biggest and most defining change, of course, had been when he had come before the court in the Old Bailey, now some six years earlier. He shook his head as he thought about those foolish and rash actions which had led to his being convicted of fraudulently obtaining books belonging to Samuel Shepherd.

What had driven him, he asked himself, to take that fateful, stupid decision that had changed his life forever? Why had he asked Shepherd's assistant for those books, knowing that the moment he set his hand to it, he was on the wrong side of the law and would face the consequences? Was it an act of desperation or despair or was it an act of youthful bravado and the consequences be damned? Even after having gained the books, he knew he could have saved himself. He could have returned them to Shepherd's chambers with Mr Clermont's compliments and no more would have been said. But no, instead, when challenged by the bookseller, Bannister, he had gone away and penned a letter, a forgery, purporting to be from William Clermont, authorising sale of the books.

You were a fool, a stupid young fool, he said to himself. *Yes, you were in distress, as you told the judge. You needed money to pay the rent, but surely there were other means, other ways to resolve that problem, even if it meant bedding the frumpy old landlady!*

He chuckled as that thought crossed his mind. *No, on second thoughts that would have been an equally unpalatable option. Yet, even being flogged for drunkenness and falsehood in Sydney Cove resulted from my own irresponsible and stupid behaviour. Well, the past is past. I've got only a year of my sentence yet to serve and I swear I'll never make such stupid mistakes again. I promise myself, from now on I'll stay on the right side of the law.*

Matthew was suddenly roused from his soul-searching introspection by the sound of two muskets being fired and the clamorous screeching of a large flock of white parrots rising from the trees in fright. Marines, hoping to procure some fresh meat, had fired on a mob of kangaroos drinking at the water's edge, but their shots had missed and the kangaroos turned and quickly escaped into the bushland. It was late afternoon and Matthew leaned over the boat to scoop up a handful of river water. He put his tongue to the water but quickly spat it out – salt water, perhaps not as salty as the harbour water at Sydney Cove, but undrinkable, nonetheless.

"How much further to Parramatta?" he asked the captain.

"Not far," came the reply, "less than an hour, I reckon."

"What do the people at the settlement do for fresh water?" Matthew asked. "The water here is still salty and brackish – it's undrinkable."

"There's a couple o' freshwater creeks flowin' int' the river," the captain replied. "Not sure whether them creeks might dry up in a drought though. You'll be 'opin' not," he added with a laugh.

A little over thirty minutes later, with the river becoming increasingly narrow, the captain pointed ahead, and Matthew saw a small clearing on the southern side of the river. The British flag hung limply from a flagpole in front of a small wooden landing deck built out over the water. Thick river reeds grew along the banks on both sides of the landing deck and one huge, picturesque eucalypt with white trunk and branches stood about twenty-five yards on the eastern side. A small gathering of rough timber-walled huts with roofs of bark formed the nucleus of a village settlement. To the west of this embryonic settlement, Matthew could see several acres of cultivated land. Beyond these, a backdrop of wooded hills encircled the settlement and formed the same blue-grey bushland vista as that which could be seen around Sydney Cove.

"Welcome t' Parramatta," the captain called as the convict crew poled the boat into position against the deck and secured her with rope. "Any of y's that wants t' be goin' back to Sydney, we'll be leaving t'morra, 'bout noon."

Matthew stepped onto the landing where a convict from the settlement was waiting.

"Matthew Everingham?" the convict asked with an Irish accent.

"That's right."

"Oi'm Will. Oi've been sent to meet y', and to take y' to yer 'ut. This way," he said, walking off.

Matthew followed Will up the small rise of the settlement and along a pathway that led past a row of huts. Near the middle of the row, Will stopped and pointed to one of the huts.

"This'll be y're 'ut," he said. "Three 'uts up that way," he said pointing, "is the kitchen. Y' ken git a bowl o' vegetable broth 'nd a crust there. The Super said t'morrow's Sund'y, so take the day to look around the place. 'e'll see 'y on Monday mornin'."

"Where will I find the Superintendent's office?" Matthew asked.

"Can't 'ardly call it an office, but y'll find 'im in the last 'ut at the end o' this row, y' will," Will said, pointing the way before turning and walking off.

On Monday morning, 19th April 1790, after a pannikin of tea and a crust of bread, Matthew made his way to the Superintendent's office, nothing more than a hut as Will had said, and introduced himself to Henry Dodd.

The two spoke of the fifty new convicts who would be arriving on the packet that afternoon and of the instructions Matthew had been given to have ten new huts built for women convicts. When Matthew mentioned there would be more women convicts on their way as soon as the next fleet arrived in Sydney Cove, Dodd decided that even more than ten huts would be needed.

"I think we'll build twenty huts, Matthew," he said. "We can let Clarke know when the first ten are completed and he can then send those who are already in Sydney. Then we'll get on with building another ten for those women who'll arrive with the next fleet. We're establishing a sewing team, so many of those women will not only be living in the huts, but also working in them."

"Those new huts for the women should be well separated from those of the male convicts," Matthew said. "Having the men and the women living in close proximity has been a problem in Sydney. I'm sure I don't need to explain the reason."

The Superintendent nodded thoughtfully. He already had a small number of women convicts at Parramatta and knew that a sudden influx of more women convicts would exacerbate an already existing problem.

"We're never going to stop fraternisation all together," he said. "But we need to do our best to ensure it's consensual and to minimise violence. I'll leave it to you to determine the best position for the women's huts."

When the extra fifty male convicts arrived on two packet boats that afternoon, Matthew allocated them to existing huts in the row where he himself lived and told them they would commence building new huts the next morning. He had decided to build what he called a "women's precinct". The new huts for the women prisoners would be built as far away from the men's huts as possible, yet still within the constraints of the settlement clearing. Thus, Matthew became part overseer, part administrator and part town planner. The twenty new huts would more than double the number of buildings at the Parramatta settlement.

Part of Matthew's administrative task, of course, was maintaining the register of convicts within the settlement. Having been thwarted by Zachariah Clarke in his attempts to keep convict records on cards, he put the idea to Superintendent Dodd at Parramatta. Dodd frowned and massaged his chin while he thought about the proposal.

"I can see merit in your idea, Matthew," he said. "Cards would be useful for keeping notations about convict skills, behaviour and the like. Yet I can also see why Mr Clarke was resistant to the change. There are two problems, as I see it."

Matthew waited in silence for him to go on.

"Firstly," he said, "I am under instruction from the governor's office to maintain a 'register'. I'm sure Mr Clarke is under the same instructions. From time to time, the governor's office asks to see the register and I'm not sure they'd be happy with a collection of cards."

He paused, gathering his thoughts before continuing.

"Secondly, and this is my main concern, a card could easily be lost and, if that happened, a convict would totally disappear for our records."

Matthew nodded.

"You're right, sir," he said. "I hadn't considered the possibility of losing a card." He paused for some time before continuing. "Perhaps we could do both – cards *and* a register. It'd mean more work for me, but I think being able to keep notes and readily access those notes would serve us well."

Dodd broke into a broad smile.

"We'll do that," he agreed. "That system might work well for us, Matthew."

Matthew scanned the register to find a convict whose skill was listed as "carpentry" and then commissioned the man, Joseph, to make four tray-like, rectangular boxes, with lids. The boxes, he told Joseph, would need to be about five inches wide and about a foot in length. He expected quite rough boxes but, when Joseph delivered them to him at the Superintendent's hut, Matthew was astonished at the quality of the workmanship. The boxes had been made with dovetailed corner joints, finished smoothly and polished with beeswax and each lid had a diamond-shaped inlay made from wood of a different colour.

"Absolutely beautiful," Matthew said, commending Joseph for his work. "Far better than I expected. You obviously take pride in your work, Joseph."

Joseph smiled at the compliment.

"I were a furniture maker in London," he said, "b'fore I fell foul o' the law, that is. Stole the boss's watch 'nd ended up growin' corn 'ere in Parramatta."

As Joseph took his leave and returned to the corn fields, Matthew decided the first card he would write would be that of Joseph. "Furniture maker", he wrote on the card, "fine craftsman".

He assigned two of the filing boxes to cards relating to the male convicts and, with a fine hot poker, he burned onto the front of one box *"Male Convicts A–Z"*. On the front of the other box, he burned the words *"Male Skills A–Z"*. The other two boxes he set aside to be filled with similar cards for the female convicts. Before long, both Matthew and Dodd came to rely exclusively on the cards, though, as instructed, the register was also maintained. The extra work to maintain both cards and register was more than compensated for by the time saved when it came to searching for convict details.

Parramatta was becoming a growth area for the colony. The fifty extra convicts Clarke had sent from Sydney worked well and, to Matthew's amazement, the twenty new huts in the women's precinct were finished within a month. He had expected the work to take twice as long and attributed the progress to the fact that convicts at Parramatta were well treated and better fed than their counterparts at Sydney Cove. Matthew, too, was beginning to feel at ease with his work at Parramatta, despite having been less than enthused when first told of his new assignment. Parramatta lacked the busyness of life in Sydney and the beauty of the harbour he had come to love, and he missed some of his friends there, particularly Thomas Hylids. Yet life in Parramatta, he decided, was not to be complained about. He got on very well with the Superintendent, and infractions by convicts at Parramatta were less frequent than amongst the convicts at Sydney Cove. It was hotter, that was true, because Parramatta got no cooling sea breeze as did Sydney. But countering that and perhaps somewhat because of it, life was more laid-back than in Sydney.

The fifty new women convicts arrived on two packet boats in late May, and Matthew moved them into ten of the new huts – five to a hut. After ascertaining their skills, if they had any, which most didn't, he assigned them to separate work groups. Some helped in the kitchen, some in the washhouse, some were assigned to cleaning duties and ten formed the nucleus of the new needlework team, mending the uniforms of officials and marines. The others, about thirty in all, worked in the fields, growing vegetables and grain crops.

The acreage under cultivation at Parramatta doubled when the hut-builders were released from that task and joined the other convicts working in the fields, and Parramatta began to be talked about everywhere as the food bowl of the colony. Moving the produce from Parramatta to Sydney, however, remained a problem, and the packet boats struggled to transport it in adequate amounts. Matthew surmised that, in Sydney, his friend Thomas Hylids was probably busy helping to build more boats.

"It'd be better if there was a road so we could move the produce by cart," Matthew said to Dodd, who nodded as he sipped his tea.

"There's something of a track," Dodd said, "and I understand efforts are being made to turn it into a viable road, but it's going to take some time."

While they waited this to happen, the packet boats continued to shuttle back and forth and move as much food produce as they could. So common was the sight of a packet boat tying up at the river landing that

Matthew and most others became blasé about their arrival and paid little attention. That was to change, however, when the packet arrived on the afternoon of Wednesday, 30th June 1790. The moment it nudged against the landing deck, a convict jumped ashore and ran into the settlement, past all the huts, yelling at the top of his voice.

"Fleet's in! Fleet's in!"

---

1. Both names are found in a list of place names compiled by Governor Arthur Phillip and others in 1791. Anon, *Vocabulary of the language of N. S. Wales in the neighbourhood of Sydney* (Native and English), c 1791. Ms 41645, Book C, School of Oriental and African Studies, University of London, London.

9

Matthew found Henry Dodd sitting at the small table in his hut, poring over the documentation sent to him on the packet boat from Sydney. He did not look happy.

"Problems?" Matthew asked.

Dodd nodded, then sat with his elbows on the table, his chin cupped in the palm of his left hand while reading from a page in his right. For a few minutes he said nothing, while Matthew waited patiently.

"The arrival of the fleet isn't going to solve many of our problems, Matthew," he said. "It may well exacerbate them."

"Surely the fleet has brought supplies?" Matthew asked.

"Some. But not what we were expecting or hoping for. Apparently, the main supply ship, *HMS Guardian*, was wrecked when she hit an iceberg in the Southern Ocean. She made it back to the Cape, but most of her supplies were lost."

Matthew was crestfallen.

"So, we'll continue on half rations?"

Dodd nodded, and again sat silently for several minutes.

"Worse still," he finally said, "not only have we received precious little in the way of supplies, but Sydney Town has been burdened with seven hundred and fifty weak and emaciated convicts. The fleet had a mortality rate of 26% during the voyage. And, on arrival at Sydney Cove, dead and dying convicts were simply cast overboard. Clarke says there are dozens of corpses floating in the harbour. Unbelievable!"

Matthew stood there, mouth agape, unable to comprehend what he was being told. On the First Fleet, of which Matthew had been part, the mortality rate had been just over 2%.

"According to Clarke, the governor is incensed," Dodd continued, "and the hospital is overwhelmed. They're expecting many of the convicts who arrived alive to die within the next week."

"They were obviously mistreated during the voyage," Matthew said. "Someone should pay for that. I hope they don't send any weak or sick convicts here. We're not equipped to deal with that."

"According to this letter from Clarke," Dodd added, picking it up again, "he'll be sending a group of female convicts in a few days' time – about twenty-five, and he says they're 'relatively healthy', whatever that means."

Matthew considered the situation for a few moments before making a suggestion.

"We've got ten empty huts in the women's precinct because we were expecting about fifty new women convicts. If we get only twenty-five, then we could accommodate them in five of those huts. The remaining five huts could be the workplace for the needlework team, meaning that they wouldn't need to work in their own accommodation huts."

"Yes," Dodd replied. "We might have to rearrange things if they send more women later, but for now, that seems like a sensible option."

"If you don't mind, sir," Matthew said, changing the subject, "I've written a letter to a man in England. I'd like you to despatch it on the packet so it can be taken back to England on one of the fleet ships."

"Didn't take you long to write a letter, Matthew. The fleet only arrived two days ago."

"Actually, I wrote it more than a year ago," Matthew replied, "probably closer to a year and a half. I've been waiting for the fleet so it could be sent."

Matthew had found himself frequently reflecting on the circumstances in his life which had brought him to this place, unsure whether these thoughts arose from a sense of guilt, remorse, self-incrimination or something else. Anger, perhaps? They had become almost compulsive, returning to torture his mind far too often. He remembered the day he had first come to Parramatta and the time he had spent considering everything as the packet passed along the river. *You were a fool, a stupid young fool,* he had said to himself that day. Yes, it was anger. He was not angry at Samuel Shepherd who had prosecuted the case against him. He was not angry at the judge who had sentenced him to seven years with transportation to this place. He was not even angry with the guards who had treated him badly during the years spent on the hulk at Woolwich. Instead – he was angry at himself. Determined to change his life, he had written the letter to Samuel Shepherd which would be delivered on one of the fleet ships when it returned to England.

> *I am resolutely determined never to leave it in their power to say I ever deviated from the strictest principle of honesty and honour, which I yet retain a sense of, however depraved I may be otherwise. I have now two years and seven months to remain a convict and then I am at liberty to act and will act as a free born Englishman ought to do, and sincerely hope I can never more abuse that liberty, too severely have I felt the effect. I am yet but young, only 19, and I think if God spares my health I shall not be one jot the worse for being transported. I have by the iron hand of experience been taught the bad effects of bad company and shall always be careful to avoid them and I think, let me be in whatever station of life, I can keep myself from being imposed upon.* [1]

Matthew handed the letter to Dodd and prayed he would be strong enough to stand by the promise he had written to Shepherd.

"So help me, God," he uttered under his breath as he left the Superintendent's hut.

A contingent of twenty-five women convicts arrived on the packet two days later. Superintendent Dodd had arranged for two marines to meet them at the boat landing and walk them up the hill towards the women's precinct. Matthew stood watching the women as they approached, dressed in filthy, tattered rags. Almost all were barefooted and, as they came closer, he could smell the filth, including faeces, and the pungent, almost acidic aroma of something else – stale vomit, perhaps? When the women gathered in front of him, he addressed them with a firm, commanding voice.

"You will live in these five huts," he said, pointing to the huts. "Organise yourselves five to a hut." The women turned immediately toward the huts, but he called out again, "Stop!" He paused, waiting for their attention, then added, "Before you enter the huts, you will be taken to the settlement store where you will be issued with convict clothing and a piece of soap. You will go directly from the store to the river and there you will bathe until you are totally clean."

There was a general murmur of dissent from the women, some of whom probably hadn't bathed for years.

"Only after you have bathed and dressed in convict clothing may you enter the huts," he said. "Is that clear?"

"What about dinner?" one woman asked from the back of the group.

"After you are dressed in convict clothes, you can go to the kitchen," he said, pointing the way. "But, don't expect anything fancy. We're all living on half-rations, and it seems we'll continue to do so for some time."

"We've bin six months on *Neptune* with a murderous crew 'nd less than 'arf-rations," a young woman called from the front of the group, "We'll survive 'ere!"

Matthew looked at her and asked her name.

"'lizabeth," she said, "'lizabeth Rymes. 'nd who might y' be?"

Matthew was a little taken aback by the young woman's boldness, yet at the same time impressed by her confident attitude.

"My name's Matthew Everingham," he said. "I am assistant to the Superintendent of Labour here at Parramatta and overseer of the convict workforce. I'll meet all of you here tomorrow morning and you'll be given your work assignments. I'll expect you to be clean."

"Cleanliness 's next t' godliness, they sezs," said Elizabeth Rymes with a smile.

Leaving the women in the care of the two marines, he smiled at her, then turned and walked away, wondering what Elizabeth Rymes might possibly know about godliness.

He had always been a stickler for personal hygiene. Even in the unsanitary conditions on *Censor* at Woolwich, he had attempted to keep himself as clean as possible. He had been trained to do so since childhood and it had served him well.

The next morning Matthew met with the women where he had left them the previous day.

Well, he thought, *if cleanliness is next to godliness as Elizabeth Rymes said, cleanliness is also a subjective measure.*

Some women had made every effort to clean themselves, including washing their hair, while others had made only token efforts. Acting on an unplanned, impulsive thought, he asked the women to go and stand in groups of five in front of their huts and, as soon as they did he smiled at his own intuition. The five cleanest women, including Elizabeth Rymes, stood together in front of one hut. The five dirtiest stood together in front of the next hut and the other women were grouped with others showing similar degrees of filth and grime.

Matthew wanted to gather as much information about each woman as he could – information that would be recorded on their individual cards. He also needed to assign each woman to a specific work group.

"Who amongst you can cook well?" he asked.

Twenty-five hands were immediately raised. Matthew pursed his lips before asking another question.

"Who amongst you can sew?"

Twenty-five hands were raised.

"Who amongst you has experience as a cleaner?"

Again, twenty-five hands were raised. Some had not even lowered their hands from the previous questions. They just kept their hands in the air.

"And, who amongst you has experience at farming, and growing vegetables?"

Those who had been keeping their hands raised through the earlier questions quickly lowered them. Not a single hand was raised.

"Working in the fields is very pleasant," he said. "You get to enjoy the sunshine every day, rather than working in a dark, damp hut."

Still, not a single hand was raised.

He had known it would come down to short, individual interviews to gather relevant information about the women and to assign them to workgroups. In fact, he already had quite a lot of information about most of them, sent in the documentation from Zachariah Clarke. In some cases, he even had transcripts of their court hearings and convictions prior to transportation. Still, he would ask questions to confirm that information and perhaps in the process ascertain whether the women were being honest with him. He also needed to make note of which hut each woman was living in. He called for one of the marines to set up a small table with two chairs in the sunshine, then said to one of the dirtiest of the women, "We'll start with you."

Matthew spent very little time assessing the first woman. Even as she sullenly came forward and sat facing him at the table, he decided she would work in the fields.

"You didn't manage to get yourself very clean," he said. "Almost seems like a waste of soap."

"I've neva used soap in me life," the woman replied. "Y' ken 'ave it back if y' want. I don't need it."

Matthew quickly assigned her to work in the vegetable garden, then called for the other women to come and sit at the table in any order. When he found Elizabeth Rymes sitting in front of him, he spent some time reading the information he already had about her, including a copy of her trial transcript from the Old Bailey.

She had been born in 1774 and arrested in Spitalfields where she was cohabiting with a John Moore, he noted, as he read the transcript. Reading further, he found that at the time of her arrest, she had eleven duplicate receipts of pawn in her pocket, so it seemed likely the theft for which she had been convicted was not her first offence, but more likely the first time she had been caught. He couldn't help the faintest of smiles when he read in the transcript that, when confronted by her accuser, the innkeeper's wife, she had said "You need not turn down the bed. There is a blanket and a sheet missing." [2]

This is a girl of some spirit and strength, Matthew thought to himself, *not one to shirk the issue even when confronted with her own wrongdoing.*

No doubt, Matthew decided, she had been accustomed since childhood to living on her wits and her physical charms to survive on the streets of London. Spitalfields was in the East End of London, near Whitechapel, where thousands of young women and men had no means of support other than to engage in petty crime as a daily way of life. Packed with cheap inns, lodging houses and bars, frequented by thieves, burglars, pickpockets, rapists, murderers and prostitutes, it was a dangerous district for respectable people and, though it was only three miles from the Middle Temple where Matthew had lived and worked, he had never been there.

Getting transported was probably the best thing that could have happened to her, he thought. *It would almost certainly have saved her from a life of prostitution.*

He asked her age, but she merely shrugged in reply. She didn't know.

"According to the information I have here, you were born in 1774," he said.

Another shrug, and then:

"So, 'ow old am I now?"

"By my reckoning, that would make you sixteen years old."

"Okay," she said. "If y' say so. I ken rememba that."

"This is a very different land than what you've been accustomed to, Elizabeth," he said, addressing her by name for the first time. She looked around the settlement clearing and nodded.

"'tis a new life in a new land," she said. "I'll make the best of it."

He eyed her carefully, trying to decide which work team he would assign her to. She was a pretty girl, he thought – a small-framed girl with an elfin-like face and with her hair cut a couple of inches above her shoulders. And she was clean which, to Matthew, meant more than anything else. She waited, looking at him with a slight smile on her face, and Matthew soon sensed she knew exactly what he was trying to decide.

"Cookhouse or sewing team?" he finally asked.

"I'll sew," she answered immediately. "I dunno nothin' 'bout cookin'."

"Yet you raised your hand when I asked who could cook well."

"Didn' everyone?" she asked with a smile that turned to a laugh. "None of 'em wants t' work in the fields."

"I noticed," he said. "And you can sew?"

"I ken learn!" she said quickly and confidently. "Can't be that 'ard. What'll we be sewin'?"

"Slops, mainly," he answered. "That's what we call convict clothing – slops. And, from time to time, the needlework team will repair uniforms and clothing for the marines and other officials."

"I ken learn that," she said. "I'm quick at learnin'."

"Very well, you'll join the needlework team."

She smiled again, this time a broad smile that made her eyes scrunch up.

"Thank y', Mista Everingham," she said, followed by yet another broad smile with scrunched up eyes.

"You don't have to call me Mister," he told her. "I'm a convict, just like you."

"Oh, yer not like me Mista Everingham," she replied. Then as she stood and turned to leave she added, "Choose the cooks carefully. I don't reckon none of 'em ken cook much."

Matthew smiled as he watched her go.

"Next!" he called.

With the women assigned to work teams, Matthew spent some days transferring his notes into the register and onto his cards. The first card he wrote was that of Elizabeth Rymes but as he wrote all the other cards, he found himself continually coming back to look again at her card which had already become well thumbed.

RYMES, Elizabeth

D.O.B   : ± 1774
Convicted   : Old Bailey, 28 Oct. 1789
Crime   : Theft (blanket & bedsheet)
Sentence   : 7 years
Ship   : Neptune, 1790
Emancipation: 28 October 1796

Offences in the colony: -

GENERAL NOTES :
    Needlework team
    Positive attitude, Confident,
    Honest? (uncertain)
    A captivating smile!

"God save me," he said to himself, as he stared at the card yet again. "Her smile has cast a spell on me. I think I've fallen in love with a thief from Spitalfields."

1. *The Letterbook of Matthew James Everingham*, pp.37-38 (extract)
   University of Melbourne Archives
   Archive number 1974.0084.05378
2. *Old Bailey Proceedings Online* (www.oldbaileyonline.org, version 8.0, October 1789, trial of JOHN MOORE ELIZABETH RYMES (t17891028-23), (accessed 15 July 2022)

10

The arrival of the Second Fleet saw the marines replaced by the red-coated soldiers of the newly formed New South Wales Corps under the command of Major Francis Grose. Most of the marines chose to return to England, though some remained in the colony and were given land grants by the governor, and a few were incorporated into the Corps. The Corps were far from an efficient, trustworthy and loyal group of soldiers – many were military deserters and civilian lawbreakers who had been given the choice of prison in England or service with the New South Wales Corps. Had the Home Office intended to establish a dishonest, exploitative and oppressive force, they could hardly have done better.

Accompanying the Corps on the Second Fleet was one Lieutenant John Macarthur, his wife Elizabeth and their infant child Edward. John Macarthur had purchased his commission as an officer of the Corps and was generally seen as an arrogant man whose only aim in life was to advance his own prosperity at the expense of others.

He had been born at Stroke Damerel, near Plymouth, in 1767, the son of an expatriate Scotsman who was a cloth trader in Plymouth. In 1783 he had moved to Devon where he lived an insignificant life for five years before gaining the lowly rank of ensign in the 68th Regiment and serving in Gibraltar. During that time, Macarthur determined on a strategy to advance his own social standing, rank and opportunity – he would purchase a commission in the newly formed New South Wales Corps and he would marry well.

With his commission secured, he was able to court and marry the well-educated Elizabeth Veale, daughter of affluent Devonshire landowners. Elizabeth, it transpired, had spent a considerable time living with her grandfather, a man obsessed with perfecting the bloodline of rams in attempts to produce fine wool – experience the young Elizabeth Macarthur would find invaluable in New South Wales, but that was still in the future.

In Sydney Cove, Macarthur was intensely disliked by all he met, including Governor Arthur Phillip. Elizabeth Macarthur, on the other hand, was received in Sydney as a fashionable socialite. An attractive and charming woman of noble birth, Elizabeth Macarthur was the first educated woman to arrive in a colony consisting mainly of convicts and other malcontents and, unlike her husband, she soon became a most welcome presence at social gatherings. She played piano and was instructed in astronomy by Lieutenant William Dawes at Dawes' Point. Some, however, considered her knowledge of astronomy to be rudimentary, even after a considerable time of instruction, and wondered whether the many hours spent at the isolated Dawes' Point were invested purely in academic pursuit.

Meanwhile, at Parramatta, the relationship between Matthew Everingham and Elizabeth Rymes had quickly developed into a full blown romance. Both had long working hours, of course, but spent as much of their free time together as they could, sometimes openly, but at other times more surreptitiously in the privacy of Matthew's hut.

He called her Beth, and they would frequently sit in the sunshine on the landing deck by the river, especially on Sundays which were work-free days. On those days, they would take their lunch to the deck, a crust of bread and perhaps a piece of cheese or salted meat, if they could get it, and spend the whole day there chatting. On one such Sunday, Matthew reflected on the earlier life of the young woman who had become his lover.

"You're a good person, Beth," he said to her. "What made you turn to thieving?"

She paused for some time before answering.

"Y' eva bin t' th' East End?" she finally asked. "T' Spitalfields or t' Whitechapel?"

Matthew shook his head.

"No," he said. "I lived and worked in the Middle Temple."

"Walkin' distance," Elizabeth nodded, "but worlds apart."

"I imagine it is," Matthew replied.

"'tis a world where y' do what y' 'ave t' do t' survive, Matthew. A dog-eat-dog sorta place."

She sat for some time, deep in thought and gazing out at the reflection of the afternoon sunshine on the surface of the river. Yet her thoughts were about Matthew, not about the river.

"And you?" she finally asked. "What about you? Y' was given a privileged life, Matthew, not like me. What made y' turn t' thievin'?"

"I'm not a thief," he replied, but she immediately raised a disbelieving eyebrow.

"Really? Word 'round 'ere is that y' got sent down f' thievin' a couple o' books."

He looked at her in disbelief, not so much at the accusation itself, but rather at the revelation. How did she know?

"Who told you that?" he asked incredulously, and she gave a slight chuckle as she replied.

"Matthew, there's no secrets amongst a few 'undred souls thrown t'getha in a small clearin' in the bush."

"Well," he said, "I was convicted of fraud, of obtaining the books under false pretences. It wasn't theft."

"What does fraud mean?" she asked. "What's false pretences?"

Matthew explained to her how he had obtained the books by falsely claiming he had been sent by his employer to borrow them, and how he had then gone on to sell the books, after forging a letter purportedly giving authority for the sale.

"And that's not thievin'?" she asked, with a smile on her face.

"Not according to the law."

She laughed at him.

"Matthew, thievin' 's one thing I know somethin' 'bout, 'nd if that's not thievin', I dunno what is! 'Tis no betta than a man sayin' 'I'm no thief, I'm a pickpocket.' Y' ken not tell me what y' did weren't thievin'."

He sat for some moments contemplating her accusation. *She's right,* he thought, *it's a fine line between fraud and theft, if there's really a difference at all.*

He considered too the commitment he had made in his letter to Samuel Shepherd and a conflict arose in his mind. He wanted to marry this girl. He had already decided that. But would he be able to live honestly, as he had promised to Shepherd, if yoked in marriage to the young woman who sat beside him, openly admitting to a life of theft?

"Well," he finally said, "those days are behind me. I've promised myself and I promise you from now on I'll be an honest man. Will you make the same promise, Beth?"

"I will," she said as she reached out to embrace him. "No more thievin'." Then, with one of those broad smiles that caused her eyes to scrunch up, she added, "or false pretences!"

The two were wed on Sunday 13th March 1791, under the huge eucalypt tree near the riverboat landing, in a ceremony solemnised by the colony's Chaplain, Rev Richard Johnson. After the short and simple marriage ceremony, witnessed by two other convicts, the newly married couple repaired alone to the landing deck. Although Elizabeth did not know it at the time, she was almost two months pregnant. After the marriage, she moved into Matthew's hut but, of course, during workdays, they were both involved in their assigned tasks.

It was on a wet and cold morning in mid-April 1791 when Elizabeth, engrossed in her task of sewing slops, was summoned by a loud, demanding and arrogant voice.

"Girl!" the man said. "Do I have to stand here all day, waiting for your attention?"

She looked up to see before her the uniformed figure of John Macarthur whom she recognised from the time she had spent with the Macarthur family on *Neptune*, though Macarthur certainly did not recognise her. He literally threw a red uniform coat of the Corps at her as she stood up, in deference to him.

"This coat has several buttons missing," he said. "Replace them!"

Elizabeth looked at the brass buttons of the coat.

"I'm sorry, sir," she said. "We don't 'ave none o' them buttons."

"Then get some girl, from the colony store here in this godforsaken place and be quick about it. I'll be back for the coat this afternoon."

"I'll try, sir," she responded, "but I think the store won't 'ave none o' them buttons either. I think them buttons 'll 'ave t' come fr'm Sydney. It'll take a couple o' days."

Macarthur stood there, almost apoplectic, before turning on his heel and exiting the hut, only to immediately re-enter and to snap at Elizabeth, "Deliver the coat to me the moment the job is done!"

"Yes, sir," Elizabeth replied, before adding under her breath, *You 'aven't changed since y' were on* Neptune. *Y're still an arrogant bastard!*

John Macarthur and his family had been sent to Parramatta at the beginning of April 1791, with Macarthur himself under instructions to assume command of the Corps in Parramatta. Yet the appointment was not to the liking of either Macarthur or his wife. John Macarthur considered it a backwater and an obscure post that would do nothing to enhance his career or his prosperity, while Elizabeth Macarthur missed the social life of Sydney Town and perhaps the tutelage of Lieutenant Dawes. The family stayed in Parramatta only three months, before Lieutenant

Macarthur bribed Major Francis Grose to secure a return posting to Sydney Cove.

"'nd good riddance t' 'em," Elizabeth remarked to Matthew, when she heard the Macarthurs were returning to Sydney. "John Macarthur's trouble, believe me, 'nd I don't reckon we've seen the last of 'im."

The time of Matthew and Elizabeth's emancipation was fast approaching. Matthew would complete his seven-year sentence on 7th July 1791 and, although Elizabeth had served less than two years of her seven-year sentence, under the laws of the colony, a female convict who was married to a male convict would receive her emancipation on the same date as her husband. They therefore had some serious decisions to make. Would they attempt to work their passage back to England on one of the transport or supply ships or would they choose to stay in the colony? Both felt that there was nothing for them back in England.

"If we stay," Matthew said, "we could apply to the governor for a land grant and become farmers."

"If we do that," Elizabeth said, "we'll lose our government 'ut and meals. 'ow would we live?"

Matthew nodded.

"We'd need to build our own house. But land grants are given together with a monthly supply of clothing and provisions, usually for a year and a half, I think. After that we'd need to be self-sufficient."

"Ken we do that?" Elizabeth asked.

"I think so," Matthew replied. "Others have, though it would certainly be hard work."

Matthew was thinking, in particular, of James Ruse, an ex-convict whom he had known when they were transported together on *Scarborough* as part of the First Fleet.

Ruse was a Cornishman who, at the age of twenty-three, had been convicted of burglary in the Cornwall Assizes and sentenced to seven years with transportation to New South Wales. He had arrived at Sydney Cove with eighteen months of his sentence remaining. On 5th September 1790, James Ruse married Elizabeth Parry, a convict who had arrived in Sydney Cove on *Lady Juliana* on 3rd June 1790.

On emancipation, Ruse became the first ex-convict to be given a land grant in New South Wales when, in response to his application, Governor Arthur Phillip gave him a parcel of land at Rose Hill. Awarding the land grant to Ruse was something of an experiment on the part of the governor who wanted to learn how long it would take an emancipist to become a self-sufficient farmer. Anxious that his experiment would succeed, Phillip provided Ruse with provisions for a year, clothing, seed, implements for tilling the land, livestock and assistance in clearing a small area of land for cultivation. By February 1791 Ruse was able to support both himself and his wife, Elizabeth.

In comparing his own situation with that of Ruse and hoping to emulate Ruse's success, however, Matthew had overlooked one important fact. Ruse had been born and raised at Launceston, Cornwall, England. He was born and bred to farming, whilst Matthew Everingham had been a copy boy in the office of a city attorney and knew absolutely nothing about farming, other than the little he may have picked up as supervisor of the workforce at Parramatta. It was to be a telling difference.

"If the gov'rnor gives us a land grant with provisions, we'll stay then," Elizabeth agreed. "If things go ag'inst us, we ken always sell the land 'nd go back t' England later."

Some emancipated convicts chose to work their passage back to England after their sentences were served, and the fact that Matthew and Elizabeth chose to stay reflected a strong and robust pioneering spirit. It would be needed.

On 8th July 1791, one day after the termination of his sentence, Matthew applied to Governor Arthur Phillip for a settler's land grant. The Governor, after reviewing Matthew's work record within the colony, decided that Matthew and his young wife were the type of people likely to make a success of their farming endeavours and granted them fifty acres at The Ponds, an area being established as an outpost of Parramatta. They were also granted provisions, including clothing, for one year and a half, grain and boxes of vegetable seeds, a tent and agricultural tools. The Ponds was a district only about four miles to the northeast of the settlement at

Parramatta, yet there was nothing but a rough and narrow sandy track linking the two.

Matthew and Elizabeth arrived at their fifty-acre allotment on the afternoon of Monday, 18th July 1791. As they stood on the rough dirt track and looked over their land, Matthew's heart sank at the sight of the heavily wooded hills with wispy columns of smoke rising from several points in their midst – the fires of Aboriginal camps. Even clearing the land was going to be a herculean task, much less cultivating it.

And there are Aboriginal groups living on our land, he thought. But then, as he gazed at the hills and at those columns of smoke, he realised something few others in the colony had ever thought about.

It's their land, he thought. *We're the intruders here.* It was a revolutionary thought. At Parramatta, Matthew had seen Aboriginal people moved off the settlement by soldiers of the Corps. On one occasion, he had witnessed an Aboriginal man shot by a soldier and he had heard of settlers and emancipated convicts, men just like himself, who had shot and driven Aboriginals off their own land. That, he knew, was a recipe for disaster, both for the Aboriginals and for the settlers.

We'd never be safe if we did that, he thought. *It'd set up an enmity between them and us. It'd probably lead to raids on our own house and put the lives of myself and Elizabeth at risk. Being successful here will need all our strength and fortitude and we're going to have to come to terms with the Aboriginals. Somehow, we must learn to co-exist with them.*

Elizabeth, by contrast, was in a state of high excitement, talking constantly about "our land", about the beauty of the hills and pointing out a small, flat piece of ground where she quickly determined "our 'ouse" would be built.

Matthew smiled at her indulgently.

She has no idea how difficult this is going to be, he thought, *but I understand her excitement. This piece of land is the only thing she's ever been able to call her own, apart from the things she stole in Spitalfields. And, in a way, we're stealing this land too.*

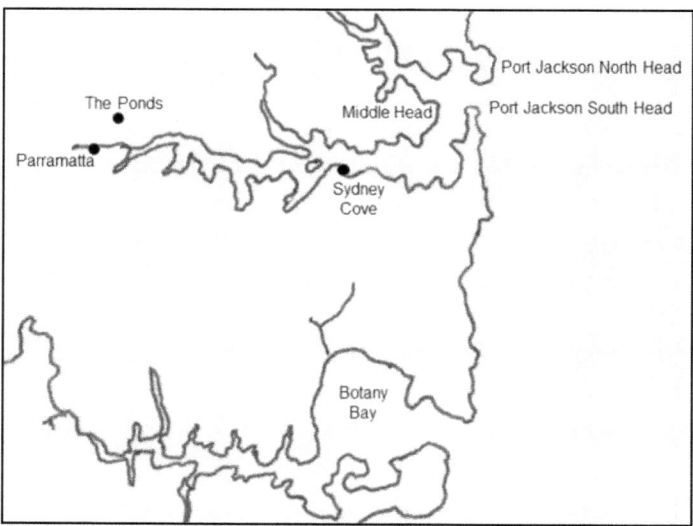

Fig1. New South Wales in the 1790s, showing location of Sydney Cove, Parramatta, The Ponds and Botany Bay.

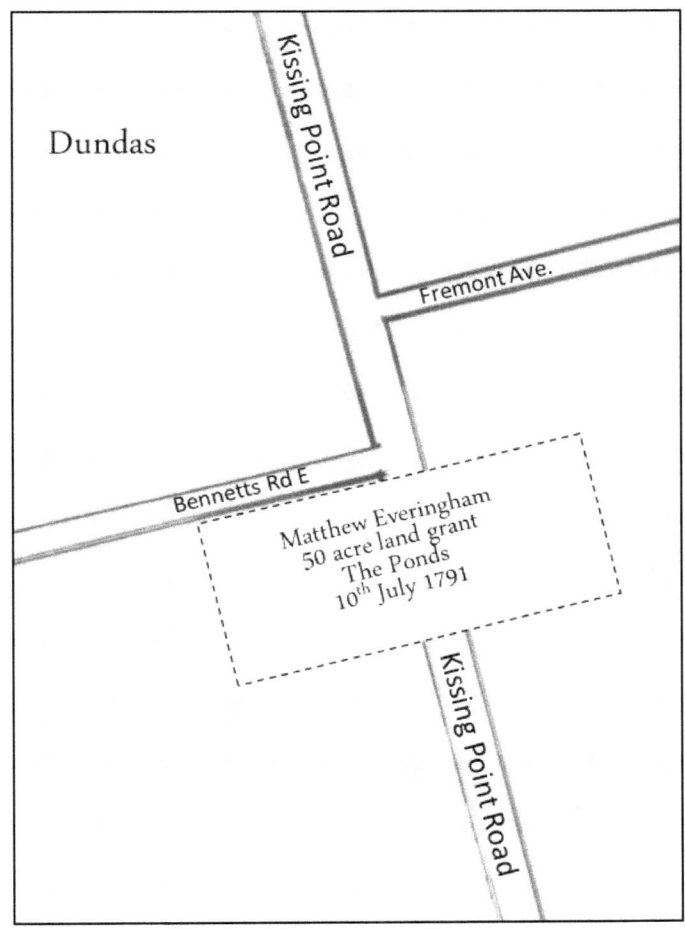

Fig2. Map showing the location of Matthew Everingham's first land grant at The Ponds, superimposed over the roads of the area now known as Dundas North. Matthew's land is now in an area of suburbia where probably few of the residents are aware of its history. Matthew's fifty-acre grant is bisected by the present-day Kissing Point Road and is adjacent to the corner of Kissing Point Road and Bennetts Road East.

11

They pitched their tent on the small piece of level ground which Elizabeth had declared would be the site for their house.

"But this is where we're gonna build our 'ouse," she protested. "We'll 'ave t' move the tent when we start t' build the 'ouse."

Matthew looked at her and smiled.

"We'll build the house around the tent," he said. "Then when the house is finished, we'll just pull down the tent and we'll be in our house."

"Y're a clever man, Matthew Everingham," she said with her trademark smile.

"Well, I'm no builder, Beth. You need to realise the house'll be nothing like you were used to in London. It'll be a simple hut, modelled on the huts we had at Parramatta."

"I don't expect no London 'ouse, Matthew. Some o' them 'ouses in Spitalfields where I lived weren't much betta than the 'uts at Parramatta anyways. This'll be the best 'ouse I've eva lived in 'cause it'll be *our* 'ouse."

The next morning, Matthew hammered pegs into the ground to mark out what would be the four corners of the house. Then he took up his axe, preparing to go into the wooded hills in search of suitable sized trees which would form the corner posts of the house.

"I'll come with y'," Elizabeth said. "I ken 'elp."

"No, you won't," Matthew told her sternly. "You're more than three months pregnant and you can't be doing that kind of work. I'll be gone all day, so you stay here and prepare dinner."

As Matthew had anticipated, it took him a full day to find four trees of appropriate size, cut them down and trim them to form the four corner posts of the house. It would take him another two days to drag them back to the site for the house. Twice during the day, he noticed a small group of Aboriginal men standing some distance off, somewhat sullenly observing him as he felled the trees. He raised his hand to acknowledge their presence but, on both occasions, the Aboriginal men quickly turned away and disappeared back into the bush.

When Matthew returned to the tent late that afternoon, dragging the first of the corner posts behind him, he was exhausted and the winter sun was setting behind the hills. It was, therefore, not until the next morning that he discovered two of the pegs marking the corners of the house had been removed and deep holes had been dug ready to receive the corner posts. He turned to Elizabeth, embraced her and thanked her, but then firmly admonished her for doing such hard work in her present condition.

How can I get through to her, he asked himself, *that she can't be doing heavy work while she's carrying a baby?*

She's so excited about getting this house built, and I can understand that, but for her own sake and for that of the baby, she simply must not do heavy work.

Before leaving to get the remaining corner posts from the hills, he reiterated to her again the need to avoid heavy work and elicited her agreement. And yet when he returned to the tent at the end of the day, he found that not only were the remaining two corner holes dug, but she had also made a start on a small vegetable garden.

"Oh, Matthew," she said to him when he admonished her again, "y' worry too much. I'm 'ealthy, 'nd we need to get them vegetables planted soon or we'll starve t' death out 'ere."

Despite Matthew's best attempts to convince his wife not to do heavy work, which even included hiding the tools on one occasion, Elizabeth continued to work on the house. Even after its completion she took to the fields and insisted on helping Matthew clear a small area of land, in preparation for sowing crops. Matthew was simply unable to stop her and she worked until well into the eighth month of her term. Sadly, that work would bring sad consequences in the coming months.

The house, when built, was a one-room hut with a dirt floor and a roof made of bark. Between the four corner posts, they used slabs of timber which Matthew cut, with much difficulty, from the hardwood of the Australian eucalypt trees. They attached a door on hinges fashioned from strips of leather and made two detachable window shutters to be put in place in the evenings or in wet weather. At one end of the hut was a small fireplace with a short chimney, but they could only ever have a small fire of coals there, for fear of burning down the house.

The day they pulled down their tent, Matthew stood observing their handiwork from a distance.

Later, he thought, *I'll build an awning across the front of the house, something like a roof over a veranda,* but he wisely kept that idea to himself, knowing that if he mentioned it Elizabeth would insist on helping.

By late-October 1791, when Elizabeth finally agreed to retreat from the fields and cease heavy work, the two of them had cleared just over an acre of land where crops would later be sown. Matthew continued to work in the fields by himself, slowly clearing more land. At times, he again observed Aboriginal men watching from a distance.

It seems they disapprove of the land being cleared and trees being felled, he thought, *but what option do I have? If we're going to stay here I need to get some land ready for crops.*

This was the situation when a marine lieutenant, Watkin Trench, arrived at The Ponds on 7th December 1791. Trench had sailed with the First Fleet on board the transport ship *Charlotte*. He had been commissioned as a marine officer but, before leaving England, he had come to a personal arrangement with the London publishing firm of Debrett to write a book describing the voyage and the development of the new colony in

New Holland. He included the following in the notes for his manuscript when he arrived at The Ponds"

> *7th December 1791. Proceeded to the settlement called The Ponds, a name which I suppose it derived from several ponds of water which are near the farms. Here reside the fourteen following settlers.*[1]

The Everinghams were one of those fourteen settlers.

> *Matthew Everingham and wife. Attorney's clerk. Fifty acres of land. Two acres under cultivation.*[2]

Since his arrival at Port Jackson, Matthew had repeatedly told authorities that, in England, he had been employed as a clerk in the chambers of Mr William Clermont, attorney at law. It was a stretch, and he knew it for, when he had worked for Clermont he had been only fourteen years of age, hardly old enough to be a clerk. He had actually been employed as a messenger boy and copy boy, making handwritten copies of legal briefs and other such documents. Nonetheless, he told Trench too that he had been an attorney's clerk. It sounded better than "copy boy" and Matthew thought it did no harm to embellish his past credentials a little.

Looking around The Ponds, Trench was clearly unimpressed with what he saw.

> *These people are to receive provisions, (the same quantity as the working convicts) clothes, and medicinal assistance, for eighteen months from the day on which they settled. To clear and cultivate the land, a hatchet, a*

> *tomahawk, two hoes, a spade and a shovel, are given to each person, whether man or woman, and a certain number of cross-cut saws among the whole. To stock their farms, two sow pigs were promised to each settler but they almost all say they have not yet received any, of which they complain loudly. They all received grain to sow and plant for the first year. They settled here in July and August last. Most of them were obliged to build their own houses; and wretched hovels three fourths of them are.* [3]

It is obvious from Trench's survey that Matthew Everingham and his wife were not amongst those whom he expected to endure as successful farmers.

> *The attorney's clerk,* Trent wrote, *I also thought out of his province: I dare believe that he finds cultivating his own land, not half so easy a task, as he formerly found that of stringing together volumes of tautology to encumber or convey away that of his neighbour.*[4]

Just two weeks after the visit of Watkin Trench, on 23rd December 1791, Elizabeth went into labour and, with Matthew assisting, gave birth to the couple's first child, a daughter whom they named Mary. From the moment of her birth, the child was small and weak. As Matthew held her in his arms, and while Elizabeth rested, he knew the child would not survive.

> *She's too small* he thought, *way too small.*

He did not speak of his concerns to Elizabeth but, with a sigh, he laid the baby down with her mother.

Live for us, little one, he thought as he watched the child suckle at her mother's breast. Yet he knew it was a vain hope.

Elizabeth nursed her baby day and night and, though she said nothing, Matthew was sure she too knew the baby would not survive. It showed in the sadness of her eyes and the tears she brushed from her cheek, hoping Matthew would not notice. Mary Everingham died on 24th January 1972, having lived just four weeks. They buried her alongside Elizabeth's vegetable garden behind their house and placed a small cross on the tiny grave. As they stood there in a tight embrace, looking at the tiny grave Elizabeth wept uncontrollably into Matthew's shoulder.

"I shoulda listened t' y', Matthew," she said between sobs, "I did too much work. The little mite didn't 'ave a chance. She were jist too small."

Matthew held her tight without saying anything. It was not the time to say, "I tried to tell you so," nor was it the time to comfort her by saying there would be more children. It was a time to let her grieve, as he himself was grieving. It was also a time, he knew, harsh though it might be, to allow her to come to an understanding in her own mind about the amount of work she could do whilst carrying a child. It was a tragic and harsh lesson to learn, but an important one.

"She were me first child 'nd I didn't know," Elizabeth said as she continued to weep. "I felt like I were 'ealthy, I felt good, I thought I could do the work, but I were wrong. I'm sorry, Matthew, I'm so sorry."

He lifted her head from his shoulder, his shirt soaked with her tears, and kissed her.

"Hush," he whispered into her ear. "We'll manage this, Beth. We've still got each other and, together, we'll get through this terrible loss."

Elizabeth grieved beyond measure for three long months. At times during the day, she would retreat to a place in the fields, far from the house, where she would lie down in the grass and weep. At other times she ventured into the bush on the hillsides and lay weeping amongst the trees. On occasions, amongst the trees, Aboriginals watched the grieving white woman. They knew why she wept, but they kept their distance and she was totally unaware of their presence. Matthew allowed her this time alone with her pain, though he worried about her state of mind and kept an eye on her from afar.

No seventeen-year-old girl should have to go through this, he thought. *Perhaps we rushed things. Perhaps I should have been firmer with her and stopped her from working. But how? Perhaps we should have returned to England, rather than settling here on this harsh land. Perhaps…Perhaps …Perhaps!*

Nights were the worst, when he would be wakened in the middle of the night by the sound of her sobbing, as she lay with her head on his chest and her tears soaking his nightshirt. On those occasions, he would hold her tight and whisper in her ear.

"There'll be other children, Beth."

After three months, the tears gradually subsided, as Elizabeth cautiously became more accepting of the loss and more pragmatic about her circumstances, almost as if feeling her way back to normality. Her trademark smile with scrunched eyes had not returned, but it seemed to Matthew that she was emerging from the grieving process a more versed and mature young woman. Nonetheless, he was surprised one day when she appeared beside him in the fields, shovel in hand.

"It's all right, Matthew," she said, in response to his enquiring look, "I'm not pregnant now so I can 'elp with the work. I've learned me lesson 'nd I won't work when I'm carryin' a child."

Matthew nodded and allowed her to work in the field alongside him, taking it as a positive sign that, for the first time, she had acknowledged the possibility of another child.

It's a start, he thought. *She'll grow stronger and wiser — the smile will return.*

The two worked side by side in the fields almost every day throughout 1792, determined to make themselves self-sufficient. In October of that year, fifteen months after taking up his land grant at The Ponds and only ten months after the visit of Watkin Trench, Matthew wrote to Samuel Shepherd in England.

> *The first six months everything seemed to run against me. My crop failed, my daughter died and my wife hung on my hands very ill and, not having any supply in time from England, the whole colony was almost starving.*

This was bad encouragement for a young beginner, but I worked on [and] encouraged myself with the old saying "when things are at the worst they will mend." And I thought they now as bad as they well could be.

I have now settled 15 months and my little farm thank God seems to promise pretty well. My wife has got pretty well and really a good one she is. I have 5 acres of India Corn, one of English wheat, about half an acre of Barley Pumkins, [sic] *melons,* [one word illegible] *in abundance, all seem to thrive well. I have two sows big with Piggs,* [sic] *some poultry and a hive of this Country's bees. They are exceedingly small. In three months, I aim to maintain myself and family independent of the public store and do the best I can for myself. Next year I hope I shall be able to maintain two men off the store. I have now one and then I shall be able to live a little comfortable.*[5]

Watkin Trench would never have believed it.

But, despite their progress at The Ponds, the colony was going through what would be called "The Hungry Years", a time when the supply of grain and vegetables grown in the colony would barely support the population. Meat was in even shorter supply, especially because officers of the Corps, men like John Macarthur, had taken large land grants and were monopolising the supply of mutton which they frequently withheld from market to force up the price. The Macarthur family had returned to Parramatta in 1792, when John Macarthur had been pressured by the Corps Commander, Major Francis Grose, to take up the appointment of Corps paymaster in Parramatta, a position which Macarthur agreed to accept only on the promise of double his Lieutenant's salary.

The officers of the New South Wales Corps gained almost total control of the colony's economy when Governor Arthur Phillip departed for England on 11th December 1972, leaving Major Francis Grose as acting Governor until the arrival of Governor John Hunter, on 11th September 1795. In every way, Grose favoured the officers of the Corps, granting them extensive land grants, large numbers of convict labourers to work the land and a monopolistic control of trade, especially that of food and rum. Arthur Phillip had prohibited the sale of rum and other spirits to convicts, but Francis Grose repealed that law the day Phillip left the colony. Thirsty convicts who had not tasted a dram of alcohol for years suddenly found themselves able to sell almost all they owned to procure a bottle of rum, and drunkenness prevailed. Soon, because of their exploitative extortion through the trade in rum, the NSW Corps became known as The Rum Corps. One of Grose's first acts as Lieutenant-Governor was to award John Macarthur a one hundred-acre grant of the best land in the colony at Rose Hill and forty convict labourers to work the land for him.

Matthew had to travel regularly to Parramatta, to collect the victuals that had been awarded to him as part of his land grant. After returning from one of those trips, he told Elizabeth how he had run into John Macarthur at the colony store.

"Don't tell me that arrogant sod's back in Parramatta?" Elizabeth exclaimed.

"He is," Matthew said, "lording it over all and sundry. He insisted the storeman check, then double check, that I was entitled to the provisions I was drawing."

"Sounds like 'im," Elizabeth said. "When we was on *Neptune* I 'eard 'im tell 'is wife 'e'd be the richest man in the colony."

Matthew nodded.

"He's well on his way to that. Everything he does and says is part of his strategy to do just that."

The 'hungry years' were difficult for Matthew and Elizabeth, as they were for almost all settlers, officers of the Corps excepted, of course. Elizabeth discovered, late in 1972, that she was pregnant again and, remembering only too well the death of her first child, readily agreed to stop working in the fields. Yet, Matthew worried about the child's survival.

I have to do everything in my power to make sure this child lives, he thought. *The loss of another child would be just too much for her, but it's going to be difficult.*

He made a decision then – when necessary, he himself would go without food and ensure that Elizabeth had enough to eat.

Little rain fell, Matthew's wheat withered and died and the corn was reduced to rustling leaves on dry stems. In early 1793, what was left of their corn crop was devoured by plagues of mice and grasshoppers. But for the victuals being drawn from the colony store in Parramatta, the small vegetable garden that Elizabeth had planted – potatoes, carrots and turnips – and an occasional kangaroo that Matthew would shoot, they would have starved.

On sunny days, Elizabeth frequently went on long walks across the fields and often into the wooded hills. At first, Matthew worried about her encountering Aboriginals, but when she told him she had seen Aboriginal men from a distance and that they had waved to her in response to her wave, he worried less. He himself had never been able to elicit a wave from them.

All I get are sullen stares, he thought, *I think it's because, for some reason, they're angry about me felling the trees.*

"I saw some Aboriginal women today," she told him after one of her walks. Matthew raised an eyebrow because it was unusual – Aboriginal women folk were rarely seen. "They was diggin' in the ground with sticks."

Matthew's interest was piqued by this news. *Why would the women be digging in the ground with sticks?*

"Where was this, Beth?"

"Down on the flat, near the pond. There were 'bout ten of 'em, women I mean."

Matthew asked Elizabeth to take him and show him the place where the women had been digging and, as they stood there looking at the disturbed soil, Elizabeth bent to pick up a sharpened stick, about two feet long.

"This looks like one of them diggin' sticks they was using," she said, handing it to Matthew, who took the stick and used it to dig up a plant growing nearby.

"Looks like some kinda potato," Elizabeth said, as Matthew brushed the soil from the roots of the plant, "but not like our potatoes. Our potatoes 're round, these 're long 'n' thin"

Matthew nodded.

"It's some kind of wild, native potato," he said. "It's obviously a food source for them and I think we should leave this area untouched for them. We'll not use this area for planting crops."

"It's some o' the best land, Matthew," Elizabeth said. "It'd be a good area f' growin' corn."

Matthew nodded again.

"But this potato is important to them, Beth. We'll leave it for them."

They left the strange potato on the ground and Matthew put the digging stick back where they had found it before they turned and walked back toward the house. As they walked away, native eyes watched them from within the dark undergrowth amongst the trees.

As Elizabeth continued with her frequent long walks, Matthew hit on an idea for a surprise project, something he hoped would lift her spirits as her pregnancy progressed. On days when she was off walking, he cut lengths of timber with a crosscut saw borrowed from his neighbour, John Anderson, and stored them out of sight amongst the trees behind the house. He did not want to assemble it until the last moment, so it would remain a surprise for her and, when all was ready, he needed only one day to assemble it fully.

"It's a lovely day," he said to her. "Are you going for your walk today?"

"I think I will," she replied. "I'm really 'oping t' make contact with them Aboriginal women. I've waved t' 'em a number of times, 'nd they wave back, but if I approach 'em, they walk off int' the trees."

"I think they're gradually getting used to us," Matthew said. "I'm sure they'll make contact when they're ready."

As soon as Elizabeth left for her walk, Matthew hurried to retrieve the cut timber from amongst the trees and set about assembling his project at the back of the house, alongside the small grave of their daughter, Mary. He had agonised in his mind about whether that was the right place for it, about whether Elizabeth would be comfortable with it there or whether the reminder of the child's death might distress her yet again. In the end, however, he decided it was the best place for it.

I can always move it if I have to, he thought.

He worked tirelessly throughout the day, sawing timber, hammering planks into place and digging holes for the foundation posts, determined to have it finished when Elizabeth returned from her walk. Late in the afternoon, he met her in front of the house.

"Come around here," he said, taking her hand and leading her to the back of the house, "I've something to show you."

She stood there looking at the small wooden construction Matthew had built, about ten feet square and only six inches high.

"You made a deck?" she asked incredulously, as she turned to look at him.

Matthew put his arm around her shoulders and nodded.

"I made it for you – for us, actually. I remember so fondly those times we spent together on the river landing deck in Parramatta. Remember how we'd sit there and talk on sunny days? There's no river here, but it's still a place we can sit and talk."

She stepped up onto the deck and sat down, facing him.

"Is the location all right?" he asked. "I can move it if you'd like."

She knew why he was asking. She didn't answer immediately but looked around at Mary's tiny grave.

"It's perfect!" she said. "Come 'nd sit with me, Matthew."

Then she broke into one of those broad smiles that always made her eyes scrunch up.

It's the first time I've seen that smile for more than a year, he thought as he stepped onto the deck. *I've missed it. God, how I've missed it!*

1. Tench, W *A Complete Account Of the Settlement At Port Jackson, In New South Wales Including An Accurate Description of the Situation of the Colony; of the Natives; and Of Its Natural Productions.*Nicol & Sewell, London 1793. P.102
2. Ibid. p.102
3. Ibid. p.101
4. Ibid. p.103
5. Everingham, M J
   The Letterbook of Matthew James Everingham
   University of Melbourne Archives
   Archive Reference: 1974:0084.05378 pp.47-48 (extract)
   (words in brackets added by the author)

12

Matthew and Elizabeth's second child was born at The Ponds on 9th June 1793, a strong and healthy little girl to whom they gave the name Sarah Elizabeth, though she would always be known as Sally. It was the coldest winter the colony had known since its inception in 1788, but the child thrived in the small house, kept warm by a relatively small fire in the fireplace.

In September 1793, Matthew and Elizabeth walked the four miles along the narrow track to Parramatta, carrying the child, where she was baptised in a granary hut by the Reverend Richard Johnson. Though Parramatta had a street named Church Street, there was no church. Foundations for a church had been laid early in 1792, but its purpose had been changed before any further construction took place and a jail had been erected on those foundations. Reverend Johnson despaired at the decision which meant he would continue to hold church services under the large tree on the banks of the river where he had married Matthew and Elizabeth or in one of the small granary huts in the event of bad weather. The planning authorities, however, agreed with the recommendation of John Macarthur who had declared the settlement in greater need of a jail than a church.

The birth of their daughter, Sally, seemed to herald the commencement of better times for Matthew and his family. He now had a convict labourer, Thomas Moran, assigned to help him cultivate the land on his farm at The Ponds. Moran was a young man, nineteen years of age, who had been convicted in Surrey and sentenced to seven years with transportation for having stolen a sheep. He was a cheerful young man, frequently singing or whistling as he went about his tasks, making light of his transportation to a distant shore.

"Gettin' sentenced t' transportation were an adventure f' me," he told Matthew. "'ow else would the likes o' me git t' see anotha part o' the world? Soon as I git me Ticket o' Leave, I'll be off t' see more o' this land."

Thomas turned out to be a good worker, and Matthew had no concerns about leaving him alone with Elizabeth and Sally when he went to Parramatta. With Thomas to help in the fields, Elizabeth could concentrate her efforts on caring for their young child and managing the small vegetable garden near the deck.

On a visit to Parramatta, Matthew noticed that pumpkins appeared to be much sought after in the vegetable market and that they brought a good price.

Pumpkins are easy to grow, he thought. *We've already got a small patch of Barley Pumpkins, though they are different and smaller than these. I'm sure we can grow these larger pumpkins, and we can extend the vegetable garden near the deck to grow them. The biggest problem will be getting them to the market here in Parramatta because of their weight, but there should be some way to overcome that.*

He bought a large pumpkin and, when he got back to The Ponds with it, he told Elizabeth of his plans.

"We'll dry the seeds and plant them in the spring," he said. "These sell well in Parramatta, and for a good price."

Elizabeth saw the problem immediately.

"That's a good idea, Matthew," she said, "but pumpkins 're 'eavy. 'ow are we gonna get 'em t' Parramatta?"

Matthew nodded thoughtfully.

"Yes, I've been thinking about that all the way home from Parramatta today," he said. "We've got the mule that John Anderson traded to us for the cow. I'm thinking I'll need to make some kind of cart for it to pull. I'm not sure what I can use for wheels yet, but Thomas and I'll sort out something."

In August of 1793, Matthew and Thomas managed to clear an extra acre of land for the planting of maize, and regular rainfall meant the spring and summer months were an excellent season for the growing of crops and pumpkins.

"We'll bring in a good harvest in the new year, Beth," Matthew said to his wife in November, "our best crop ever."

"Will it be 'nough t' pay off our debts, Matthew?"

"That'll depend a little on the price at market," he replied. "The damn Rum Corps are still manipulating prices, but we should be able to pay off most of our debts."

"I swear t' God I could kill that John Macarthur 'nd all 'is greedy officers," Elizabeth exclaimed. "'The Gentlemen', they call 'emselves. Hah! That's a laugh!"

Matthew laughed within himself but managed to keep a stern expression on his face.

"I agree with your description of Macarthur and his ilk, Beth, but let's have no talk of killing even though I know you don't mean it literally. It's better for us to always speak well of others."

"'tis a pity 'e don't feel the same way," Elizabeth replied, with one of her broad, trademark smiles. "'e wouldn' last a minute in Spitalfields."

At this, Matthew was no longer able to hold his stern countenance.

"I dare say I wouldn't last a minute in Spitalfields either," he said, and they both laughed.

Notwithstanding the fact that the Rum Corps was still exploiting settlers and that the colony in general continued to struggle through The Hungry Years, Matthew and Elizabeth were managing quite well at The Ponds. They were, to a large extent, isolated from the mainstream settlements of the colony and thus from the exploitation of the Rum Corps. They ground their maize to make porridge and they had plenty of vegetables. Their small brood of hens provided eggs to supplement their diet, but meat was a rarity, except for the occasions when Matthew was able to shoot a kangaroo. They had ceased to draw victuals from the colony store, it being more than eighteen months since the land had been granted to them, and at market they bought only flour, sugar and tea. Even flour was bought only rarely, as something of a treat – most of the time Elizabeth used ground corn to make cornbread. With clothes no longer being supplied by the colony store, Elizabeth spent many hours mending tears in their clothes and adding patches, often made from flour bags or sugar bags.

"Jist as well I learn'd t' sew at Parramatta," she said looking up from her stitching with a grin.

Matthew smiled, remembering how as assistant to the Superintendent at Parramatta, he had assigned her to the needlework team after she'd told him "I dunno nothin' 'bout cooking."

"Just as well you learned to cook, too," he replied. "Otherwise, we'd be eating raw vegetables."

She rewarded him with one of those broad smiles he loved so much.

The harvest of January 1794 fulfilled Matthew's expectation and was their best ever. Thomas and Matthew had built a cart for taking the produce to market in Parramatta. The track from The Ponds to Parramatta had been widened and improved – not yet what one would call a road, but at least the mule was able to drag the cart to the market. When Matthew and

Thomas got to Parramatta with a load of produce, Matthew would stay and try to sell it for the best price, while Thomas would take the mule and return to The Ponds for another load. On a good day, when the track was not muddy, they could manage three trips a day – two loads of corn cobs and one load of pumpkins.

By September 1794, Matthew and Thomas had cleared 11 acres of land, although preparing the ground for the planting of the spring crops would prove difficult. Most of the fields had been inundated in July of that year when the Parramatta River flooded. The rising river caused the Subiaco Creek to spill into The Ponds Creek which then flooded Matthew's fields, cutting them off from Parramatta and making the muddy ground all but impossible to prepare for sowing. Still, they counted their blessings because their house stood on higher, dry ground and because they had sufficient supplies of vegetables. Matthew was philosophical about the situation.

Plagues, floods and droughts, he thought. *It'll probably always be thus in this harsh land, though hopefully the governor's efforts will free us from the greed of Macarthur's Rum Corps. The hand of God makes life here difficult enough for us, without the self-interests of that lot.*

Matthew stood in front of his house, looking across his fields to the Parramatta River and the small but growing settlement of Parramatta. Beyond Parramatta and running in a line from north to south, as far as the eye could see, rose the formidable Blue Mountains which no white man had yet crossed.

"Y're lookin' at them mountains ag'in," Thomas said. "I've seen y' lookin' at 'em a lot."

"Yes," Matthew said. "I can't help wondering what's on the other side."

"Some people say there's a big inland sea," Thomas replied. "Some even say China's jist on the other side o' the mountains."

Matthew allowed himself a short chuckle.

"Well, I can tell you it's not China, Thomas," he said. "I think there's probably really good, flat farmland though – good for growing crops or for raising herds of cattle, or sheep."

"'nd 'ow do y' reckon y'd get a 'erd o' cattle over them mountains?" Thomas asked. "Even a man can't git over 'em. Y' couldn't possibly drive a 'erd o' cattle across 'em."

Matthew nodded.

"Yes, that's how it is now, Thomas, but one day it'll open up. Someone'll find a way over those mountains."

And it could be me, he thought, though he didn't give voice to those thoughts. *Why not? It'd be well worth trying, for I'm sure the governor would reward the first man across those mountains with a large grant of good land. But this is not the time for me to attempt that. Beth's pregnant again and the child will be born around May or June next year. Perhaps after that I can look for the way to cross the mountains.*

The Aboriginal presence at The Ponds was increasing during the mid-1790s, and word amongst the neighbours was that a settler living about a mile from Matthew's property had shot two Aboriginals in an attempt to drive all Aboriginals off his property. In retaliation, Aboriginal warriors had raided farms, setting fire to crops and houses, and spearing settlers. Matthew shook his head when his immediate neighbour, Curtis Brown, told him this news.

That's not the answer, he thought. *Of course, the Aboriginals will retaliate if threatened or treated badly. And perhaps we should expect resistance from them anyway. After all, we invaded their country, not that I or the other convicts had any say in the matter. Still, it's reasonable that they see us as invaders. Any settler who doesn't attempt to get on with the Aboriginals is asking for trouble.*

"We've had no trouble from them, Curtis," he said. "We don't bother them and they don't bother us. I see them walking across our fields from time to time. Mostly they ignore us, but there've been a few occasions when one or two of them have raised their arms to acknowledge our presence. They've never approached us."

"You've been lucky, Matthew," Curtis replied. "They've taken corn cobs out of my fields and they raided John Anderson's house while he and his wife were in Parramatta recently. Apparently, they set fire to his crops and stole flour, sugar and potatoes from his house."

"Well, we try to accommodate them where we can, Curtis. They take some corn cobs from my fields too but, really, how much corn are they going to take? We can allow that, and there's a patch of ground down by the pond where their women dig some kind of wild potato from the ground, so we set that part of the property aside for them, rather than sow maize there. As I see it, learning to live with them is the way to avoid trouble."

Curtis Brown raised an eyebrow and looked at Matthew sceptically. It was not an approach that he or indeed any other settlers in the area had considered and, to him, it seemed a foolhardy way to live.

"Each to his own, I guess, Matthew," he said. "I reckon it's hard enough providing for my own family in this land, without pandering to heathen savages."

Matthew nodded, realising he was not going to change Curtis' attitude, and the two men agreed to differ.

Matthew and Elizabeth's third child was born at The Ponds on 23rd May 1795, a healthy baby boy to whom they gave the same name as his father, Matthew James Everingham (II). Two months after the birth, Matthew and Elizabeth took their young son and their toddler Sarah in the vegetable cart drawn by the mule to Parramatta for Matthew Jnr's baptism. The baby boy was baptised there by a new assistant chaplain, Reverend Samuel Marsden. Marsden had arrived in the colony on the *William* on 10th March 1794, after being recommended by William Wilberforce, British politician, philanthropist and ardent slave trade abolitionist, to be assistant chaplain to Reverend Richard Johnson, who Matthew and Elizabeth knew so well. By June 1795, Johnson was largely restricting his work to the settlement at Sydney Cove and Marsden was conducting church services and events such as marriages and baptisms at Parramatta.

On their way home to the Ponds after the baptism in Parramatta, Matthew and Elizabeth fell into discussion about the two chaplains.

They liked and respected Reverend Marsden, but there was no doubting they had a special affinity with Reverend Richard Johnson, and their ties with Johnson went well beyond the fact he had married them and had baptised Sally. Johnson had arrived on the First Fleet. Although he had sailed on the *Golden Grove* on that voyage, at Rio de Janeiro and at the Cape, he had held services on other ships, including *Scarborough*, and that is where Matthew had first met him.

Reverend Johnson was highly respected by Governor Arthur Phillip, but when Phillip left the colony in December 1792 and Lieutenant-Governor Francis Grose assumed control, Johnson fell into disfavour. Grose attacked Johnson over the length of the Sunday morning services and about his insistence on enforcing Arthur Phillip's regulation demanding church attendance for convicts. To Grose, that was simply a waste of convict working hours. By the time Reverend Marsden arrived in 1794, Johnson was locked in almost constant, serious quarrels with Grose and with his crony, John Macarthur, both of whom took to referring to Johnson as "that Methodist", a label which Johnson resented because, of course, he was a Church of England clergyman, not a Methodist.

Matthew Everingham admired any man who attempted to stand up to Francis Grose, and even more so one who stood up to John Macarthur. But, for Matthew, the thing that sealed his admiration of Reverend Richard Johnson was the name the chaplain had given to his daughter. Johnson and his wife, who had sailed on the First Fleet with him, had two children. The first, born in 1790, was a daughter to whom they gave the name Milbah – an Aboriginal name.

"Reverend Johnson is such a godly and honourable man," Matthew said to Elizabeth as they drove the cart back to The Ponds, "and I respect him very highly. To give an Aboriginal name to one's first-born child says a lot about his attitude towards the Aboriginals. It shows him to be a man of compassion and goodwill, and I think he's been treated very badly by the authorities in this colony. He deserves better."

"Y' spend a lot o' time lookin' at them mountains," Elizabeth said to Matthew one day as they sat on the deck in the spring sunshine. "Y're gonna go 'nd try t' find a way across 'em, aren't y'?"

Matthew looked at her in surprise for, whilst it had indeed been on his mind, it was not something he had even suggested to his wife.

Perhaps Thomas has said something to her, he thought.

"What are you now, a mind-reader?" he asked, smiling.

"I know y' well, Matthew," she responded with her trademark smile. "I ken tell what y're thinkin'. When are y' plannin' on goin'?"

"Soon," he said. "We've got a new governor and I'm sure Governor Hunter would handsomely reward the first man across those mountains. There are just a few things I have to think through before I attempt it. Leaving you here alone with the children while I'm gone is my main concern."

"I ken manage, Matthew," Elizabeth replied. "Thomas 'll be 'ere, so I'd feel quite safe, but I'd worry 'bout y' out there on them mountains. If y' go, y' must take others with y'."

"I'm working on that," he said. "There are two men in Parramatta who arrived with me on the First Fleet. We've had some discussions about forming a team."

"So, yer plannin's pretty well advanced?" Elizabeth asked.

Matthew nodded.

"Yes, but we've still a few things to decide on," he said. "We want to talk to some others who have tried and failed to cross the mountains, to see if we can pick up any pointers from them."

"That's a good idea, Matthew. But when y' go, please be careful. I need y' t' come back t' me."

On 30th October 1795, Matthew Everingham, William Reid and John Ramsey set out from Parramatta on an expedition to find a route across the Blue Mountains. Reid and Ramsey had arrived with Matthew on the First Fleet, and now, almost eight years later, the three were setting out together on yet another unknown journey. Each man carried a knapsack on his back with about forty pounds of provisions. Each also carried a musket and ammunition. [1]

On the first day, they covered twenty-seven miles, arriving late in the day at a place called Richmond Hill on the banks of the Hawkesbury River, where they were given accommodation for the night in a settler's hut. They crossed the Hawkesbury the next morning and, for the next several days, tried to find a route into the mountains, time and time again coming up against unpassable cliff faces and precipices.

Matthew would later write to Samuel Shepherd:

> *Having two excellent pocket compasses with us there was no danger of losing ourselves tho treading on ground to all appearance where human foot never trod before.*[2]

At noon on the third day, they found themselves on the summit of a mountain which they named Mount Collins, in honour of Lieutenant-Colonel David Collins, Judge Advocate of the colony, and there they found a bush which Matthew believed was a formerly unknown species – one which he described as "bearing a flower the colour and smell much resembling lavender". Remembering Samuel Shepherd, his advocate and supporter in England, Matthew drank to Shepherd's good health and named the bush "Shepherd's Bush".[3] From atop Mount Collins, they could look eastward and observe the coastal plain all the way to the coast, with the sea rolling against the shore and the Hawkesbury River with all its windings through the low country.[4] To the west, of course, they could see only ridge after ridge of formidable mountains. They slept wherever they could find cover and some warmth, often in hollow trees or in natural caves within the cliffs.

The party found themselves climbing and descending mountains time and time again, only to be confronted with yet another line of mountains rising before them, always higher than the previous, and with the way forward frequently denied them by impassable chasms. The bush was so close they could scarcely force their way through it[5] and the danger of taking a step forward only to fall over a high precipice was ever present.

After many days, they reached a line of mountains they named the "Western Mountains" to distinguish them from the Blue Mountains. From the top of these mountains, Matthew described the view to the west as yet more lower ridges of mountains and beyond that "a picturesque view of open country with few trees", to the south "a level champagne of land", to the north "nothing but mountain ridges rising behind till they are buried in the clouds".[6] To the east, of course, their view was blocked by the ridges they had traversed of the Blue Mountains.

From the top of what Matthew believed to be the highest mountain in the chain he had named the Western Mountains, their objective was literally within sight, although there remained yet other ridges of the

Western Mountains between them and the open plains to the west. But they could go no further because their provisions had been exhausted and, had they carried on, they most certainly would have perished. Reluctantly, they returned to Parramatta, following their same outward route. The last three days, they were totally without provisions, and Matthew was without shoes, which he lamented was "worse than the loss of victuals".[7]

Matthew returned to The Ponds on 14th November 1795 after having been away for fifteen days. Yet when he sat down with Elizabeth on the deck to talk about the expedition, he said very little about the hardships they had faced. He said little about their exhaustion, about the lack of provisions or about the painful days of walking through the bush without shoes. Rather, he spoke of the expedition as having been something of a sublime spiritual experience. He told her how the grandeur of the mountains had impressed upon him the power and the majesty of the God by whom all things are made.

"One night, Beth," he told her, "we slept in a huge rock cavern whilst a storm raged outside with such ferocity, thunder and lightning that I was reduced to a feeling of total insignificance before the God of all creation. I found myself drawn to the outside of the cavern to stand in the soaking rain and to take in the wonder of God's almighty power. Never before have I experienced such unfathomable awe and admiration before the power and majesty of God."

Later, in describing this event in his letter to Samuel Shepherd dated 30th August 1796, Matthew would write:

> *Never in my life was my soul struck with such awful admiration. The echoing of the thunder about those terrible rocks and mountains was sublimely grand…... It at last ceased and became quite calm. The rest of the night, tho we were very tired, was not spent in sleep, but in descanting accord to our little ability on the awfulness and majesty of the supreme being and our own littleness and insignificance while we stood trembling under a rock at the very terror of his sounds.*[8]

1. Matthew Everingham, writing to Samuel Shepherd in a letter dated 30th August 1796.
   The Letterbook of Matthew James Everingham, p.15 (extract)
   University of Melbourne Archives. Archive number 1974.0084.05378
2. Ibid., p.18
3. Ibid., pp. 20-21
4. Ibid., p.19
5. Ibid., p.26
6. Ibid., pp.27-28
7. Ibid., p.29
8. Ibid. p.25

13

By mid-1797, the Everingham family had spent six years struggling to support themselves on their land grant at The Ponds – an area that was by then becoming known as The Field of Mars. With the help of their convict labourer, Thomas Moran, their cultivated fields had sometimes produced good crops but at other times had been destroyed by plagues, floods and fires. The vegetable garden had been extended and in good years produced sizeable harvests of pumpkins, carrots, turnips and potatoes which Matthew was able to sell at market in Parramatta. Yet life continued to be a struggle and the Rum Corps continued to make that struggle even more difficult than it needed to be. Despite good intentions, Governor Hunter had not been able to curb the exploitative practices of the Corps officers.

A devastating bushfire had swept through The Field of Mars in April 1797, destroying the Everingham home along with many others and had left them near-destitute and with mounting debts. With the help of their neighbours, their house had been rebuilt – a two roomed wattle and daub house – but a winter with very little rainfall then left the ground dry and devoid even of grass. In summer, the thin topsoil cracked making the sowing of crops almost impossible and perhaps even futile.

Unless rain falls soon, Matthew thought, *there'll be no point in sowing crops this year.*

Yet no significant rain fell for many months and an extended drought meant there would be very little to harvest in the new year. The Everinghams, along with all other settlers in the area, faced an uncertain future as all were brought close to starvation levels.

"There aren't even any kangaroos to shoot," Matthew lamented to Elizabeth who was now pregnant again. "There were plenty here six months ago, but now it seems they've all moved on, looking for better pasture. Can't blame them for that – there's not a blade of grass here for them to eat."

"We'll be oright, Matthew," she replied. "We always are."

It was into such difficult circumstances that Matthew and Elizabeth welcomed their next child, a son, to whom they gave the name William, born 8th August 1797.

The small Everingham family and the other settlers at The Field of Mars were not the only ones feeling the impact of the drought on their diminished food supplies. The Aboriginals, too, were finding it difficult to survive. They too suffered from the absence of kangaroos, and the ground where their yams usually grew had dried out, causing the yams to wither and die. It was only by killing and eating snakes, lizards and an occasional fish they might spear in Subiaco Creek that they were able to survive.

Although Elizabeth had occasionally been the one able to elicit friendly waves from the Aboriginals, it was Matthew with whom they first made contact, perhaps realising the role of male hegemony within white families of the time. It was in mid-1798 when a small group of Aboriginal men first approached Matthew as he attempted to dig in his hard, barren fields. Using sign language, they made it clear to him that they were hungry and in need of food. Matthew sympathised with them – times were tough for everyone and he knew he had little food to offer them. He spread his arms indicating his dry and barren fields in a gesture of despair but then, seeing the hopelessness in their eyes, he beckoned to them to follow him to the house. He would give them what little he could.

Flour was one commodity that could be procured from the colony store in Parramatta, though prices were high. To purchase flour, however, meant increasing debt, because it needed to be bought on credit and, more often, Elizabeth would grind corn to make cornbread damper. For their family, most meals consisted of a weak vegetable broth and a crust of damper. Matthew gave the Aboriginals a cornbread damper Elizabeth had baked that morning and a flour bag with several potatoes and a couple of carrots. The Aboriginals accepted what was given to them, nodded in a gesture of thanks, then turned and walked away. Matthew and Elizabeth stood in front of their house, watching them go – Elizabeth nursing William on her hip, Sally standing beside her and Mathew Jnr peeping from behind his mother's skirt.

"Well, that's our first real contact with 'em," Elizabeth said. "It's taken a while."

Matthew nodded, as he watched the Aboriginal men disappear into the bush at the end of his fields.

"It's taken more than time," he said. "It's taken a genuine need for food. I'm sure they'll be back."

"Did y' see 'ow thin they was?" Elizabeth asked. "They was so thin y' could see their rib bones, 'nd their legs 'nd arms was so thin too."

"They're desperate," Matthew said. "When we can, we'll give them what we can spare. When we've nothing to give, we'll just have to hope they understand."

Elizabeth had also a number of parallel, horizontal scars across the chests and arms of the Aboriginal men, seemingly the result of deep cuts.

"I've heard about their practice of scarring themselves," Matthew said when Elizabeth raised the matter. "They cut themselves and rub some kind of pigment into the wounds to make the scars proud and noticeable."

"Why do y' reckon they'd do that t' 'emselves?" Elizabeth asked.

"It seems to be a cultural practice," Matthew replied, "and the scars could tell the story of a person's life – coming of age, an individual's status within the tribe, pain, courage and perhaps the sorrow of bereavement. Their womenfolk do it too, so I've been told."

Elizabeth shuddered and her face curled into a grimace.

"I sure am glad I'm not an Aboriginal woman," she said. "Must be awfully painful."

Visits by groups of Aboriginals asking for food continued periodically throughout the latter half of 1798 and into the autumn of 1799. After the first few visits it was mainly the Aboriginal womenfolk who came asking for food, though they did not come as often as Matthew expected. It seemed they respected and understood the fact that the settlers, like them, were surviving on scant food provisions and they only came when they were absolutely desperate. They always gave the Aboriginals a damper – even on occasions persuading them to stay and wait while Elizabeth prepared one. Most of the time, other than a damper, the Everinghams had little more to offer them. Elizabeth had fallen into the habit of taking the women inside to get or to make a damper, while Matthew searched the parched vegetable garden for something else they could give to the women. He was quite surprised to discover that Elizabeth, perhaps through spending more time with the Aboriginal women, was beginning to pick up parts of their language. She had learned their names and words such as *yuru* (hungry), *gurung* (child), *bidja* (here), *gunya* (house), *warrawi* (stand) and *ngalawa* (sit).

On a visit in February 1799, the Aboriginal women brought with them a number of small children – two boys and a girl whom Elizabeth though were probably about six or seven years of age, all three with distended bellies and with hungry flies crawling over their eyes and their sad little faces. One of the younger women carried a small baby wrapped in soft, white bark that looked like powdery paper. She held the baby out to Elizabeth, urging her to take and hold it in its blanket of soft bark, but, when Elizabeth took the baby in her arms and pulled back the soft covering of bark, she was immediately overcome with emotion. She quickly handed the baby back to its mother and, sobbing uncontrollably fled the house and ran straight into

Matthew's arms. Matthew took hold of her and embraced her tightly.

"That baby's so weak, it'll not live 'till t'morra," she sobbed, her tears wetting Matthew's shirt. "'ow many more childr'n 'ave they got like that? We 'ave t' give 'em whateva we ken, Matthew."

Matthew continued to hold her tightly and spoke softly to her.

"This is a harsh land," he said, "but they're strong people. Their ancestors have probably been living here for thousands of years."

"But some of 'em are dying, Matthew."

"Yes," he said "These are very difficult times, and some white settlers will die too. We'll do whatever we can to help them, but I wish we could do more. Now, go back in there and give them the damper and this small bag of potatoes."

With tears still running down her cheeks, Elizabeth handed the damper and the small bag of potatoes to the women and embraced the mother of the emaciated baby.

"Didjurigura" they said to her as they turned to leave, *"Didjurigura."*

As they left the house they said the same to Matthew – *"Didjurigura."*

Matthew looked at Elizabeth enquiringly.

"I dunno what that means," she said. "They said the same t' me. Maybe it means 'thanks', I'm not sure."

The winter of 1799 brought much needed rain, and green shoots began to show promise in the vegetable garden. Matthew and Thomas immediately began preparing the fields for spring planting, and everyone's spirits seemed to lift. The Aboriginal women still visited from time to time, but not so much to ask for food, although Elizabeth still gave them a damper on each visit. There was even one occasion when they brought a large fish as a gift to Elizabeth.

"*Maugra*" the women said as they handed the fish to her. "*Maugra.*"

Maugra, Elizabeth thought – "fish".

"*Didjurigura,*" she said as she accepted the fish and the Aboriginal women smiled broadly.

Yes, she thought, Didjurigura must mean "thank you".

By the beginning of November, things were generally looking more positive for the Everingham family. The maize and wheat fields showed promise of a small and much needed harvest in the new year, if occasional rain continued to eventuate. Meanwhile, Matthew and Thomas had been able to resume regular trips to Parramatta with cart loads of pumpkins which Matthew sold at market. The pumpkin sales allowed him to purchase other basic necessities in Parramatta, though they were insufficient to make a start on paying down the debts he had accumulated during the drought.

"Will the maize 'nd wheat 'arvest be enuf t' pay off our debts, Matthew?" Elizabeth asked as they stood looking over the fields in late November.

Matthew shook his head and reflected on the simplicity of Elizabeth's thinking. He had kept an account of what they had borrowed and balanced that against what he expected to recoup from the small harvest to come and from future pumpkin sales. Yet he knew such numbers were incomprehensible to Elizabeth.

She understands the concept of debt, I know that, he thought, *but numbers are meaningless to her. She knows we'll need to pay our creditors when we can, but, in her mind, the extent of our debt is something vague and ill-defined. Still, I wouldn't want her any other way. I love her for what she is.*

"No," he said. "It'll allow us to make a start on reducing our debts, but life's going to remain a struggle. It'll take more than one small harvest to clear our debts."

"We'll be oright, Matthew," she replied with her usual optimism. "We always are."

Another young Everingham was born on 9th December 1799 – a healthy boy to whom they gave the name George.

"Welcome to the Everingham family, George," Matthew said as he nursed his newborn son, "even though you'll be another mouth to feed."

"Don't say it like that, Matthew," Elizabeth scolded. "Every child's a blessin'."

Matthew smiled at her and looked again at his newborn son.

"I didn't mean it the way it sounded, Beth. You know I love every one of our children, and George'll grow up to be a fine young man. I'm just constantly thinking about reducing our level of debt."

"Well, 'e won't eat much f' a while, Matthew," she said with one of her broad smiles. "I've got enuf milk f' 'im."

The first year of the new century ushered in a period of more dependable weather with regular but not excessive rainfall and, for the next two years, the settlers at The Field of Mars, or The Ponds as Matthew continued to call it, would be spared destructive plagues, fires and floods. Yet, for the Everingham family, and probably for most of the other settlers in the area, this became a period of static stagnation when little progress towards more sustainable farming was achieved. Gradually, Matthew and Elizabeth were able to clear their debts and Matthew worked hard with Thomas to bring more acres of his land under cultivation but he was becoming increasingly disillusioned with life at The Ponds. The problem, Matthew realised, was the thin topsoil there. The older fields which had been under cultivation for some years were becoming sterile.

To the surprise of their neighbours and the chagrin of some, relations with the indigenous people continued to be amicable. Elizabeth now found she was able to visit the Aboriginal women digging for yams near the pond, without them fleeing at her approach. She was learning more and more words from the local Aboriginal language – Darug – but meaningful communication remained difficult. Elizabeth would often carry young George down to the pond to visit the Aboriginal women, usually accompanied by eight-year-old Sally and six-year-old Matthew Jnr. At first, Matthew was apprehensive about Elizabeth's growing familiarity with the Aboriginal women, but after he himself had visited them at the pond on a couple of occasions he assuaged his concerns by keeping an eye on these meetings from a distance. There was one particular woman amongst the Aboriginals to whom Elizabeth had taken quite a liking – a young woman named Mali – and it was clear that the feeling was mutual, despite the frustrations each of them felt because of the language difficulties.

Yet, despite Elizabeth's growing relationship with the Aboriginal women, it was Matthew who was met by a small group of Aboriginal men carrying spears, as he exited the house one morning. One of the Aboriginal men reached out and took Matthew's hand, pulling at it.

"Gawi!" he said, "Gawi!"

"What does he want, Beth?" Matthew asked his wife.

"Gawi! Gawi!" the man said, tugging again at Matthew's hand.

"They want y' t' go somewhere with 'em," Elizabeth said. "Gawi means 'Come'."

"Where to?"

"I dunno, Matthew. Maybe t' their camp, but I really dunno."

Matthew hesitated, casting an eye at his musket which leaned against the front wall of the house, but quickly realised resorting to the use of the musket would be futile. If these Aboriginal men meant to harm him, they could already have done so.

"I think y' ken trust 'em, Matthew," Elizabeth said. "If they want y' t' go t' their camp, y' should think it a great honour. I wish it was me they's wantin' t' take t' their camp."

"Well, it seems you're not invited, Beth. And if it were you they wanted to take, I wouldn't allow it."

"Go, Matthew! Go with 'em. I know y' ken trust 'em."

Feeling he had no option, Matthew reluctantly allowed himself to be led away, turning back to call to Thomas, "Take care of Beth and the children!"

It was late in the afternoon when the Aboriginal men brought Matthew back to the house. He immediately went inside and came out carrying a damper, but, before giving it to them, he spoke to Elizabeth.

"What's that word that means 'thank you', Beth?" he asked quietly, drawing her aside.

"*Didjurigura,*" Elizabeth spoke quietly to him, "*Did-juri-gura.*"

He turned and handed the damper to one of the Aboriginal men.

"Didjurigura," he said, *"Didjurigura."*

Matthew and Elizabeth watched as the Aboriginals turned and left, but Elizabeth could hardly contain her excitement.

"I wanna know all 'bout it!" she said. "Tell me!"

"It was fascinating," Matthew said. "I'll tell you all about it at dinner time."

"So?" Elizabeth said the moment they sat down to eat dinner. "Tell me 'bout it. Where do they live?"

Matthew talked slowly about his experience, making sure the older children were listening. He thought it important that they too should learn as much as they could about the Aboriginals.

'Well, they live in small shelters made of bark," he started, putting down his wooden spoon to make a tent shape with his hands, "*miri-miri* they call the shelters. The camp is amongst the trees, a bit over a mile from here, I reckon."

"There were about fifty of them, maybe sixty, but they seem to live in small groups of about fifteen. Maybe they're family groups, I'm not sure. Each group has their own fireplace – that could be a safety measure,

I suppose. One big fire for a large group would probably be dangerous and cause the fire to get out of control. The place where they camp is quite smoky with all of those little fires. The men who came to get me took me to sit around their small fireplace and some from the other groups came over to where I was sitting. They talked to the men who had taken me there, but they didn't sit around the fireplace with us – it was as if they had come to visit, just to get a look at me. I couldn't understand what they were saying, of course, but they showed great interest in me, sometimes pointing at me but not in any angry way. I'm sure they just came over to get a closer look at the strange white man."

Elizabeth and the children were fascinated and listened in silence.

"I think they probably move around a bit," Matthew continued, "because, on the way to their camp, we passed what was obviously another campsite with those bark shelters and fireplaces, but it had been abandoned. Perhaps they go back there from time to time – I'm not sure about that."

"Was there women 'nd chil'ren there, at their camp?" Elizabeth asked.

"There were," Matthew replied. "The children were very interested in me, coming to stare at me like someone from a far country, which I guess I am to them. But the women kept their distance. They mainly came to the fireplace to prepare food."

"They gave y' food?" Sally asked.

Matthew nodded.

"They did," he said. "We ate some of those wild potatoes we've seen them digging from around the pond. They cooked them in the hot coals of the fireplace. Actually, they tasted more like turnips than potatoes – *'midny'* they call them, or maybe *'midiny'*. Something like that anyway."

"Yeah, *'midiny'*," Elizabeth said. "The women diggin' for 'em near the pond told me that's what they's called."

"And they cooked a big lizard," Matthew said.

"A lizard?" Elizabeth exclaimed with a lift of her eyebrows.

"Yes, one of those huge lizards, about three feet in length, the kind we sometimes see in our fields. They baked it on the hot coals in their fireplace."

"And you et some of that?" William asked, his face curling into a grimace and his eyes scrunching shut.

"Ate, William, not et," Matthew corrected his son. "Yes, I did eat some of the lizard. I think it would have been rude to have refused. Anyway, I figured if they were eating it then it couldn't do me any harm. Actually, it wasn't bad – it tasted a bit like chicken."

"Eew!" Sally, Matthew Jnr and William cried in unison.

"Don't worry, chil'ren," Elizabeth said with a broad smile. "We aint gonna be eatin' no lizards in this 'ouse."

"On the way back here," Matthew continued, "they stopped and made a point of showing me some large trees. I'm not sure what that was all about, but they touched the trees with the flat of their hands and then they touched themselves on their chests in the same way. It seemed they were telling me the trees were important to them. In some way, I think that may have been the sole reason they took me to their camp. And I'm sure it had something to do with the reason they seemed to be angry at us when we felled the trees for our fields."

"Well," Elizabeth said, "next time, I wanna go with y'."

But there would be no 'next time'. The Aboriginals seemed to have made their point. They had been content to take Matthew to their camp on one occasion and did not ask him to go with them again.

By late-1801 Matthew had persuaded Elizabeth they would be better off selling the land at The Ponds and moving further north to the district known as "The Hawkesbury".

"People are saying the land up there is more fertile and better for growing crops," Matthew told her.

"Is there a settlemen' town there?" Elizabeth asked, "Like Parramatta?"

"There's a small developing settlement," Matthew replied. "Green Hills, it's called. Much smaller than Parramatta at this stage. We'll apply for a land grant, though I imagine we'll be given land some distance from Green Hills."

" 'nd Thomas'll go with us?" Elizabeth asked.

"No. We'd be losing Thomas soon anyway – he'll get his Ticket of Leave in January and he'll be leaving to seek paid work. It'll be good for him and we'll wish him well. I'll write a letter of recommendation for him."

"Will we git anotha lab'rer t' replace 'im?" Elizabeth asked.

Matthew nodded.

"I'm sure we will, maybe two," he said. But I think maybe we'd be better off waiting until we get settled in the Hawkesbury. We can do without a labourer for a couple of months and make application for new labourers when we get there. There's no sense in getting new labours and then moving them all the way to the Hawkesbury. I'll miss Thomas though. He's been a good worker and a friend."

"I'm gonna miss them Aboriginals 'ere too," Elizabeth said. "Let's 'ope the new owner o' the land treats 'em well."

In January 1802, officials of the colonial government toured the district to compile a muster of all settlers and their land holdings. At The Ponds, the muster recorded that Matthew Everingham, wife and four children held fifty acres, seventeen of which were under cultivation – thirteen acres of wheat and maize and four acres of vegetables (mostly pumpkins). He also had a mule, a cow, 10 pigs, a brood of hens, a musket and a pistol.

"We won't be here much longer," Matthew told the muster official. "We're going to move up to the Hawkesbury as soon as we can sell this property."

"Which part of the Hawkesbury will you be heading to?" the official asked.

"I'm thinking a district called Portland Head, up towards Wiseman's Ferry," Matthew replied. "I hear the land there is fertile so we'll try to rent a property there, then apply to the governor for a land grant."

The official raised his eyebrows in surprise.

"That's a tough and lawless district," he said. "A lot of the settlers there are frequently attacked by hostile natives, not to mention escaped convicts. You'll need to be prepared for that."

Matthew nodded – grateful Elizabeth was not within earshot. He knew the dangers and he knew he was taking something of a risk in moving his family to the Hawkesbury. Yet he remained optimistic and confident in his belief that it would be a good move for them.

"Yes, Portland Head and Wiseman's Ferry are pretty much the frontier of this colony, but we've managed to live amicably with the natives here at The Ponds. Hopefully we'll be able to do the same there."

"Well, good luck," said the muster official. "I read in the *Gazette* about the leader of a tribe of murderous natives near Portland Head. 'Branch Jack', they're calling him, apparently because he hails from the district around the branch of the Hawkesbury and the Colo Rivers. Watch out for him!"

"Appreciate your advice," Matthew said as the muster official turned to leave.

"What were that all 'bout?" Elizabeth asked as she re-joined Matthew at the front of the house.

Matthew shrugged and gave her a smile, indicating it was nothing important.

"Just small talk," he said. "He was asking about which district we intend to move to."

The fifty-acre land grant at The Ponds was sold to Andrew Hume in April 1802 and, as they loaded their scant possessions onto the cart, ready for their move to the Hawkesbury, Matthew stood for a moment holding the reins of the mule and taking one last look around the property as he reflected on the time they had spent there. It had taken every ounce of his strength and fortitude to stay on that land for those eleven years.

I did my best, he thought, *and I couldn't have done it without Beth. We worked hard to produce crops from sterile soil, we struggled to provide for our growing family through times of severe drought and through times when our crops were reduced to stubble by plagues of mice and grasshoppers. We've seen our house destroyed by bushfire and we rebuilt it. We've lived through "The Hungry Years", and we've struggled to survive against the exploitation of the Rum Corps.*

He put a foot on the wheel and climbed up into the cart, settling himself beside Elizabeth, with the children behind him in the tray, and readied himself to drive the mule forward.

We've known three Governors, he thought – *Arthur Philip, John Hunter and the current Governor Philip Gidley King, and we've lived through the disastrous transitional Governorship of Lieutenant-Governor Francis Grose who, along with his crony John Macarthur, changed the colony forever – and not for the better.*

He turned in his seat to look at their four children – Sally, aged nine, Matthew Jnr, aged seven, William, aged five and little George, aged two.

It's been tough for them too, he thought. *It's time fortune smiled on us. Perhaps we'll find it in the Hawkesbury.*

Then, resolutely looking down the road ahead, he flicked the reins and called on the mule to move forward.

14

The journey from The Ponds to Green Hills, later to be named Windsor, would have taken about eight hours in good conditions, but April 1802 was not the best of conditions. Recent rains had reduced the road, if it could ever have been called a road, to a muddy track, with deep wheel ruts into which the cart frequently sank and became bogged. Time and time again, Matthew, Elizabeth and the older children had to lift and push the cart out of the mud and urge the mule forward. By mid-afternoon, all of them, especially the mule, were exhausted. Matthew knew the risks of camping overnight by the side of the road, but he was faced with no alternative.

Green Hills is probably only another hour away, maybe an hour and a half, but, if we try to push the mule forward any further, we'll kill it, he thought, *and that'd be a disaster.*

"We'll camp here tonight," he told Elizabeth. "We'll unhitch the mule so she can rest and we'll unload the cart so you and the children can sleep in the tray. I'll sleep on the ground alongside the road."

He expected he was going to get precious little sleep – at least that was his intent. The risk of attacks by natives or escaped convicts was very real and Matthew intended to remain as alert as possible throughout the night. He took up his musket which he had taken to calling "Bess" and lay down with it beside the front wheel of the cart. Despite his best intentions to remain alert, he was soon fast asleep, with Bess wrapped in his arms.

Morning brought sunshine and Matthew, having been awakened by the laughter of the children playing nearby, rose to his feet and went slightly into the bush to relieve himself. Turning, he found Matthew Jnr backing the mule into the shafts of the cart and Elizabeth sitting up in the cart, rubbing the sleep from her eyes and then combing her hair with her fingers.

"Mornin', Matthew," she said. "Did y' sleep well?"

"I was awake most of the night," Matthew lied, "keeping watch over you all."

Elizabeth nodded, then broke into one of her broad smiles that made her eyes scrunch up.

"Did y' know that y' snore while y're awake 'nd watchin' over us?" she asked.

Matthew realised he'd been caught out and smiled sheepishly.

"Well," he said, "I might have dozed off momentarily, I suppose."

The remaining part of their journey to Green Hills was much easier than the first day's journey. The closer they got to Green Hills, the more the track improved – the last couple of miles actually being made firm by compacted gravel. The people of Green Hills, it seemed, were proud of their settlement.

As they drew closer, they noticed extensive wheat fields, the best they had ever seen, and on the edge of the fields a fine, double storeyed house made from red bricks, with a shingled roof.

"'e's done well f' 'imself, whoeva 'e is," Elizabeth said, gazing at the fine fields and the red brick house.

"It wouldn't surprise me," Matthew said, "if he's an officer of the Rum Corps – one of Macarthur's cronies. Not many other people in the colony could afford a property like that."

They found themselves separated from Green Hills by a wide creek which they would later learn was called South Creek. A pathway led along the south bank of the creek and eventually they came to a place where a floating pontoon bridge gave passage to the other side, and to the Green Hills township. The bridge, which appeared to be the only way to cross the creek, was a toll bridge manned by a toll collector. It would cost twelve pence for the family and their cart to cross the bridge he informed them. As Matthew paid the toll he asked the toll collector about the red brick house and the fine wheat fields.

"That's what people around here call The Red House Farm," he replied. "The bricks they make here in Green Hills are red in colour, because of the local clay. That house belongs to Mr Andrew Thompson. He's an ex-convict, well known and well liked in these parts – a captain of industry, you might say."

The toll collector did not add that the toll bridge on which they would cross the creek was also owned by Andrew Thompson. Matthew thought further about the fine, red brick house and its extensive fields and wondered how an ex-convict, like himself, had been able to better himself to become a "captain of industry", in the words of the toll collector, and to own such a fine house. Little did he imagine that he and his family would one day live in that very house, though he would not own it.

In Green Hills, Matthew made arrangements to rent a fifteen-acre farm at Portland Head – a district which would later be called Sackville Reach.

"Y'll find that seven acres of the land's bin cleared f' crop plantin'," the owner assured him, "'nd there's a small 'ouse. Y've probably 'eard the river floods now 'nd then, but y'll be oright b'cause the 'ouse's on high ground."

Realising that the younger children needed a good night's rest before continuing the journey to Portland Head, they took a room for one night at a cheap inn. Elizabeth and the children rested there during the afternoon, while Matthew headed off to the Colonial Lands Office. There he submitted an application for a fifty-acre land grant at Portland Head and for two convict labourers to help work it. He was fully aware that the colonial government never made quick decisions on such matters and that it could be a year or more before he received his land.

The next morning, they crossed the Hawkesbury River at Green Hills on a ferry owned by Andrew Thompson and headed north following a rough map given to them by the property owner, to the location of their rented farm at Portland Head, eventually finding it adjacent to one arm of a large U-shaped bend in the river.

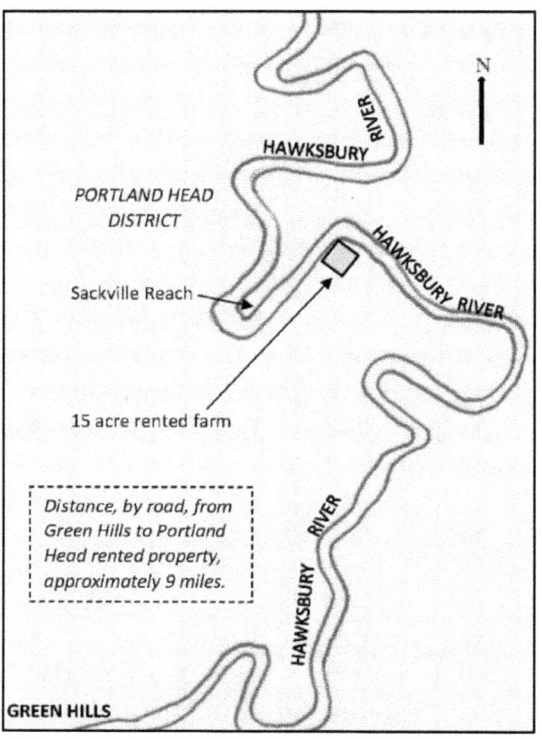

The Everingham family settled in well at Portland Head. The house was bigger than they expected – a three roomed slab house with a bark roof, a dirt floor and a small awning type veranda in front of it. Matthew was pleased to find that the owner in Green Hills had been honest, when he had assured them that seven acres had been cleared for fields.

I'm not sure it's seven acres, he thought. *It might be a bit less, maybe five or six, but it's enough. If it hadn't been cleared, we'd have moved on. There's no way I would have cleared another man's land for him.*

When Matthew spoke to the children about assigning chores to each of them, Sally quickly declared that feeding the hens and collecting the eggs would be one of hers.

"I'll do other chores too," she said, "but the hens are mine!"

Matthew smiled. He remembered how Elizabeth had enjoyed caring for the hens at The Ponds. Indeed, she had told him how caring for the hens on the voyage to Botany Bay in 1790 on board *Neptune* was the one enjoyable part of an horrendous journey. He remembered too how Elizabeth had taught Sally, then a toddler, to feed the hens and collect the eggs at The Ponds and he knew Elizabeth too would be pleased that Sally still wanted to look after their brood of hens.

For the Everingham children, as with all children of pioneer families trying to eke out a living in this inhospitable land, daily life revolved very much around chores, and there were plenty to go around. As the eldest child, Sally willingly took on more than her fair share. She would help William carry water from the river, for the younger children were not permitted to go near the river unless supervised either by Sally or by one of their parents. She would wash the clothes and, in the evenings, would sit by the fire with Elizabeth and learn how to make repairs to torn clothing.

Matthew Jnr's main chores were to chop wood and to help his father in the fields and, if Sally had any free time, she too would help in the fields. Matthew Jnr and Sally washed the dishes after the evening meal and William was learning to lay the fire and to clean the fireplace the next morning. Elizabeth, pregnant again, restricted herself to caring for the toddler, George, and preparing meals.

In the evenings, after the dishes had been washed, Matthew would call Sally, Matthew Jnr and William back to the table where he would teach them reading and writing.

I should have taught Beth to read and write when we were young, he thought, *when we first met, though she seems happy without knowing those skills. Probably it's more important for a man than a woman, but I'll teach Sally as well – she'll probably marry some man who is illiterate and literacy skills will be useful to her.*

Matthew had written several short stories in simple language for the children and he drew crude illustrations to complement the sentences. Elizabeth had stitched the pages together to form small booklets.

He wrote sentences and drew pictures from his own experience – the voyage to Botany Bay on *Scarborough* with the First Fleet, tents and the early settlement at Sydney Cove, meeting Elizabeth at Parramatta and life at The Ponds. The pictures he drew were relevant to each booklet – the tall ships, African natives coming alongside at The Cape trying to sell fruit, images of kangaroos, Aboriginal people at The Ponds and their camp he had visited.

The favourite booklet amongst the children, particularly the boys, was the booklet about the voyage with the First Fleet.

"Tell us again about the ship and about the harbour in Africa," they would plead. But, although he knew their literacy skills would never be at a high level of proficiency, he was nonetheless determined to teach his children as best he could.

"No," he would say when they asked for those stories, "*you* tell me about the ship. Look here at this sentence. Read the words one letter at a time. What does that word say?" he'd ask, pointing to the words.

When he was satisfied with the evening's lesson, he would reward them with stories about the voyage on *Scarborough* – the singing of the sailors as they climbed high into the rigging, the salty spray carried by the wind as the ship forged its way through almost every wave, the visits by Captain Arthur Phillip when he came on board *Scarborough* from his flagship at Rio and at The Cape. The one thing he never talked about to his children, or to anyone else, was his life in England before his transportation. That was a different life.

During the year spent at the rented fifteen-acre-farm, there were signs of increasing unrest and tensions between the white settlers and the local Aboriginals, though no news of any outright conflicts came to Matthew's ears. He had found yam beds and signs of digging by the river and, as had been his practice at The Ponds, he determined to leave that ground untouched. Furthermore, with the rented land already cleared for cropping, Matthew had no reason to fell more trees and he felt sure the Aboriginals would have been pleased about that. Yet stories of skirmishes between the settlers and groups of Aboriginals persisted – tensions and conflicts were brewing below the surface and the two races remained wary of each other.

It was a cold afternoon in mid-winter 1802 when Sally and Matthew Jnr came running back to the house calling for their father's attention.

"Pa," Sally said excitedly, "come and see the hands we found."

"Hands?" Matthew asked in alarm, thinking the children must have found the remains of human bodies. "What hands? Where?"

"Pictures, Pa," said Matthew Jnr breathlessly. "Come and see."

Elizabeth, overhearing the children's excitement, decided she too wanted to see these "hands", so Sally and Matthew Jnr led the whole family to an area several hundred yards behind the house where they had been collecting firewood.

"It's over there, Pa," Matthew Jnr said excitedly, pointing to a rock face below a wide overhang.

They approached, rapt in awe and amazement, Matthew with his hand over his mouth as he stood there taking in the vista on the rock face. Hands – dozens of hands – imposed in red and brown ochre on the limestone wall. Matthew was speechless, until one of the children spoke.

"Let's draw our hands too," William said.

"No!" Matthew said quickly and with authority. "We mustn't touch this. Never touch it in any way, children."

They stared at him questioningly, not really understanding. Matthew himself did not fully understand what he was looking at, yet he knew it was something of great importance.

"These drawings are very old," he said, "hundreds of years old, perhaps thousands of years. I think this place is probably very important to the Aboriginals – maybe a reminder of their ancestors. They may consider it a sacred place, maybe something like a cemetery. We must respect it and not touch it."

They returned to the house, and speculation about the purpose of "the hands" was the only topic of conversation during and after dinner. During the family's remaining time on the rented farm, Matthew would often return to the rockface to stare at the hands, unaware of the dark eyes watching him from the undergrowth of the bush.

On 7th November 1802, Matthew and Elizabeth welcomed the newest member of the Everingham family, a healthy daughter to whom they gave the name Ann. Matthew was now thirty-five years of age and Elizabeth thirty-one.

Despite Matthew's best efforts to co-exist with the local Aboriginals – his setting aside the yam beds, his insistence that their rock art be honoured, plus the fact that he was not felling trees – the tense undercurrent of mutual misunderstanding persisted and remained a constant threat to settlers in the district. They longed for the kind of relationship they had established with the Aboriginals at The Ponds, but thus far there had been no real contact with any of the local natives and no opportunity for Elizabeth to use even her limited knowledge of their language.

"They might not even understand you here, Beth," Matthew told her. "It's likely that different tribes in different districts each have their own language. You might have to start over again and learn new words."

"I ken do that, Matthew," she replied. "I jist 'ope we git t' meet some of 'em soon. I wanna ask 'em 'bout them hands."

Matthew looked at his wife, a slight frown crossing his face – a frown of uncertainty.

"I'm not sure that'd be a good idea, Beth," he said. "I think it's probably a very important place to them – perhaps a place they consider very private. We'll have to decide whether to talk about the hands if and when we meet any of them."

Yet, Matthew was pleased he had brought his family to Portland Head. His fields there were proving more successful than at The Ponds because the soil was rich and fertile and his crops thrived. But the settlers who had been there for some years spoke of the disastrous flood of 1799 washing away farms, houses, bridges, ferries and livestock, three years before the Everingham family had moved to Portland Head. The river had risen more than fifteen feet overnight, they said, and whilst that worried Matthew, he decided it must surely be an exaggeration. Despite the threat of floods and Aboriginal hostility, people like Matthew had still flocked to the district and, by 1803, nearly a thousand people lived and farmed along the Hawkesbury between Green Hills and Portland Head.

I think we'll be all right here, he thought. *We're fortunate this small farm is on high ground. It'd take a rise in the river of more than fifteen feet to reach our fields, and the house is even higher.*

Still, he watched the river and the clouds daily, praying that his judgment was correct and that his good fortune would continue.

Matthew periodically made the four-hour journey to Green Hills with his cart to pick up supplies and sometimes take a load of pumpkins for sale at the Green Hills market. On returning from one of those trips near the end of May 1803, he greeted Elizabeth with a smile and waving a piece of paper.

"We've got our own grant of fifty acres," he said, "granted to us on 3rd April, and with two convict labourers to help work it."

"'ave y' seen it, Matthew?" she asked.

"Yes. It's not far from here, just a mile downstream. I called there on the way home from Green Hills to look at it and left the two convict labourers there, with instructions to build a house for us and a hut for themselves. We'll move there as soon as the house is ready."

"Ken y' trust them convicts not t' run off?" Elizabeth asked.

"Well," Matthew said, thoughtfully, "they seem like good men, though I've only known them half a day. But just like Thomas at The Ponds, we'll supply them with food and clothing drawn from the colony storehouse in Green Hills until they get their Ticket of Leave. They know if they run off, they'll not get that, and they'll become outlaws. So, in a way, they're dependent on us. I think they'll stay and work."

Elizabeth nodded, and Matthew continued to think about his two convict labourers alone on his land grant a mile away.

"Even if they were working here and living with us," he continued, "they could still run off. I wouldn't be able to stop them. But, as long as they get fed, I think they'll stay."

"'nd what's the land like?"

The smile dissipated from Matthew's face, replaced by a kind of half-grimace.

"It's not perfect," he said. "Part of it is low lying ground likely to flood. The high ground where the house will be built is an area with some huge rocks, some as big as houses. Still, there's an area of good ground we can clear for crops, hopefully above any flood line."

Over the course of the next several weeks, Matthew moved some of their belongings to the new farm. One day, he took the cart loaded with his shovels, axes, saws and other agricultural implements, most of which would be of use to the convicts building the family's house and their own hut. He and Matthew Jnr spent a day at the new land grant building a fenced yard for his pigs. Then the next day, the two of them drove the pigs down the very rough track to the new property and secured them in the fenced yard. Near the house, they built a pen for the hens and Matthew Jnr, with William, moved the hens to their new home just days before the family was ready to move.

As they prepared to move to their new land grant, Matthew decided to make one last visit to the rockface with the ancient painting of hands. While he stood there gazing at it his mind went to what, if anything, he should do about it.

I'm still in awe of this place, he thought. *Should I tell the owner of the land about it? No, he doesn't strike me as the kind of man who'd respect it. Should I tell the government authorities about it? If I do, what would they do about it? There's no way to know what they'd do. They might even try to cut that rockface out and take it away – maybe even send it to England.*

In the end, he decided to do nothing and walked away, hoping the place would remain undiscovered by other settlers.

The Everingham family moved onto their new fifty-acre land grant at Portland Head at the beginning of July 1803.

15

Matthew's two convict labourers on the fifty-acre land grant at Portland Head had a great deal in common. Both were Irish and both spoke with a lilting Irish brogue. Both were twenty-three years of age, both had made their way to London and both had fallen foul of the law there. Both were convicted of theft in the Old Bailey and both sentenced to seven years with transportation to the penal colony in New South Wales. Their lives in Ireland, however, had been quite different.

Owen Maguire had been raised in a peasant family on a potato farm in County Limerick, a rural area of southwest Ireland. From there he had made his way to Dublin and then to London where he was convicted of stealing a coat and sentenced to seven years transportation. A gregarious man whose only possession was a fiddle brought with him from England when transported, agriculture was in his blood.

His compatriot was Lawrence Byrne – "Call me Larry," he said – a Dublin man who had followed his father into the family business as a cobbler and worker of leather goods. An amiable man, though perhaps lacking some of the bonhomie of Owen Maguire, his leather working skills would be useful to Matthew from time to time, but he knew little about farming techniques.

As had been the case with Thomas Moran, their previous labourer at The Ponds, Matthew would be able to draw victuals for the two from the colony store in Green Hills until such time as they gained their Ticket of Leave – Owen on 1st March 1805 and Larry three months later on 1st June 1805.

The two had worked well together to build the house for the family and the hut for themselves. By the time the family moved to their new land, Owen and Larry had even made a start on clearing land for the planting of crops.

As Matthew and Elizabeth sat eating lunch with the two labourers, Elizabeth turned to Larry with a request.

"Do y' reckon y' could make some shoes f' the chil'ren?" she asked. "They's growing so fast we need some new shoes f' 'em, 'specially f' Sally 'nd Matthew Jnr. We ken pass their shoes down t' the younger chil'ren, but new shoes f' the older chil'ren are so expensive."

Larry looked a little non-plussed before finally responding.

"Oi've never made shoes, Missus Everingham," he replied. "Oi s'ppose oi could turn me mind t' it, but dey'd be rough, t' be sure 'nd be certain dey would. Not like duh good, new shoes y' could buy in duh store."

It was now Elizabeth's turn to look surprised.

"I thought y' was a cobbler?" she asked, but it was Matthew who intervened with an explanation.

"Cobblers don't make shoes, Beth," he explained. "Cobblers only repair shoes."

"Aye, dats duh truth of it, f' sure 'nd be certain," Larry added. "Back in Oiland, we cobblers were even forbidden fr'm working wid new leather. We 'ad t' use old leather t' make repairs. A shoemaker 'd be very insulted if y' ever called 'im a cobbler, 'e would. But oi'll try me 'and at making shoes f' the children if y' want."

Matthew winked at Larry.

"See what you can do, Larry," he said.

It was Owen who pointed out to Matthew the advantages and drawbacks of the huge rocks behind the house.

"Those rocks'll shelter duh house fr'm strong westerly winds, Mattew" he said, "and might even 'elp protect duh house from fire. But de're also a perfect 'iding place 'nd a shield f' any Aboriginals dat might try t' attack duh house, and oi hear dat around 'ere duh natives are quite restless."

Matthew eyed the rocks with renewed disquiet. He too had heard of conflicts between the white settlers and the Aboriginal people of the district, though he still hoped to establish an amicable relationship with them such as they had enjoyed at The Ponds.

"Well, we can't do anything about the rocks," he said. "Most of them are even bigger than the house so we'll be grateful for the windbreak and just hope we can get on well with the Aboriginals."

It would prove to be a vain hope.

Soon after the establishment of the settlement at Sydney Cove in 1788, the Governor, Captain Arthur Phillip had charted the lower reaches of the Hawkesbury from its mouth at Broken Bay upstream for a distance of about twenty miles. Phillip named the river after Lord Hawkesbury, President of the Privy Council Standing Committee on Trade. Meanwhile, Lieutenant Watkin Trench, the same Watkin Trench who had visited the Everingham farm at The Ponds, set off to walk inland from Sydney towards the Blue Mountains. At the foot of the mountains, Trench discovered a large river which he named the Nepean after Evan Nepean, the Under Secretary of State at the Home Office and a close personal friend of Arthur Phillip. It took about three years for the government to realise that the Nepean and the Hawkesbury were one and the same – the Nepean was the upper reaches of the Hawkesbury.

The headwaters of the Nepean River rise about sixty miles south of Sydney and about ten miles from the coast. The river flows north through the Nepean Gorge, forming the western edge of the Sydney settlement. Near Yarramundi, at its confluence with the Grose River, the Nepean becomes the Hawkesbury River. The indigenous Darug and Darkinjung people who lived, and still live, along the Nepean-Hawkesbury River course had always known it to be one river and call it Deerubbin. It forms a striking landscape, especially north of Green Hills (Windsor) where the river course cuts through deep sandstone gorges, through Portland Head and north as far as Wisemans Ferry, before turning east and heading to the ocean at Broken Bay.

The indigenous people of the Hawkesbury-Nepean at first hoped these new white people were mere interlopers who might eventually move on. They would, perhaps, have been prepared to share access to the land with the newcomers, but, finding themselves driven further and further away from their ancestral lands and their staple food sources, especially the yam beds on the riverbanks, they were being forced into a situation of near starvation, with no option but to resist.

The white settlers and their government were clearly not interested in sharing anything. The settlers considered themselves to be the owners of land given or sold to them by their colonial government. They would protect that land, if necessary – and often unnecessarily – by firing on Aboriginals who crossed or attempted to procure food from their land. Yet, to the indigenous people, any concept of "land ownership" was, and is, totally alien and inconceivable.

Thus, from 1794 until 1819, the Deerubbin became the site of one of the longest and most brutal frontier wars the colony would experience – a series of wars between the British Empire and the resisting indigenous peoples – wars which became known as "The Frontier Wars". Portland Head was at the very centre of those conflicts. The Everingham family together with their convict labourers had taken up residence in a war zone.

In May 1804, an Aboriginal raiding party attacked the Everingham farm, coming from behind the huge rocks at the rear of the house while Larry Byrnes was on an errand in Green Hills and while Matthew, Elizabeth and their other servant, Owen Maguire, were in the fields inspecting the maize crop. All three were speared, although none were mortally wounded. Their five children at the time – Sally (aged 11), Matthew Jnr (aged 9), William (aged 7), George (aged 4) and Ann (aged 18 months) – were ignored by the raiders and not molested in any way. The houses were plundered and set on fire, yet it seemed to Matthew that, rather than killing the entire family, which they could easily have done, the raiders were more interested in taking the readily removable produce of their land, including the hens.

It's a warning, Matthew thought. *They just want us to go away. Yet, what can I do? Where can I go? I didn't ask to come to this country, but now, like all settlers, I can only stay here and try to learn to live with these people.*

It was true – in part. Matthew had not asked to come to this country, but when given the opportunity to return to England upon his emancipation in 1791, he had chosen to stay and take a land grant. He could still leave, now, and take his family back to England, if he wished. Thus, in a way, he had chosen to become complicit in the ongoing dispossession of Aboriginal land. That, however, was an issue of which he was seemingly unaware, notwithstanding the fact that he was somewhat more enlightened about relationships with the indigenous people than most of his compatriots.

At the time of the Aboriginal attack on his property, Matthew was unaware of similar raids on the property of a neighbour, John Howe, and on that of other settlers in the immediate district. When the report of those attacks, along with the report of the attack on his own property, appeared in *The Sydney Gazette & New South Wales Advertiser*, Matthew read it out to Elizabeth.

We are concerned to state that a few of the Natives have again manifested an inclination to hostility, and already proceed to acts of abominable outrage. Report at the present juncture confines their ravages and barbarity to Portland Head where Mr Matthew Everingham, settler, his wife, and a servant are said to have been speared; as is also Mr John Howe, settler, near the above spot. The house and out-houses of the former were plundered and afterwards set on fire, but the spear wounds received are not accompanied with any mortal appearance. Several other settlers in this neighbourhood have suffered very considerably in being robbed of their clothing, flock, and grain. On Thursday evening, shortly after the accounts arrived, HIS EXCELLENCY dispatched a file of Troopers to the Magistrate at Hawkesbury, with instructions promptly to adopt such measures as the exigency of the case required. The settlers and constables of that settlement went to the succour of the other settlers at Portland Head; as no provocation appears to have been given the Natives in that quarter, and as the Natives in the other districts are still on the domesticated footing they have been for the last two years, it is hoped the exertions that are making [sic] *to keep them in that state, will have the desired effect without proceeding to further extremities.*[1]

"Are we gonna be safe, 'ere, Matthew?" Elizabeth asked, when he finished reading the report.

Matthew sipped at his pannikin of tea several times and considered the question for a few moments before replying.

"I think we will, Beth," he finally said. "The fact of the matter is that, when they attacked our house, they could have killed us. They could have killed all of us, but they chose not to."

"So, they was jist too lazy t' chase us int' the field 'nd finish us off? 'nd maybe they jist like chil'ren. Maybe that's why they didn' 'arm the chil'ren?"

Matthew released a long sigh and took another sip of his tea. He knew Elizabeth could be right. Yet he believed that he had little choice but to stay on this land, so he needed to reassure her.

"I think the attack was a warning to us, Beth. Perhaps an expression of anger towards us."

"What 'ave we done t' make 'em angry, Matthew? Nothin'! We've left patches o' their *midiny*, those wild potatoes, for 'em down by the river, jist like we did at The Ponds"

"Yes, but we cut down the trees," he said. "Remember how the Aboriginals at The Ponds were angry because we felled the trees? I think that's why these people here are angry at us. Fortunately, we don't need to fell any more trees, so perhaps they won't bother us again. We'll stay here, Beth. We'll try and get on with them. There's nothing else we can do."

"I 'ope y're right, Matthew," Elizabeth said as she picked up baby Ann and carried her through to the bedroom.

Whether it was because Matthew's assurances were based on correct assumptions or whether they were just lucky, the Everingham Farm was not subjected to any further attacks. Matthew and Elizabeth frequently sighted groups of Aboriginals walking across their fields and even at times stealing corn cobs from the maize field, but there was no direct contact. Matthew sometimes waved to the Aboriginals but, although it was obvious they had seen him, there was no wave of recognition in return.

Attacks on the properties of other settlers, however, continued up and down the Hawkesbury, in some cases perpetrated by gangs of Aboriginals who joined together to form large attack parties. One such gang formed in a location around the confluence of the Hawkesbury and the Colo Rivers under the leadership of the Aboriginal warrior known as Branch Jack, the man about whom Matthew had been warned before leaving The Ponds. By the beginning of 1805, Branch Jack and his band were becoming increasingly hostile towards settlers along the Hawkesbury.

In April 1805, they attacked and killed a settler and former trooper of The New South Wales Corps named John Llewellyn. *The Sydney Gazette & New South Wales Advertiser* reported on it thus:

> *With inexpressible concern we have to recount a series of barbarities lately practised by a banditti of these people, inhabiting the out-skirts of Hawkesbury. Last Wednesday night a fellow known by the name of Branch Jack went to the farm of John Llewellyn,*

> *one of the Military settlers, who was at dinner with his labouring servant in a field; he was invited to partake of the fare; and after sharing in the repast, found means to get the settler's musket and powder horn in his possession, with which he made off with a loud yell, which was returned by about 20 others that had before concealed themselves, but now came forward, and discharged several spears at the unfortunate men, two of which entered the master's breast, who fell immediately, two others passing between the servants legs. The latter requesting to know their motive for the barbarous assault, was answered by a flight of spears, one of which penetrated his shoulder, and another one of his groins. After he had fallen the natives closed upon him, and thrice struck him on the head with a tomahawk, each blow occasioning a dreadful wound.*[2]

The same issue of the *Gazette* went on to report on yet another attack by Branch Jack and his gang.

> *On the same day another event of the same horrible kind took place at the branch, within three miles of the above. The farmhouse of T. Adlam was set on fire by a body of natives supposed to be the same; and after the alarm had been given, a search was made for the settler and his man, but they had shared a merciless fate, a part of their Relicks being found among the ashes, and the remainder scattered piecemeal, to become the prey of prowling animals and carnivorous birds; from which circumstance it is*

> *probably conjectured, that after the ill-fated people had been inhumanly murdered, their limbs were severed and wantonly scattered.*[3]

In the midst of such unsettled times, on 10th June 1805, Elizabeth gave birth to another daughter whom they named after her mother – Elizabeth (II). Less than a week later, Aboriginals attacked the farm of John Cuddy, an Everingham neighbour. Again, *The Sydney Gazette & New South Wales Advertiser* reported the attack.

> *Last Sunday the natives did considerable damage on Cuddy's farm at Portland Head; and continuing to menace the neighbouring settlers, information was forwarded to the Magistrate at Hawkesbury; who immediately dispatched a party to apprehend if possible the principal aggressors; but the banditti, perhaps apprehensive of their danger, had dispersed before the party arrived.*[4]

The next issue of the *Gazette*, on 23rd June 1805 reported yet another attack on a settler's farm, this one belonging to William Knight. Knight's farm, known as Knight's Retreat, would later be purchased by Matthew's son, Matthew Jnr, and an Everingham family burial plot would be established on that farm. Matthew's wife Elizabeth would be buried there, but Matthew himself would not, as his death would predate his son's purchase of the farm. But all of this was well in the future, and Matthew was oblivious to it as he read the *Gazette's* report.

> *The natives on Saturday last stripped the farmhouse of William Knight, settler at Boston's Reach Portland Head. At about half past three in the afternoon none were visible, and the settler went with his man into an adjoining field; but were not many paces from the house before they were alarmed with the shouts of a number, who were rushing in at the door, under cover of about a dozen, who with spears shipped, cut off their communication. Branch Jack brought out the settler's musket, and calling him by name, assured him they were by no means apprehensive of the consequences; they then plundered the place, and carried off every article they could find, of bedding, wearing apparel, tea & sugar, meat, and such to an amount which the sufferers declare one hundred pounds sterling would not replace.*[5]

Branch Jack was finally brought undone during an audacious attack on a river trading boat, the *Hawkesbury*, belonging to Andrew Thompson, although Thompson was not on board at the time. Driven off by musket fire, the warriors dived overboard and attempted to swim ashore but the crew, firing muskets from the boat, shot several of them, including Branch Jack who died on the banks of the Deerubbin, his ancestral home.

Even without their leader, however, the branch warriors continued their war on the farms of white settlers along the Hawkesbury. Week after week, for more than ten years, every issue of the *Gazette* carried reports of at least one attack during the preceding week. And the *Gazette* made no attempt to humanise the indigenous people or to suggest they may have some rightful claim to the land they fought for. In various issues of the Gazette, the Aboriginals were described as "savages, villains, barbarous wretches, miscreants, indolent and vicious hordes" and, in one issue in January 1806, as "an unhappy race of the least envied beings in existence".[6]

If the indigenous people were incapable of understanding the concept of land ownership, the colonists were incapable of understanding the Aboriginals' ingratitude for all the perceived benefits the colonists believed they were bringing to them.

Reporting the "outrages" of Aboriginal attacks on the farms of settlers, the *Gazette* would write:

> *It is sometimes contended, that these outrages are only 'acts of retaliation' for injuries received; but such a persuasion must be allowed to yield to observation and experience to the contrary. Should it at any time appear that an individual amenable to the law abuses by maltreatment any of these people, the offence is immediately investigated, and the slightest act of injustice treated with even greater rigour than it would have been had the complaint proceeded from a European. The natives are themselves perfectly aware of the protection they owe to the Government and its Officers; and seldom suffer an occasion to escape of representing the slightest grievance…*

> *The benefits they daily receive from the settlers and other inhabitants are on the other hand boundless and should lay claim to every grateful return, which can extend no further than to a passive forbearance from rapacity…*

> *And nothing further need be said to refute a notion of their being actuated to enormity by a principle of resentment, than the bare recollection that those enormities are periodical in their commencement, at every season when they may despoil the settler of his crop and reap by stealth and open violence the produce of a tract they are themselves too indolent to cultivate.*[7]

The Aboriginal people frequently set fire to the settlers' crops because they knew the colony was short of food. Thus, burning the crops, the Aboriginals believed, or hoped, would force the invaders to abandon the land. In some places that tactic worked – in other places it did not.

From the reports of the *Gazette* in the first decade of the 19th century, a reader would be led to conclude that any notion of the indigenous people suffering dispossession of their lands and loss of access to their food sources should be considered of little consequence. Because the Aboriginal people were not engaging in broad-acre farming of the land, the colonists believed, and the *Gazette* reported, that the land held little if any value to the natives. Yet nothing could have been further from the truth, because the Aboriginals, as hunter-gatherers, depended entirely upon the land for their subsistence and survival. Theirs was a lifestyle in which all food was obtained by gathering edible wild plants and by hunting wild animals and fish. It was a lifestyle which stood in contrast to the agricultural endeavours of the colonists who engaged in cultivating crops and raising domesticated animals for food production, yet the Aboriginal lifestyle was no less dependent upon access to the land.

The colonists, however, believed their system of agriculture to be a superior evolution of the hunter-gatherer lifestyle, and the *Gazette* frequently published reports describing the Aboriginals as being simply too indolent to cultivate the land. Indeed, the *Gazette* repeatedly carried reports declaring that, even if it could be shown that any dispossession had occurred, the Aboriginal people should be eternally grateful for such dispossession and indebted for all the perceived benefits brought by colonisation. Sadly, in some parts of the Australian community, such sentiments would still hold sway more than two centuries later.

Yet, despite the growing enmity between the Aboriginals and the white settlers, it would not be the Aboriginals who would force Matthew and his family off their land at Portland Head, but nature itself. The second half of 1805, commencing soon after the birth of the Everinghams' daughter, Elizabeth (II), ushered in an extended period of difficult and uncertain times – long periods of severe droughts, alternating with flooding rains. The drought commencing in July 1805 caused the dry soil to crack and reduced the maize crops to little more than lifeless, creaking stems and dry leaves. Matthew and Elizabeth hoped they might just be able to collect a small harvest of dry and emaciated corn cobs in the new year, but they also knew that, even if things went well, 1806 would be a year of destitution and that they would struggle to survive – literally.

And things did not go well! In March 1806, as the maize struggled to produce even a little corn, nature turned against them again and drought turned to flooding rain, sweeping away their crops before they were able to gather even the small harvest they hoped for. Yet, at least the Everingham house was spared the flood because it had been built on the highest part of their land. Others along the Hawkesbury were less fortunate. Many drowned, whilst others were left clinging to trees and rooftops until they could be rescued by boats, many of which belonged to Andrew Thompson.

Reduced to destitution and near-starvation, Matthew had no alternative than to incur ever increasing debt, as the family procured the bare essentials for survival on credit in Green Hills. Governor Philip Gidley King had done his best to curb the excesses of the Rum Corps but, like governors before him, he had been thwarted in those efforts. The officers of the Corps, including John Macarthur, continued to manipulate the market and exploit the settlers. Matthew avoided dealing with the Colonial Store and with the officers of the Rum Corps whenever possible and incurred most of his debt with the more reasonable Green Hills general store, owned by Andrew Thompson.

On 12th August 1806, while the Everingham family were struggling to sow seed for a new crop in Portland Head, Governor Philip Gidley King departed the colony, handing over the Governorship to Captain William Bligh RN who assumed the position of Governor the next day. Ironically, the spring and summer of 1806-1807 would prove to be a very good season for farming in the Hawkesbury, but Matthew and Elizabeth had been forced to buy their seed on credit and, with an eye on their mounting debt, they purchased and sowed only a small amount of seed. The harvest in January 1807 would be a good one, but too small to make any noticeable improvement to their debt level.

Politically, too, this first decade, the first decade of the nineteenth century was a time of instability. The new Governor, William Bligh, had come to the colony with a determination to bring the officers of the New South Wales Corps to heel. A strong-willed man, as evidenced by his experience when the crew of his ship, *HMS Bounty*, had mutinied in the South Pacific and set him and some loyalists afloat in a small open boat, Bligh had been specifically appointed Governor of the colony because of his reputation as a strong disciplinarian.

He had been given full authority by the Colonial Office in London to do whatever necessary to end the Corps' dominance and manipulation of the colony's economy. It was the makings of a serious conflict between the officers of the Corps and the Governor, and Bligh was not the kind of man to back down.

Throughout 1807, Bligh became increasingly involved in confrontations with the Corps and, in particular with John Macarthur, dismissing some officers of the Corps from government positions and refusing to issue further land grants to officers who were already large landholders.

From a distance, Matthew and other settlers along the Hawkesbury cheered Bligh on – he had become the champion of the small landholders.

"More strength to him!" Matthew declared to Elizabeth. "This governor will turn the tables on those so-called Gentlemen, mark my words. His appointment is the best thing that could have happened to this colony."

Not everyone in the colony agreed with Matthew's sentiments – Macarthur and his cronies in the Rum Corps railed constantly against Bligh and looked for any opportunity to have him removed.

In December 1807, Bligh ordered the arrest of Macarthur and charged him with assisting a convict to escape the colony on his schooner, *Parramatta*. The judiciary, consisting of six officers of the NSW Corps, dismissed the case, leaving the Judge Advocate unable to proceed. On 26th January 1808, Bligh attempted to again have Macarthur arrested. Macarthur appealed to his crony, Major George Johnston, commander of the NSW Corps, who then marched almost the entire Corps to Government House where, under direction from Macarthur, he arrested Governor William Bligh in an act of treason which became known as The Rum Rebellion. Bligh and his widowed daughter, Mary Putland, were held under arrest in Government House, while Macarthur and his lackey, Johnston, declared the military had assumed control of the colony to end the tyrannical, despotic and inept rule of a man unfit to be governor.

Johnston promoted himself to Lieutenant-Colonel and assumed the post of Lieutenant-Governor of the Colony of New South Wales. It was twenty years to the day since Arthur Phillip had raised the English flag at Sydney Cove. It was also the only time, and would remain the only time, a military coup would change an Australian government.

The Sydney Gazette and New South Wales Advertiser had absolutely nothing to say about this. No issue of the *Gazette* was printed between 30th August 1807 and 15th May 1808 because of a lack of paper – or so it was said – notwithstanding the claim of the publisher and printer of the *Gazette*, one George Howe, that there was plenty of paper in the government store.

The *Gazette*, first published on 5th March 1803, was considered an official weekly medium for the publication of government proclamations and general advertisements. Its masthead included the words "Published by Authority", a clear indication that any news carried in its pages was subject to close government censorship. Thus, the independence of the *Gazette* was very much slanted towards presenting the official point of view of the authorities. In some instances, the censorship may well have been invoked to withhold information.

Thus, in January 1808, a cynical person might well question the excuse that there was a shortage of paper and might have concluded the *Gazette* had been shut down by government decree, because of political intrigues and machinations which would ultimately lead to the coup on 26th January 1808.

With no issues of the *Gazette*, most people in the Hawkesbury district knew little about the true state of affairs in Sydney and gossip spread like wildfire.

"Governor Bligh's been hanged," some claimed.

"John Macarthur has fled the colony," others countered.

"Macarthur's the new Governor," some insisted.

In Green Hills and along the Hawkesbury, chaos ruled unchecked, fuelled by unfounded gossip. Some hot-headed settlers talked of taking up arms against the Corps with the intention of "rescuing" Governor Bligh and reinstating him to his office. Some even spoke of assassinating John Macarthur – boasts that were no doubt energised by not a small degree of intoxication. The jubilant Corps officers in Green Hills erected mock gallows in the small township, lit large bonfires and burned an effigy of Bligh before the gallows, giving rise to the rumour that Bligh had been hanged.

Because Macarthur had resigned his commission as an officer of the New South Wales Corps, Johnston appointed him Secretary of the Colony, a position created specifically for Macarthur and one which gave him effective control over the affairs of the colony. Realising the situation was volatile, particularly in the Hawkesbury, and perhaps having been told of threats to assassinate him, Macarthur's first act in his new role was to order the disarming of the populace, forcing all settlers to surrender their firearms. If talk amongst the settlers of taking up arms to oppose the Corps and to reinstate the Governor had been anything more than bravado, it soon dissipated. Without their firearms the moment had passed and the opportunity was lost.

John Macarthur dismissed Andrew Thompson from his position as Chief Constable of the Hawkesbury and replaced him with one of his own supporters, Richard Fitzgerald, who showed "remarkable activity and regular conduct", as Macarthur put it.[8] Fitzgerald had been appointed by Governor John Hunter as Superintendent of Public Agriculture in Toongabbie, but in June 1804, Governor Philip Gidley King had dismissed him from that post for "neglect of duty".[9] The charge of "neglect of duty" appealed to John Macarthur who liked people with a disposition to turn a blind eye to things, and Richard Fitzgerald, thereafter, served as the "faithful factor" of John Macarthur.[10]

Yet another supporter and appointee of the Johnston-Macarthur regime was Robert Fitz who had assumed a low-level appointment as deputy-commissary after arriving in the colony on *Sinclair* in August 1806. Fitz complained to the Colonial Office in October 1807 of Governor William Bligh's despotic measures and, when Bligh was deposed in January 1808, Fitz supported the rebel regime. After assuming command, Johnston ordered Fitz and other commissariat officers to make a deposition on the activities of ex-Governor Bligh. Fitz asserted Bligh had been supplied with clothing for his servants free of charge, had appropriated for himself wine and spirits which had been intended for the hospital and had procured other articles from the bonded store for his own personal use,[11] all of which the Governor was fully entitled to do. Yet, Fitz was just the kind of supporter Johnston and Macarthur liked, so Johnston appointed him as collector of the debts due to the government and allowed to retain two and a half per cent of all monies collected.[12] A short time later, on 23rd April, he was appointed superintendent of the government livestock and stores.[13] A military monopoly had returned to the colonial stores and, with Fitz in charge, the settlers had little hope of disposing of their grain at a reasonable price.

Like all small farmers along the Hawkesbury, Matthew was also feeling socially and politically isolated and he made more frequent trips to Green Hills, in an attempt to better acquaint himself with political developments. Most of his fragmentary information he got from Andrew Thompson who was a regular visitor to Sydney Town and who, in fact, had been in Sydney contesting a legal matter before the court on the day of the coup.

"Are you telling me the military has overthrown the governor and we now live under martial law?" he asked of Andrew Thompson.

Thompson nodded.

"I'm afraid so, Matthew. The military, and John Macarthur in particular, have been trying to get rid of Bligh since the day he arrived."

"That's treason!" Matthew exclaimed. "Johnston and Macarthur should be shot! If they'd tried to do something like this in England, the executioner would have their heads before the day was out."

"True enough, Matthew," Thompson replied, "but this is not England. It'll be six months before word of this event reaches England and another six months for their response to reach us. Perhaps the Colonial Office in London will find a way to restore order and reinstate the Governor or perhaps they'll just appoint a new governor."

"And in the meantime?" Matthew asked, knowing the answer.

"In the meantime," Thompson replied, "Governor Bligh will remain under arrest and The Gentlemen will run this colony. There's little doubt they'll further entrench themselves and accrue even more privileges to themselves before the Colonial Office restores order."

"God, help us!" Matthew exclaimed in despair.

1. *Sydney Gazette & New South Wales Advertiser*, 3 June 1804, p.3
2. *Sydney Gazette &New South Wales Advertiser*, 21 April 1805, p.2
3. Ibid
4. *Sydney Gazette & New South Wales Advertiser*, 16 June 1805, p.2
5. *Sydney Gazette & New South Wales Advertiser*, 23 June 1805, p.2
6. *Sydney Gazette & New South Wales Advertiser*, 12 January 1806, p.1
7. *Sydney Gazette &New South Wales Advertiser*, 21 April 1805, p.2
8. MacLaurin, E.C.B. *Australian Dictionary of Biography*, Volume 1, 1966; https://adb.anu.edu.au/biography/fitzgerald-richard-2048 (accessed July 2022)
9. Ibid
10. Ibid
11. Parsons, V. *Australian Dictionary of Biography*, Volume 1, 1966; https://adb.anu.edu.au/biography/fitz-robert-2046 (accessed July 2022)
12. Ibid
13. Ibid

16

On 28th January 1808, just two days after the deposing of Governor Bligh, Robert Fitz and Thomas Hobby drew up an address to the rebel government, purportedly from the Hawkesbury settlers, declaring their support for the overthrow of Bligh and expressing gratitude to the Corps, and to Johnston in particular, for putting an end to Bligh's "despotic governance". They then set about coercing and intimidating the settlers of Green Hills and the Hawkesbury into signing their fanciful address. Settlers along the Hawkesbury were threatened, if they refused, that their assigned labourers would be withdrawn, that land grants could be revoked and that even imprisonment might follow. Along with most settlers in the Hawkesbury, Matthew Everingham signed the document under duress.

"What else could I do?" Matthew said when Andrew Thompson asked whether he had signed.

"You did the right thing, Matthew," Thompson told him. "Right now, The Gentlemen rule the colony, but bide your time, the wheel will turn – that address will be recognised as the worthless piece of paper it is."

Matthew grimaced and shook his head in despair.

"If it doesn't turn quickly I'll be ruined by their exploitation. I can't sell my crop other than for a dram of their alcohol."

"Bring your crop to me, Matthew," Thompson said. "I'll give you a fair price for it."

Thompson had, in fact, found his dismissal from the position of Chief Constable had given him more time to concentrate on his own business concerns and he continued to prosper. As the largest grain grower and the wealthiest settler in the colony, Thompson was too heavily involved in the economic life of the colony to be severely impacted by the iron-like grip of the Corps officers, and they resented his fair dealings with the small landholders. Then, just as Thompson had told Matthew, the wheel began to turn against the Corps – slowly, spasmodically and without clear direction, effected primarily by Johnston's personal sense of insecurity. Johnston had been used by John Macarthur and had got himself injudiciously involved in a situation that was spiralling out of control – and he knew it.

Wishing to extricate himself from this situation, in April 1808, Johnston appealed to Lieutenant-Colonel William Paterson, the administrator of the settlement at Port Dalrymple, later to be named Launceston, to come from Van Diemen's Land to Sydney and assume control of the colony of New South Wales. Paterson, who was no admirer of Johnston, had no desire to become involved in the mess of Johnston's making and remained at Port Dalrymple.

On 28th July 1808, Lieutenant-Colonel Joseph Foveaux unexpectedly arrived in Sydney from England. Foveaux had formerly been the administrator of the settlement at Norfolk Island but had been forced to return to England for a time because of ill health. Arriving in

Sydney, Foveaux found Major George Johnston in command of the colony and Governor William Bligh under arrest. Outranking Johnston, and, to Johnston's great relief, Foveaux was faced with the unenviable task of either reinstating Bligh or taking control of the colony himself pending further orders from London. He chose the latter course of action and, perhaps aware of his precarious situation, set about making minor reforms. He dismissed John Macarthur from his role as Colonial Secretary, much to the delight of the settlers with small land holdings, prohibited the illicit trade in liquor with limited success and made some judicious land grants, including a town grant to Andrew Thompson in a part of Sydney later to be named Macquarie Place.

The Sydney Gazette & New South Wales Advertiser had re-commenced publication in mid-May 1808 and, just three days after the arrival of Foveaux, the issue of 31st July 1808 carried a proclamation by him. The proclamation, appearing as the lead article on page one of the *Gazette*, announced Foveaux's assumption of command and spoke of the "suspension" of Governor Bligh, six months earlier.

> *Sydney, July 30, 1808. Proclamation.*
> *JOSEPH FOVEAUX.*
> *As the Government of this Colony has been upwards of six months out of the hands of William Bligh, Esquire; and as the circumstances attending his Suspension have been fully submitted to his Majesty's Ministers, who alone are competent to decide, Lieutenant-Governor Foveaux conceives it to be beyond his authority to judge*

between Captain Bligh and the Officer whom he found in the actual command of the Colony.

In assuming the administration of the Government until His Majesty's pleasure shall be known, LIEUTENANT-GOVERNOR FOVEAUX is determined to adopt such measures as he deems to be most effectual for the preservation of the public tranquillity, and the security of public and private property; and to follow, in the discharge of the arduous duties imposed upon him, a system of the strictest economy, and the most impartial justice between persons of every description. All reports, communications, and other correspondences relative to Public Business, are to be transmitted to James Finucane, Esq who is appointed Secretary to Lieutenant-Governor Foveaux.
God Save the King.
By Command of His Honour the Lieutenant-Governor.
James Finucane, Secretary.[1]

Like Johnston before him, however, Foveaux soon found command of the Colony of New South Wales to be a poisoned chalice. Finally, Lieutenant Colonel-William Paterson relented, in response to Foveaux's constant urgings, and sailed from Port Dalrymple to Sydney, arriving on 9th January 1809 to assume command as Lieutenant-Governor of the colony. Paterson's first act was to arrest Johnston and Macarthur and ship them off to England to face trial on charges of sedition. Governor Bligh continued to be held under house arrest for some time, before being put in command of *HMS Porpoise* and ordered to sail to

England. Instead, Bligh sailed *HMS Porpoise* to Hobart in Van Diemen's Land where he sought support from the Lieutenant-Governor of Van Diemen's land, Colonel David Collins. Collins refused to help Bligh and detained him in Hobart aboard *HMS Porpoise* on the Derwent River, until the arrival of Governor Lachlan Macquarie in Sydney in January 1810.

Meanwhile, as political machinations continued in Sydney Town, at Portland Head, life was all about survival. For the Everingham family, this became increasingly difficult when they lost their assigned convict labourers. Both labourers working on Matthew's property in Portland Head were given their Ticket of Leave in 1808. Owen Maguire received his Ticket on 1st March 1808, though he magnanimously stayed and helped sow the next crop in the spring of that year. Larry Byrnes received his on 1st June 1808 and immediately left to look for paid work, as he was entitled to do. One new labourer, Charlie Harrison, was assigned to work Matthew's fields, with the promise from the Commissary of Labour that a second would soon be assigned.

Matthew, with the help of his boys and Charlie Harrison, brought in a good harvest in January 1809 – enough to pay down some of his debt, though not all. The rest of 1809, however, brought disaster and ruin, not only to the Everingham family, but to all settlers along the Hawkesbury. It was the wettest year any of the settlers could remember and the river broke its banks in April of that year, flooding their fields which were ready for ploughing in preparation for sowing the spring crop. Just as the fields were drying out, almost to a state in which they could be ploughed, it happened again near the end of May and the settlers began to wonder whether they would get a crop sown at all that year.

From Matthew's perspective, notwithstanding the ongoing difficulties caused by the weather, at least it was promising that the Lieutenant-Governor was making some efforts to alleviate the impact of the floods and ongoing rain on the Hawkesbury settlers.

"It looks like we might get another assigned worker," Matthew said, as he sat reading the *Gazette* after dinner.

"Y' think so?" Elizabeth said. "They 'aven't even replaced one o' the workers we lost when they got their Ticket o' Leave last year."

Matthew nodded, knowing Elizabeth was right. Despite his regular applications, only one of their two former workers had been replaced.

"It seems like the floods may have forced their hand. Listen to this," he said, reading from the *Gazette*.

> *All Persons having Three Male Prisoners off the Store, and who have not Ten Acres of Land sown or ready to be sown with Wheat, are hereby ordered immediately to return one of them to the Principal Superintendants [sic] in their respective Neighbourhoods, in order that they may assist the Settlers and Cultivators on the Banks of the Hawkesbury, in adopting means for lessening the Evils to be apprehended from Inundation. The Acting*

Commissary has received directions to issue a Suit of Slops to each Prisoner on his arrival at the Hawkesbury.

By Command of His Honor the Lieutenant- Governor,
James FINUCANE, Secretary
Head Quarters, Sydney,
May 30, 1809. [2]

"People 'll always find ways t' avoid givin' up their workers," Elizabeth said. "They's greedy 'nd they'll think nothin' o' the needs of others."

Matthew nodded, knowing she was right yet again.

"You're probably right, Beth," he said.

And indeed, she was. Very few additional workers were allocated to settlers along the Hawkesbury, and none to the Everingham farm.

Matthew had been fortunate in bringing in his harvest in January of 1809, but many others who had left their crops in the ground with a view to harvesting a little later were ruined, when the prolonged wet weather set in. In consequence, by late July, the reduced wheat harvest was having a deleterious effect on the supply of food within the colony. In particular, bread, the staple food of the colony, was in short supply and the Lieutenant-Governor introduced measures intended to lessen the demand for it – a reduction in the daily working hours of convict labourers. His edict was carried in *The Sydney Gazette & New South Wales Advertiser* on 23rd July 1809.

In consequence of the present reduced Ration of Grain and the shortness of the days, the Servants employed in Public Labour will leave off Work at One O' Clock until further Orders.

By Command of His Honor the Lieutenant- Governor,
James FINUCANE, Secretary
Head Quarters, Sydney,
July 20, 1809. [3]

The reduction in working hours made little difference to Matthew. With his fields still waterlogged, there was little work to be done anyway, and he spent many hours sitting under the veranda awning of his house sipping tea, smoking his pipe and chatting with his sons and with Charlie Harrison, as they watched yet more rain falling – not heavy rain, but enough to prevent the fields drying out.

Sitting there chatting on the evening of 26th July, just after sunset, Matthew and Charlie were stunned and terrified when the fields were suddenly lit by an enormous flash of lightening, followed instantaneously by a clap of thunder that literally shook the house. Immediately, the heavens opened and discharged a deluge of almost biblical proportions, forcing them both inside, even though they had been sitting under the cover of the veranda's awning. They were not to know it at the time, but the deluge was being released upon the whole Hawkesbury catchment area, from the Richmond Lowlands, upstream from Green Hills, right down to the mouth of the Hawkesbury at Broken Bay.

The river rose rapidly and swept away everything in its path. By Sunday 31st July, many settlers along the river, particularly between Green Hills and Wisemans Ferry, had lost everything – in some cases their very lives. Matthew and Elizabeth's house was built on the highest part of their land, but still the river came within a few feet of inundating and probably washing away their home. Almost everything else was lost – fences, their small granary where they stored their precious threshed wheat and corn, their tool-shed and most of their livestock, including their fifteen pigs and four of their five cows. Only their one horse, a mule and a cow managed to find higher ground and survive the cataclysmic flood. It would not be until the second week of September that the river eventually receded to something appropriating normal levels, leaving behind a large amount of debris for Matthew and Charlie Harrison to clear from the sodden fields – fallen trees, the remains of houses washed down from further upstream, animal carcasses and even several human bodies – white settlers and Aboriginals. The Darug people along the Deerubbin may have remembered worse floods or may have been told ancestral narratives about such events but, for the white settlers, this had certainly been the worst flood since the establishment of the colony.

This disastrous flood of July-August 1809, of course, only exacerbated the shortage of grain and bread within the colony and the Lieutenant-Governor appealed to all settlers, even in Sydney Town, to grow vegetables as a measure for alleviating food shortages.

> *As a distressing Scarcity of Grain must inevitably ensue from the late Inundations of the Hawkesbury and George's River, which there is reason to fear have been more extensively destructive than on any former occasion, the Lieutenant-Governor most earnestly enjoins every Person possessed of a Garden to raise as great a quantity of Vegetables as possible; by which means the consumption of Bread will be much reduced, and the evils to be apprehended from the dreadful calamities by which we have twice in the space of two months been visited, be thereby considerably alleviated.* [4]

As Matthew read that report from the *Gazette* to Elizabeth, he paused for a few moments before continuing.

"Listen to this, Beth," he said. "This sounds a little encouraging."

> *To deter any Inhabitant of this Colony from attempting a Monopoly of Grain, or any other species of Provisions, with a view of selling again at an exorbitant advance, the Lieutenant-Governor is determined most strictly to enforce the several Laws enacted for the protection of the People from the extortion of Forestallers, Ingrossers or Regrators; and he pledges himself to the Public, that the most unremitting vigilance in the detection, and the most rigorous measures for the punishment of crimes of so detestible [sic] a nature, will be exercised by every branch of the Executive Authority.*
> *By Command of His Honor the Lieutenant- Governor, James FINUCANE, Secretary. August 5, 1809.* [5]

"What do them words mean, Matthew? Them words 'bout people usin' extortion?" Elizabeth asked.

Matthew looked at the report again and read from it.

"'Forestallers, Ingrossers or Regrators'," he read. "A forestaller is a person who anticipates what's going to happen with market prices and then purchases goods before others can, to force up the market price. 'Ingrosser' is just another word for the same person. I'm not exactly sure what a 'regrator' is. I don't think I've seen that word before, but I imagine it's another word for a person who manipulates the market for his own profit."

"Well, let's 'ope the gov'nor's as good as 'is word and 'e does clamp down on 'em." Elizabeth responded. "'tis 'bout time someone put an end t' the way them Gentlemen is manipulating the market,"

And yet, despite the vaguely encouraging words of the *Gazette's* report, a pall of disillusionment and despair had descended upon the Everingham family, including the children who were uncharacteristically quiet and listless. They knew they were fortunate to have been left alive by the flood but unsure that fortunate was indeed the right word. Great floods leave devastation in their wake – both physical devastation to towns, settlements and infrastructure as well as devastation of the mental psyche – sometimes making it all but impossible for people to resume their daily lives as if nothing had happened. For many, if the flood had claimed the life of a family member or of a close neighbour, there is a time of bereavement. Those plucked from rooftops or from trees sometimes feel an overwhelming sense of relief and gratitude to their rescuers, yet others just fall into a bottomless pit of joyless melancholy and self-pity. For others facing the rebuilding of their homes and the infrastructure of their farms, the task can be overwhelming. Then there is the stench – rotting grain, animal carcasses and human bodies. Even the waterlogged ground itself exhales the foul smell of death.

For Matthew and Elizabeth, the pall of despair and despondency that descended upon them was partly caused by the cumulative emotional burden of battling for many years against droughts, floods, fires, plagues, exploitation at the hands of the Corps officers and Aboriginal attacks. The disastrous flood, it seemed, had been the straw that had broken the camel's back.

Matthew knew he was lacking energy, empathy and motivation to get anything done and he went about the task of helping Charlie Harrison clear the land of debris without any real sense of consciousness.

It feels like I'm sleepwalking, he thought. *Awake enough to interact with Charlie and with those around me and to do things in an almost instinctive and mindless way. Yet I never feel fully present in the tasks to be done.*

He recognised, too, that Elizabeth was struggling emotionally, perhaps even more so than himself. Pregnant again, she had told Matthew she could not see a future for the child she was carrying or for those she already had. The future, short term and long term, were almost illusionary to her. She was not suicidal, just unable to see a positive future.

"I feel like I've stopped strugglin' 'nd I'm jist lyin' 'ere watching the world 'nd all around me while I drown," she told Matthew. "'tis like I don't belong 'ere anymore."

It was most uncharacteristic of her. Even in his own weakened emotional state, Matthew worried, for the first time, about his wife's ability to survive. Clearly, although they did not have the terminology to define it as such, they had both sunk into a state of deep, clinical depression which would continue until their circumstances changed.

On the evening of Christmas Day 1809, Portland Head was beset by yet another fierce storm, with lightning, thunder and torrential rain. With the storm raging around their small house and with Sally assisting as midwife, Elizabeth gave birth to another child, a boy whom they would call James.

As she rested, and while Sally stood nursing the newborn child, Elizabeth called Matthew to her side.

"Matthew," she said, "I ken not stay 'ere any longer."

1. *Sydney Gazette & New South Wales Advertiser*, 31 July 1808, p.1
2. *Sydney Gazette & New South Wales Advertiser*, 18 June 1809, p.1
3. *Sydney Gazette & New South Wales Advertiser*, 23 July 1809, p.1
4. *Sydney Gazette & New South Wales Advertiser*, 6 August 1809, p.1
5. Ibid

17

On 28th December 1809 the storeship *Dromedary*, escorted by *HMS Hindostan*, arrived at Port Jackson. On board was the newly appointed Governor of New South Wales, Major-General Lachlan Macquarie, and the newly formed 73rd Regiment of Foot. In an inauguration ceremony at Government House on New Year's Day 1810, Lachlan Macquarie was sworn in as the fifth Governor of the Colony of New South Wales. At his inauguration ceremony, Macquarie forcefully conveyed the strong disapproval of the British Government concerning the deposing of his predecessor, Governor William Bligh, and expressed his personal hope that any dissonance or schisms resulting from that action could now give ground to a more harmonious relationship between all classes. The 73rd Regiment of Foot, he announced, would relieve the officers and men of the New South Wales Corps, a small number of whom would be allowed remain in the colony as settlers, whilst most would be repatriated to England.

Macquarie found the early months of his governorship complicated by the return of William Bligh who sailed *HMS Porpoise* from Hobart to Sydney, ostensibly to gather evidence for the trial of Johnston and Macarthur in England, but perhaps also hoping Macquarie would reinstate him as governor. Having two governors in the settlement caused some discordance and Macquarie had to assert his authority as the most recently appointed governor. It would not be until 12th May 1810 that Bligh would eventually depart to England. The delay, however, was not of Bligh's making. Macquarie had decided that the now disbanded New South Wales Corps would sail with him on *HMS Porpoise*. The process of preparing the officers, men and families of the Corps for departure and the administrative tasks involved in the handover to the 73rd Regiment of Foot took some months.

Meanwhile, at Portland Head, the arrival and swearing in of the new governor had gone virtually unnoticed by Matthew Everingham who, in his state of depression, was obsessed with finding a way to save his family from their hopeless situation. Clutching at straws, he decided he would attempt to sell the property to Andrew Thompson, the one person he knew who would have the means to purchase it. Thompson was not only the wealthiest settler in the colony. He was also a man with a reputation for helping those in need whenever he could. During the floods of 1806 and 1809, at great peril to his own life, Thompson had spent many days in and on the water, rescuing many souls who otherwise must surely have perished.

A week after Matthew approached him, on 10th January, Thompson arrived at Matthew's Portland Head property to inspect it. One look at the property and the family was enough for him to appreciate their grievous circumstances.

"No, Matthew," he said, "I won't buy the property from you. It's not a good prospect."

Matthew's heart sank, his distress and despondency clearly visible on his face. Elizabeth began to weep.

"But," Thompson continued, "I'll make you an offer."

They waited silently for him to continue.

"I doubt you'll be able to sell this place, but if you do get an offer, any offer, take it. If you can't sell it, lease it to a tenant. Then move your family to Green Hills. You and your family need to get off this land."

"I can't afford to live in Green Hills."

"You haven't heard my offer yet, Matthew," Thompson said. "I have a small farm lying idle, close to my Red House Farm. The house might be a bit of a squeeze with your large family, but you can live there at a nominal rent. Your boys and your labourer could grow vegetables there, for sale in the Green Hills market, and I'll give you paid work either in my Green Hills store or with the loading and unloading of my boats on the Green Hills wharf. If you can get some rent from this property, that too will add to your income and make things more comfortable for you."

Elizabeth was totally overcome with emotion when she heard Thompson's magnanimous offer. She sank to her knees, her hands clasped over her face, and wept uncontrollably. Matthew stood next to her, tears in his eyes too, and placed a comforting hand on her shoulder. He was lost for words and it was some time before he was able to speak.

"Why would you do such a thing for us, Mr Thompson?" he asked. "What are we that you should be so generous to us?"

"You're a good man Matthew," he said. "I've known that for some time. You and your wife and your children are in need, great need. There doesn't have to be another reason."

Matthew reached out to shake Thompson's hand and then embraced him tightly.

"Thank you," he said through his tears. "Thank you."

A few weeks later, the Portland Head farm was leased to a convict with his Ticket of Leave and the Everingham family loaded their meagre belongings on their wagon for the move to Green Hills. On 1st February 1810, they left for Green Hills – Elizabeth, baby James and some of the younger children riding in the wagon drawn by their only horse, and with the rest of the family walking. The mule, now quite old and capable of little work, was packaged as part of the lease agreement to the new tenant. As the wagon and the small family group drew away from Portland Head, Sally, Matthew Jnr and William looked back at the farm where they had lived for the past seven years. Elizabeth did not look back. She had seen more than enough of that farm.

On arrival at Green Hills, they were met by Andrew Thompson who took them to the small farm at West Hill, near his Red House Farm. They arrived there to find a small stone house of three rooms with a stone floor and a loft over one half of the house. Though small for a family of nine, it was the most substantial house in which the Everingham family had ever lived. To Elizabeth, it was palatial and it took all her sense of propriety to stop herself from throwing her arms around Andrew Thompson and kissing him.

The next day, Thompson sent a team of men to construct a slab hut for Charlie Harrison, and Matthew walked into Green Hills to report for work at Thompson's general store. Thompson had decided, however, that Matthew could best be employed supervising the loading and unloading of his fleet of four river boats which were constantly plying a busy trade between Green Hills and Sydney, occasionally venturing as far as Tahiti in the South Pacific and to Hobart in Van Diemen's Land. When none of the boats were present in Green Hills, Matthew was kept busy managing bills of lading for the next shipment and liaising with settlers who were shipping goods to Sydney or receiving goods ordered from Sydney. It was only on rare occasions that he had time to work in the general store.

Back at the small farm, Matthew Jnr, now aged fourteen, William, aged twelve, and George, aged eleven, worked with Charlie Harrison to prepare a small field for planting maize and wheat – sufficient only for the family's personal needs and not for sale. Just three weeks after their move to the Green Hills farm, Charlie Harrison was given his Ticket of Leave and left immediately to find paid work. With Andrew Thompson's help, Matthew quickly made application for a replacement convict labourer – in fact, he asked for two, but was given only one. Charles Weston replaced Charlie Harrison – "Charlie Number Two" the Everingham children called him. Meanwhile Sally, aged sixteen, assisted her mother in preparing an extensive vegetable garden where they would grow pumpkins, potatoes and turnips for the Green Hills market.

It was six months before Andrew Thompson started to deduct a small rent for the farm from Matthew's wages, by which time the family was well established on the small farm near Green Hills. Freed from the constant anguish of floods, droughts and possible Aboriginal attacks at the remote Portland Head farm, they were able to look forward to a brighter future.

Matthew was fully aware that Elizabeth considered Andrew Thompson to be nothing short of a messiah, and in many ways he was. Matthew too was very grateful that Thompson had come to their aid and rescued them from dire circumstances, as indeed he had done for numerous other settlers, particularly in the wake of the recent disastrous floods. In Green Hills, Thompson was feted as a magnanimous philanthropist and a hero for saving many settlers from drowning. Matthew got on very well with him and took his advice on many matters. Yet he knew there was a more nefarious side to Thompson, for he remembered reading in the *Gazette* how Thompson, as Chief Constable, had led a team to massacre eight Darug Aboriginals, including the tribal leader, Yaraguwayi.[1] That same issue of the *Gazette*, Matthew recalled, had reported that the Thompson-led expedition had been assisted by native guides *"with a contempt of their brethren and with no other desire of reward than a promise of being permitted to seize and retain a wife a-piece."*[2]

Aware of the high esteem in which Elizabeth held Andrew Thompson and of the general improvement in her emotional and mental condition since relocating to Green Hills, Matthew kept his thoughts about Thompson's involvement in the massacre to himself.

Yet, more than two centuries later, others would write of Thompson's darker side.³

The Darug people along the Hawkesbury, it is true, did frequently attack settlers and attempt to drive them off what they knew to be their ancestral lands, primarily because, without access to their traditional food sources, the Darug were being reduced to a state of starvation. In Matthew's view, some kind of accommodating agreement needed to be reached between the Darug and the white settlers, but to pursue them with the sole intent of massacring them seemed to him an inhumane and unnecessary response. He was troubled by the attitude of the *Gazette's* writers in articles which openly declared the intention of white settlers to murder the indigenous people – those whom the *Gazette* frequently referred to as "indolent wretches", "bandits", "miscreants" and "savages".

Meanwhile, at Government House in Sydney, Governor Lachlan Macquarie began turning his attention to the necessary reforms for compliance with his commission from the Colonial Office – to restore confidence, improve morals, encourage marriages, improve education, prohibit the use of alcohol and increase agriculture.⁴ As a first measure, just four days after his arrival in Sydney, Macquarie rescinded the appointments of all government officials who had been appointed by the revolutionary or rebel government, including Lieutenant-Governor Foveaux's appointment of Archibald Bell to the position of Hawkesbury Magistrate and that of Richard Fitzgerald as Chief Constable of the Hawkesbury. Most of the former officials who had been dismissed by the revolutionary government were reinstated, one exception being Andrew Thompson who was not reinstated as Chief Constable of the Hawkesbury because Macquarie was planning a higher office for him.

At the same time, Macquarie commanded all other acts of the revolutionary government to be annulled – all trials, convictions, pardons and land grants. This was a setback for Matthew, for the Lieutenant-Governor during that period, Colonel William Paterson, had approved a land grant to Matthew of 180 acres in the Kurrajong district, known as Richmond Hill. Matthew now found himself having to re-petition for that land grant and, perhaps because the Everingham family had not yet moved onto the land, it would take the new governor some years to approve the grant.

In Green Hills, with his life and his equilibrium having returned to something like normal and with a more promising future ahead, Matthew resumed his interest in the reports of *The Sydney Gazette & New South Wales Advertiser* – and there were plenty of interesting reports to be read. Almost every issue of the *Gazette* commenced with a proclamation from the new governor, as the lead item on page one.

The 14th January issue of the *Gazette* led the way with a convoluted proclamation from the governor in long and rambling sentences concerning the acts of magistrates, constables and jailors who had held office during the time of the revolutionary government.

Proclamation

By His Excellency Lachlan Macquarie, Esquire, Captain General and Governor in Chief of His Majesty's Territory of New South Wales and its Dependencies, &c. &c. &c.

His Excellency the Governor, anxious to promote the Tranquillity of the Colony, to prevent improper and malicious Litigation, and particularly to protect those Persons who, since the Arrest and Removal of William Bligh, Esquire, late Captain General and Governor in Chief of the Territory of New South Wales and its Dependencies, have acted as Magistrates, Constables, or Jailors in any or every Part of this Colony, under Appointments and Commissions made and granted by Persons not having lawful Right or Authority to make or grant the same, from any vexatious or frivolous Prosecutions or Actions at Law, publicly Commands all Persons to take Notice, that in Pursuance of the Authorities in this Behalf vested in HIM by His Most Gracious Majesty, and for the Purposes abovementioned, hereby grants to such Magistrates, Jailors, and Constables, full, and free Indemnity from all Prosecutions, and Suits at Law whatsoever, that might be brought against them, for all Acts, Orders, Warrants, Commitments, Fines, Punishments, and Proceedings whatever, that have been performed, ordered, executed, or imposed by them since the Arrest and Removal aforesaid, the same not being otherwise illegal or informal than in having been ordered and imposed by

Virtue of Powers or Commissions granted by Persons not authorised by Law to grant the same. [5]

"Good God!" Matthew said to himself. "That's all one sentence! The man writes in a manner that few in the colony would understand." Matthew had to read that section of the proclamation several times before gaining even a rudimentary understanding of the governor's intent. He paused to consider it before reading on.

And His Excellency hereby prohibits all His Majesty's Subjects whatever of this Colony, from commencing any Prosecution or Suit at Law against such Magistrates, Jailors, and Constables, for any such Acts done by them in Virtue of such Authority as aforesaid, the same not being otherwise illegal and informal than as aforesaid. And in Case any such Prosecutions or Suits at Law as, are herein before prohibited shall be commenced or instituted in any of the Courts of Law, established in this Colony, against such Magistrates, Jailors, and Constables as aforesaid, notwithstanding the Injunctions to the contrary contained in this Proclamation, His Excellency hereby Commands to the Deputy Judge Advocate of the Colony to enter, or cause to be entered, a Verdict of Not Guilty, or a Verdict for the Defendant or Defendants (as the case may be) in such Prosecutions or Suits at Law, with full Costs of Suit, to be recovered by the usual Course and Practice of the Law established in this Colony.[5]

Matthew shook his head and again needed to read the entire proclamation several times, in an attempt to clarify the governor's words.

"Have you read this?" he asked Andrew Thompson. "I'm finding it hard to understand. What do you think it means?"

"It means," Thompson replied, "that those who were appointed as magistrates, jailers or constables during the time in which Johnston, Foveaux and Paterson ruled the colony cannot be charged or tried with any offences they may have committed in the execution of their duties."

Matthew even had to ask Thompson to clarify his answer before he fully understood the governor's intent.

"That seems strange," Matthew said, "given he's dismissed them all from their posts."

"He dismissed them because they had been appointed by persons without authority to make such appointments, not because they themselves had done anything wrong, though they may well have."

"Well, I hope the governor learns to write a little more clearly for the common man in future," Matthew said, folding the *Gazette* and going back to his work.

Governor Macquarie's Proclamations continued apace and with little ease in the convoluted nature of his words and the length of his rambling sentences. On 17th February, the *Gazette* led with a proclamation limiting the number of public houses in the colony, justifying the new limits by speaking of the *"great and unnecessary Number of Licensed Houses for Retailing Wines and Spirituous Liquors cannot fail of being productive of the most mischievous and baneful Effects on the Morals and Industry of the lower Part of the Community."* [6]

One week later, on 24th February, the Governor turned his attention to addressing what he considered to be *"the scandalous and pernicious Custom so generally and shamelessly adopted throughout this Territory, of Persons of different Sexes COHABITING and living together, unsanctioned by the legal Ties of MATRIMONY."* He went on to state, in a proclamation of more than eight hundred words, that *"such Practices are a Scandal to RELIGION, to Decency, and to all Good GOVERNMENT."* [7]

Matthew took this one home and Elizabeth chuckled as he read it to her.

"Good luck t' 'im with that one," she said. "I don't reckon that proclamation would make much difference t' this colony if it were signed by the Lord 'imself. Still, I s'pose we 'ave to give the gov'nor some credit f' trying t' make things more decent."

Notwithstanding Elizabeth's reservations, the Governor's proclamation did have some positive effect on the incidence of marriage within the colony, perhaps because, in his usual tangled and sometimes unfathomable style, he had managed to convince some in the colony that the courts would not entertain financial or property claims by women whose de-facto partner should die intestate.

> *And whereas also, frequent Applications have been made on the part of divers Women, to the Court of Civil Jurisdiction, for the Grant of letters of Administration of the Goods and Effects of Persons dying intestate, on the sole Ground of having lived for a Number of Years with the Deceased in a State of illegal and criminal Intercourse; His Excellency the Governor, anxious to promote the Interests of Virtue (upon which those of Society must ever rest), by the Encouragement of lawful Marriage to preserve Morality and Decorum, and to protect the innocent Sufferers from the Consequences of such Practices; and hoping that the frequency of such Connexions may be in a great Measure owing to an Ignorance of the Calamity which will probably result from them; and that a more extended Knowledge of this Circumstance may be the Means of checking the Formation of such engagements in future, feels it his Duty hereby publicly to make known to the INHABITANTS of this Colony that the mere Circumstance of illegal Cohabitation (for whatever Length of Time) with any Man, confers no valid Title upon the Woman to the Goods and Effects of such Person, in Case he should die intestate.*[8]

"He's attempting to change the morality of the colony," Matthew remarked to Andrew Thompson.

"Actually," Thompson replied, "he's attempting to change the *immorality* of the colony. I know the

Governor personally. and he's a very moral and religious man." Then he added, with a smile, "A fellow Scot, of course."

To say that he was a personal acquaintance of the new governor was something of an understatement on the part of Andrew Thompson. Almost from the moment of his arrival in the colony, the new governor had sought out and befriended Thompson who was at that point in time the wealthiest settler in the colony. Whether Macquarie's interest in and befriending of Andrew Thompson was because he was a fellow Scot, whether it was because he, Thompson, had not been a supporter of the revolutionary government of Paterson et-al, although he had clearly benefited from that regime, whether it was because of Thompson's knowledge and familiarity with the business affairs of the colony, or whether it was purely a pecuniary interest in Thompson's wealth was unclear. Many, however, believed it was the latter, as the governor grew increasingly close to Thompson, heeding his advice and counsel.

On 14th January 1810, Macquarie appointed Thompson to the position of Justice of the Peace and Chief Magistrate of the Hawkesbury. It was the first time an ex-convict had been placed in a position of such authority – as Magistrate, Thompson had authority to order imprisonment and/or flogging of those who transgressed the law, be they convicts, emancipated ex-convicts or free-born settlers. The relationship between Thompson and the governor grew tighter every day, and whenever Andrew Thompson was in Sydney, he was invited to dine with Lachlan and Elizabeth Macquarie at Government House.

On 24th February 1810, on the recommendation of Andrew Thompson, Matthew Everingham was granted a "Licence to retail Wines and Spiritous Liquors".[9] Under the conditions of that licence, and pursuant with the governor's proclamation limiting the number of public houses, Matthew obtained the wines and spirits from Sydney, shipped them to Green Hills on the Thompson boats and retailed them through the Thompson general store, together with beer from the South Creek brewery. The governor's earlier proclamation limiting the number of "licenced houses", of course, forbade him from becoming a publican. At about the same time, again on Thompson's recommendation, Matthew made application for the position of District Constable, but it would be some years before the governor offered it to him and it would not be in Windsor.

Sadly, Thompson's relationship with the governor and the authority he drew from that relationship would not last long. Thompson was in poor health, largely because of his heroic efforts in and on the water rescuing settlers during the flood crises of 1806 and 1809. Because of his declining health, in 1810, Thompson appointed one John Howe both as executor of his will and as financial manager of the Thompson business empire. Part of Howe's role in that position was to collect rents and to recoup monies from people with outstanding debts to Thompson. Thus, Howe was a regular caller at the Everingham farm.

Matthew knew John Howe well – Howe had lived on a property neighbouring Matthew's land grant at Portland Head. He had arrived in the colony on 13th June 1802 on board *Coromandel*, a convict transport ship that also carried a small number of free settlers, including Howe, his wife Frances and their young daughter, Mary. Frances Howe would die only three months after arriving in Sydney and was buried at Parramatta. A short time later, Howe remarried, then he, his daughter and his new wife took up residence on the property at Portland Head before later moving to Green Hills.

Andrew Thompson passed away at his Red House Farm in Green Hills on 22nd October 1810 at only 37 years of age. At Thompson's funeral, Matthew walked with many others, including John Howe and the local brewer, Richard Woodbury, behind the horse-drawn hearse, as the cortège made its way to the cemetery of St Matthew's Church in Green Hills where Thompson's coffin was buried with great ceremony. Thompson had been unmarried and without descendants and, in his will, he had bequeathed twenty-five percent of his estate to his friend, Governor Lachlan Macquarie who, three years later, would place a large and wordy memorial headstone on Andrew Thompson's grave.

Perhaps in an attempt to legitimise what by that time had become Macquarie's ever-increasing wealth within the colony and to offer some sense of transparency, the wording on Thompson's memorial headstone includes a statement relating to that bequest.

> *In consequence of Mr. Thompson's good conduct, Governor Macquarie appointed him Justice of the*

> *Peace. This act, which restored him to that rank in society which he had lost, made so deep an impression on his grateful heart as to induce him to bequeath to the Governor one-fourth of his fortune.*

Both Matthew and Elizabeth were aware that the death of their benefactor had made their future at Green Hills more than a little precarious.

"I think y' should go 'nd talk t' Mista Howe," Elizabeth said. "We need t' find out what it means f' us."

Matthew agreed and, two days later, approached John Howe.

"The passing of Mr Thompson leaves us wondering whether my job on the wharfs is secure and whether we'll still be able to stay on Mr Thompson's small farm."

John Howe nodded.

"Mr Thompson had no family or heirs in this country," Howe said. "We'll need to contact his family in Scotland, before determining what to do with his estate. That's going to take some time, so, for the foreseeable future, Matthew, I don't see any change to existing circumstances is necessary."

"That's not a long-term guarantee, Beth," Matthew told his wife. "It could all change at any moment, if the executors of Mr Thompson's estate move to sell off his assets."

Though living in precarious circumstances, 1810 was a more than satisfactory year in other ways for Matthew Everingham and his family. The small income received from retailing wines, spirits and beer through the Thompson general store, the rent from the Portland Head property, Matthew's wages from the Thompson estate and the ever-increasing sales of their vegetables at the Green Hills market meant the family was managing without purchases on credit for the first time in many years. Matthew managed to pay off all his debts and even stashed away a little money for unforeseen circumstances. He was not the only person in the colony accumulating capital for future contingencies.

Governor Lachlan Macquarie was also amassing considerable personal wealth. The Governor would leave an indelible mark on the history of New South Wales. He would be responsible for social and economic reforms which played a crucial role in transforming New South Wales from a penal colony to a free settlement and he would be well remembered for his efforts. Two hundred years later, there would barely be a town or a city within the State of New South Wales without a Macquarie Street and/or a Lachlan Street. His name would also be remembered in the naming of Macquarie Place (Sydney), Lake Macquarie, Macquarie Pier (Newcastle), Macquarie Pass (in the Illawarra), Macquarie Island (between Tasmania and Antarctica) and the associated Macquarie Ridge tectonic plate, Macquarie Lighthouse, the Macquarie River which passes through Bathurst, Wellington and Dubbo before discharging into the Macquarie Marshes, the Lachlan River and, of course, the City of Port Macquarie which Macquarie founded in 1821 and in all humility named after himself. The Sydney suburbs of Macquarie Park and Macquarie Links are named after Governor Lachlan Macquarie, as are numerous churches through New South Wales and the Division of Macquarie (one of the first 75 Divisions of the Australian House of Representatives, created for the Australian Parliament in 1901). The Macquarie University, Macquarie Bank, Macquarie Hospital (Sydney), and a great many other institutions remind Australians of the role he played in shaping Australian society. In Scotland, the inscription on his grave declares him to be "The Father of Australia".

In the first week of December 1810, Governor Lachlan Macquarie visited Green Hills, ostensibly as part of an "evaluation of the colony", though the more sceptical settlers in the Hawkesbury believed the visit had more to do with inspecting the Thompson properties, of which he now owned twenty five percent. On his way to Green Hills, he visited outlying areas and founded the settlements of Wilberforce, Richmond and Pitt Town. On declaring the foundation of those settlement areas, Macquarie made public announcements, urging the settlers of the Hawkesbury region to escape their flood-prone land grants and to resettle in his newly declared 'Macquarie Towns', a suggestion which was all but impossible for the settlers whose only capital was their existing land grants along the Hawkesbury in places like Portland Head.

Then, on 8th December 1810, Macquarie arrived in Green Hills and the Everingham family joined in local community celebrations when the Governor declared the settlement township of Green Hills would henceforth be known as Windsor. Had Matthew been aware of the difficulties Macquarie would cause him in future years he may well have decided not to join in welcoming the Governor. But in 1810, Lachlan Macquarie was still viewed by the people of Windsor and of the Hawkesbury as a deliverer from the rule of the Johnston-Macarthur-Patterson-Foveaux regime of the revolutionary government.

Ten days later, on 17th December 1810, the family celebrated again when Matthew and Elizabeth's eldest daughter, Sarah Elizabeth, known as Sally, married the local brewer, Richard Woodbury, at St Matthew's [Church of England] Church in Windsor. Matthew, at first, had been opposed to the match on the grounds that Richard Woodbury was an ex-convict while Sally was a free-born citizen of the colony, but, under pressure from his wife and realising Sally was ardent in her attachment to Richard Woodbury, he put his prejudices aside and gave the couple his blessing. One week after the marriage of Sally and Richard Woodbury, Elizabeth learned she was once again pregnant. The child to be born about August 1811 would be her ninth child.

Macquarie, meanwhile, was already becoming frustrated with the rejection of what he believed to be his benevolent policies for co-existing with the indigenous people. Like Arthur Phillip, Macquarie had arrived in New South Wales with the objective of establishing a friendly and peaceful relationship with the Aboriginals but neither Phillip nor Macquarie were able to, nor did they want to, deviate from policies predicated upon British control, and ownership of the land they had invaded. As Aboriginal peoples resisted the invasion of their lands, the colonial government forced them further and further away from white settlements which, in places, gave rise to the outbreak of frontier wars. Like Phillip before him, it would not be long before Macquarie resorted to military might with accompanying atrocities including murders, decapitations and the hanging of Aboriginal corpses from trees in prominent places, in an attempt to terrorise the Aboriginals into submission to British rule.[10]

1. *Sydney Gazette & New South Wales Advertiser*, 12 May 1805, p. 2
2. Ibid
3. Power, Julie, quoting indigenous author Jasmine Seymour. *Sydney Morning Herald*, 26 March, 2021, p.3, in an article titled *Putting Aboriginal names and places back on the map starts by the river.*
4. Hall, A. *Andrew Thompson: From Boy Convict to Wealthiest Settler in Colonial Australia.* EHS Publication, Nedlands WA, 2021, p.225
5. *Sydney Gazette & New South Wales Advertiser*, 14 January 1810, p. 1
6. *Sydney Gazette & New South Wales Advertiser*, 17 February 1810, p. 1
7. *Sydney Gazette & New South Wales Advertiser*, 24 February 1810, p. 1
8. Ibid
9. *Sydney Gazette & New South Wales Advertiser*, 17 February 1810, p.2
10. Macquarie, Lachlan. *Diary 10 April 1816 - 1 July 1818..* Original held in the Mitchell Library, Sydney.
    ML Ref: A773 pp.1-8. [Microfilm Reel CY301 Frames #237-245].

General Note: The Governor's proclamations make use of some archaic words and spellings though they were probably in common use at the time. More often, however, the proclamations and other reports/advertisements appearing in the *Sydney Gazette & New South Wales Advertiser* include capitalisation which today's reader would consider unnecessary or incorrect. However, the extracts are presented exactly as they appeared in the original issues of the *Gazette*.

18

When Richard Woodbury became part of the Everingham extended family, he was managing Henry Kable's brewery at South Creek, Windsor – a brewery which had been established by the late Andrew Thompson and which had, until its sale to Kable, been part of Thompson's business empire. In England, Richard had worked as a brewer, but he had been convicted of stealing from his employer six gallons of brandy valued at £6 and was then sentenced to seven years imprisonment with transportation to New South Wales. He had arrived at Sydney Cove on *Fortune* in 1806 and was immediately sent to the government farm at Castle Hill where he worked as a field labourer, until Thompson selected him as assigned labour to work in his South Creek brewery near Green Hills. Richard and Sarah (Sally), after their marriage, lived in a small cottage built on the back of the brewery at South Creek, within walking distance of Matthew and Elizabeth's small, rented farm.

Shortly after Thompson's untimely death, when John Howe had assured Matthew there would be no change to existing circumstances "for the foreseeable future", he was being deliberately vague. As chief executor of the estate, he suspected he would be instructed by Thompson's heirs in Scotland to sell all of Thompson's properties and businesses but, until he heard from them, he would wait. In the meantime, he would sell at auction all of Thompson's carriages, harnesses, livestock, agricultural tools etc and lease out all of Thompson's property. On 9th February 1811, Howe placed an advertisement in *The Sydney Gazette & New South Wales Advertiser* listing items for sale at auction.

> FOR SALE BY AUCTION.
> BY MR. HOWE,
> At Windsor on Monday the 11th of February, and following Days, until the whole of the residue of the valuable Goods and Effects of the late ANDREW THOMPSON, Esq is sold :
>
> THE following Articles, comprising a large quantity of tanned leather for shoes and harness, saddles and bridles, horse and bullock harness, men and women's shoes, shoemakers' tools and flax, a new curricle harness compleat, springs and iron work compleat for a curricle, saddle trees of all descriptions, a valuable assortment of medicines, good Brazil and leaf tobacco, iron pots, frying ditto, large quantities of salt, rozin, copperas and brimstone, tin lead pipes, smiths' tools and empty casks, a wagon, timber carriage, and chains, several carts, ploughs and agricultural tools a quantity of bricks and building timber, buffalo-hides and kangaroo skins (not tanned). Also, a number of cart and saddle horses, mares with foals by their sides, several fine working bullocks, pigs, sheep, and goats. For the accommodation of Purchasers, the whole will be put up and sold in small lots; and all Purchases above £10 will be allowed Six Months Credit on giving approved Security and paying a Deposit or 25 per cent. in Sterling Money or Wheat at Government Price.[1]

Matthew Everingham attended the auction, together with Elizabeth, and made significant purchases. He bought, on a twenty-five percent deposit and the remainder on credit, copperas and twenty-four flints at 19 shillings, a pair of iron chains and a pair of traces at 13s, a lot of shoe-makers shoes at £1-15-0, twenty four sheets of tin at 14s, half a gross of fruit knives at £1-1-0, a basket of tobacco at £3-7-0, a steel rat trap at 8s6d, and four hundredweight of salt.[2]

"Why are we buyin' all this stuff, 'nd on credit at that?" Elizabeth asked.

"I'm getting ready to move to our Kurrajong property," Matthew replied.

"We don't 'ave no Kurrajong property.'Twas revoked by Gov'nor Macquarie b'cause it'd bin granted t' us by them in the rebel government after they got rid o' Gov'nor Bligh."

"Yes, but I've reapplied for the land. Andrew Thompson, God rest his soul, told me the governor would certainly reinstate our right to the land. It's only a matter of time."

Matthew was quite right. It would be a matter of time – a long time. Yet, convinced that the family would soon be moving to the Kurrajong property, he began putting his affairs in order. Part of that was a renewed effort to sell the fifty-acre property at Portland Head. In the same issue of the *Gazette* advertising the auction of Andrew Thompson's moveable effects, Matthew offered the Portland Head flood-prone property for sale.

> *To be sold, a Fifty-acre Farm, most eligibly situate at Portland Head, 18 acres of which are clear, now Leased at £30 per Annum and expires next January, it containing a fine Orchard full of choice Fruit trees, with shingled Dwelling and Out-house thereon. Twelve Months Credit will be given for half the Purchase money, or Horned Cattle will be taken for the whole at a fair Valuation. -*
>
> *For further information, apply to, Mr. Matthew Everingham, Windsor or Mr, Edward Lamb, Sydney, where the Terms will be made Known.*[3]

When Matthew read the advertisement to Elizabeth, his wife broke into a broad smile.

"Sounds too good t' sell," she said. "'Most eligibly situate at Portland Head'." She broke into a laugh. "Well, 'eligibly situate' I s'ppose, if y' like floods!"

Matthew was aware his description of the Portland Head farm was being economical with the truth to some extent – to a great extent, in Elizabeth's opinion – yet he was desperate to sell it.

"What's it that people say 'bout makin' them wild lilies look good?"

Matthew allowed himself a chuckle.

"Gilding the lily," he said. "That's what they say. And yes, I suppose I've made it sound better than it is. Hopefully it'll be to somebody's liking."

It turned out not to be so and, despite Matthew's effusive hyperbole in the advertisement, the property remained unsold.

In 1811, John Howe, the chief executor of the Thompson estate, gained an appointment as licensed auctioneer at Windsor but was not in a position to auction the Thompson properties because, to the governor's mounting frustration, he was still waiting on instructions from Thompson's relatives in Scotland. He did, however, call at the small Everingham farm to make Matthew and Elizabeth an offer.

"Matthew," he said as he sat around the table with them, "we're going to offer the Red House Farm for lease. We've been waiting almost six months to hear from Andrew Thompson's family in Scotland. There's no point in allowing that excellent farm to sit idle, while we wait for word from them."

Matthew sipped at his tea and nodded, a slight frown on his brow, not knowing what this had to do with him.

"You've been a good servant to Andrew Thompson," Howe continued. "We'd like to offer you the opportunity to move to the Red House Farm."

Matthew was taken aback. He remembered his first sighting of the Red House Farm when he and his family had first crossed it on their journey from The Ponds to Portland Head ten years earlier in 1802. It had fine wheat and maize fields, the best he had ever seen, and he remembered the grand two-storeyed home with its distinctive red bricks. He had never dreamed he would be able to live in such a house.

"I don't think we'd be able to afford that," he replied to Howe.

"'Ow much would be the rent?" Elizabeth asked.

"Sixty pounds per year."

Matthew shook his head.

"We thank you for your kind offer, Mr Howe," he said, "but we can't afford that."

"Think about it, Matthew," Howe continued. "You're paying thirty pounds a year rent on this small farm. The Red House Farm offers you opportunities to more than double your income."

Matthew looked at him questioningly, with eyebrow raised.

"There are extensive fields for cultivation – your oldest son could work those fields with your assigned labourer. There are extensive pastures, and I know you don't have much stock except for the herd of goats I sold to you at auction last year, but you could take in the stock of other settlers who need agistment for their herds. You could even offer your other sons as herdsmen – you'd be getting paid both for the agistment of the cattle and for the labour of your sons. Then, there's the tannery on the farm – that could be leased out too. I'm sure you would more than make up the rent differential. Still, if you don't want to, I'm not here to force your hand."

" 'nd what would 'appen if y' decide t' sell the Red 'ouse Farm?" Elizabeth asked. "We'd be without a 'ome."

"That's true," Howe replied. "But, then again, that would also be the case if you decide to stay here. This farm could be sold too when we hear from Mr Thompson's heirs in Scotland."

"I'd like a day or two to think about all this," Matthew said. "I also need to consider the fact that we're waiting on the governor to approve a land grant for us at Kurrajong."

"Hmm, well, I wouldn't hold my breath waiting on the governor, Matthew. But of course, take some time to weigh up your options. Come and see me when you've made a decision."

The next day, Matthew and Elizabeth walked over to the Red House Farm to take a look. Behind the main two-storeyed house, they found granaries, stables, stores and another single-storeyed dwelling.

"That small 'ouse 'd be a good place f' Charlie t' live," Elizabeth said, before turning back to view the main house. "I could never 'ave imagined meself living in a' house like that."

Some distance away from the house, they found the tannery yards that appeared to be in excellent condition, with their own sheds and stores attached.

"We'd have to find someone to lease the tannery," Matthew said. "I don't know anything about that process – I don't even know how many men would be needed to operate it."

"Yeah, but there's plenty o' kangaroo skins and cattle hides being turned int' leather goods. I 'ear they're even bringin' in seal skins they git from somewhere in the ocean. Someone 'll want t' rent the tannery."

Matthew stood for some time, considering the choice he faced.

"I imagine if we decide to move here, we'll be locked into a lease agreement of at least twelve months," he said. "That means if we get the Kurrajong grant during that time we'd have to delay moving there."

"We ken do that, Matthew. Anyways, Mr Howe don't seem too 'opeful 'bout the Gov'nor givin' us that land grant."

Matthew recognised Elizabeth's strong desire to make the move into the Red House Farm. He could see that, after the years of hardship living at The Ponds and at Portland Head, it was a dream come true for her to live in such a luxurious house with plenty of room for their large family. Yet he knew too that Elizabeth had little concept about financial issues and he worried about being able to meet the rent of £60 per year. In the end, his love for Elizabeth swayed his decision.

"We'll do it!" he said. "I'll go and tell Mr Howe tomorrow morning."

Elizabeth broke into one of her broad smiles that made her eyes scrunch up, then embraced him tightly.

"Thank y', Matthew," she said.

The Everingham family moved to the Red House Farm in mid-February 1811 and, on 2nd March of that year, Matthew placed an advertisement in *The Sydney Gazette & New South Wales Advertiser* offering agistment on extensive pasture with a herdsman to attend them, at a cost of 1s per week per head.[4] He received some applications for agistment, though he would have liked more, and the Everingham's second son, William aged fifteen years, took up duties as the promised herdsman. In May 1811, the tannery was let after another advertisement in the *Gazette*[5] and added further to Matthew's overall income. His wages from his continued employment in Windsor at the Thompson store and in managing shipping invoices, together with the small rent from the Portland Head farm, the fees received for agistment, the rent from the tannery and the money which Matthew Jnr and Charlie Number Two managed to reap from their fields at the Red House Farm meant the family was getting by financially, but barely. The £60 per year rent on the Red House Farm, as Matthew had anticipated, was stretching them to the limit, and debts were mounting – he had not yet been able to pay the debt for the items he had purchased at auction from the Thompson estate in February of the previous year.

The property at Portland Head had again been ravaged by flood in February 1811, and in March, the tenant had quit and walked off the land, depriving Matthew and Elizabeth of that small but important portion of their income. Although Matthew and his family at the Red House Farm were spared the ravages of the 1811 flood, apart from some minor inundation of the wheat fields, many others along the Hawkesbury were less fortunate and many, especially those already in debt to the Thompson estate, found themselves ruined. The Executors of the Thompson estate, acting on instructions from Governor Macquarie who was a twenty-five percent holder of the estate, sold up the debtors and the Governor personally profited by their losses. This would be the reason the government-censored *Gazette* did not report on the flood until mid-April – seven weeks after the event.

Matthew wondered when fortune would turn against him and when he might find himself in a similar position to those who had been ruined by the recent flood. As a consequence, he became increasingly frugal with his expenditure. In late-June 1811, he placed another advertisement in the *Gazette* stating that a stray horse had been found on his property. The owners, the advertisement said, could claim the horse but would be required to pay "expenses".

FOUND ASTRAY, on the West-Hill (formerly called the Red-House) Farm, at Hawkesbury, a Roan Horse, with black mane, tail, and feet. The Owners may have the same by paying Expenses, on application to Matthew Everingham, at the above Farm.[6]

Claiming reparations for the grass that the horse may have eaten was a little extreme, some would say even miserly, but it reflected Matthew's parsimonious attitude and practices at the time.

On 6th August 1811, Elizabeth gave birth to another daughter whom they named Maria. Six weeks later, on 21st September that same year, Sarah (Sally) Woodbury gave birth to her first-born, a son whom they named Richard Jnr. Richard Woodbury Jnr was baptised together with his aunt, Maria Everingham, on 12th October 1811 at St Matthew's Church, Windsor.

Throughout the latter half of 1811 and the first half of 1812, the Everingham family's debt continued to climb and Matthew was not surprised when John Howe confronted him about it at the beginning of May 1812.

"I'm sorry, Matthew," he said, "but we're coming under increasing pressure from the governor to recoup debts owing to the Thompson estate. As you know, the governor owns twenty-five percent of it. That's the reason we had to sell up the debtors after last year's flood. It was a ruthless action and not one I approved of, but I was given no choice in the matter."

"And now it's my turn," Matthew said.

Howe nodded sadly.

"I'm afraid it is, Matthew. You're behind in your rent and you haven't paid for items you bought at auction. I'm under pressure to sell you up."

"I understand," Matthew said, nodding. "It's the £60 per year rent on the Red House Farm that's done me in. I probably should've chosen not to move here when you offered it to me."

"You may be right, Matthew, and I'm sorry for my part in urging you to do so. I thought it would work out better for you."

The next week, all of Matthew's stock and personal effects were offered for sale by auction in an advertisement appearing in *The Sydney Gazette & New South Wales Advertiser.*

FOR SALE AT AUCTION

16th May
At the Public Market Place in the town of Windsor at One in the Afternoon, The Provost Marshal will proceed to sell by Public Auction, 51 Goats and 10 Sheep, the Property of Matthew Everingham. Immediately after the above, at the Farm in the present Occupation of the said Matthew Everingham, 2 Bullocks, 1 Cow, 1 Calf, 13 Pigs, a Quantity of Corn in Stack, and Chaff, sundry Articles of Household Furniture, a Cart, and a Quantity of Poultry (unless the Execution thereon be previously superseded). [7]

Elizabeth wept as Matthew read the advertisement to her.

"They're takin' everything, Matthew," she cried, "even our furniture. We'll be left with nothin'. What's gonna become of us?"

Matthew wrapped his arms around her and held her tightly as he struggled to find words to console her.

"We'll move to a smaller farm with a lower rent," he said. "We'll start again with nothing, but we've done that before – we can do it again."

Elizabeth continued to weep within her husband's embrace.

Some five miles away, in Windsor, Richard Woodbury was reading that same advertisement from the *Gazette* to his wife, Matthew's daughter, Sally.

"We have to help them, Richard," Sally said, herself close to tears. "Maybe they can move in here and live with us?"

Richard shook his head before replying.

"There's nine of them, Sal, and another on the way and you yourself are pregnant. We'll have another child of our own before years' end. There's no way we could all squeeze into this little cottage."

"We have to do something!" Sally cried.

"We will, Sal. I think we can probably cover your parents' debts. It'll stretch our finances, but I think we can manage it. I'll go and talk to John Howe this afternoon."

Thus, Matthew and Elizabeth's son-in-law came to their rescue at the eleventh-hour, preventing the sale of their every belonging. With their debts cleared and with their rent paid up to date, and with Matthew determining not to make future purchases on credit, the Everingham family decided to stay in the Red House Farm and to concentrate on maximising their income from it. It was a difficult time for the family, but they would stay there until the end of 1813, notwithstanding the fact that, twice more during that period, Richard Woodbury would have to come to their aid. The second Woodbury child was born to Sally and Richard on 2nd December 1812 – a daughter who they named after her grandmother, Elizabeth.

1. *Sydney Gazette & New South Wales Advertiser*, 9 Feb 1811, p.1
2. Ross, V. *Matthew Everingham – A First Fleeter and his Times*, Library of Australian History, Sydney,1980, p.119
3. *Sydney Gazette & New South Wales Advertiser*, 9 Feb 1811, p.2
4. *Sydney Gazette & New South Wales Advertiser*, 2 Mar 1811 p.2
5. *Sydney Gazette & New South Wales Advertiser* 4 May 1811 p.2
6. *Sydney Gazette & New South Wales Advertiser, 22 June 1811 p.2*
7. *Sydney Gazette & New South Wales Advertiser*, 9 May 1812 p.4

19

The Everingham's tenuous situation was exacerbated in January 1814 when the executors of the Andrew Thompson estate, at the persistent urging of Governor Macquarie, gave up waiting for advice from the Thompson heirs in Scotland and moved to offer for sale all real estate of the Thompson estate, including the Red House Farm. All of this property was disposed of successfully and promptly, earning auctioneer John Howe the gratitude of Governor Macquarie.[1]

With no other option, the Everingham family were faced with moving back to the Portland Head district, the Kurrajong land grant still not having been approved by a less than sympathetic governor. Yet, when the matter of returning to Portland Head was discussed, Elizabeth all but refused to return to the fifty-acre flood-prone farm where they had lived before moving to Windsor. Matthew knew the mere thought of returning to that property filled his wife with dread and he remembered her fragile state of mind, and his own, which had driven them to leave that property four years earlier.

I can't do that to her, he thought, *especially with another baby on the way. I think to do that would risk pushing her to the point of despair, from which she might not recover. Besides, I don't think I can face that farm myself.*

He found that the small fifteen-acre government farm at Portland Head was available for rent – the same farm they had lived on when they had arrived in the district following their move from The Ponds. It was quite close to their fifty-acre property, yet on high ground where Matthew had never known it to flood. The family moved back to the small fifteen-acre farm at the beginning of February 1814. At the suggestion of Matthew Jnr, he and William moved to the nearby fifty-acre farm, knowing it was flood-prone, in an attempt to farm both properties and thus increase family income. Matthew leased the larger property to Matthew Jnr on a peppercorn lease – a technicality which allowed his son to apply for convict labour assistance.

On 20th July 1814, Elizabeth gave birth to a healthy boy whom they named John. Over the past twenty-three years, the couple had welcomed ten children into their family. Elizabeth was now forty years of age and John was to be her last child.

1814 seemed to be something of a turning point for Matthew and Elizabeth and, over the next few years, providence finally began smiling on the family. Even nature itself complied, with no floods, bushfires or plagues for several years. Good harvests were brought in, both on Matthew's small farm and on the larger property where Matthew Jnr and his brother William were proving to be better farmers than their father.

It was also in September 1814 that Matthew received confirmation of his appointment as District Constable. His application had been pending for such an extended period he had all but forgotten about it. Now it posed the question as to whether he really wanted it. Originally, of course, he had applied for the position of District Constable at Green Hills-Windsor – a position which he had never received. However, the application had remained active ever since and it had been the move back to Portland Head which had resulted his being offered the appointment. Apparently, the government believed they had no need of an additional District Constable in Windsor, whereas Portland Head, a more remote area, did need someone to help maintain law and order. Matthew discussed the offer with Elizabeth.

"It'll be a more difficult job here at Portland Head than it would have been in Windsor, Beth. It could mean I'd need to be away for days at a time."

"Me 'nd the children ken manage that, Matthew, but only if y' want t' do it," Elizabeth said. "'ow much does it pay?"

"It's not a salaried position, Beth. It comes with the provision of government rations for the family and clothing for you and me and up to two children."

"That's a good allowance, Matthew. I s'ppose we'd still need t' buy some food 'nd clothes f' the older children, but it'd save us quite a bit. Is it a dangerous job?"

Matthew shrugged. Although he did not really know the answer to that question, he suspected that, at times, it could indeed prove dangerous. However, he did not want to worry Elizabeth with those thoughts and, eventually, they decided he would accept the position. They found the government provisions which came with the position had a greater impact on their overall income than had been expected and Matthew was able to make a start on repaying his son-in-law, Richard

Woodbury, for the assistance given to him back in mid-1812.

One month later, Matthew and Elizabeth gained another grandchild when a son was born to Sally and Richard Woodbury on 24th October. Sally named the child William.

"Great name for him!" declared William Everingham, Sally's brother and the child's uncle.

Meanwhile, directly across the river from the fifty-acre property being farmed by William and his older brother, Matthew Jnr, was a farm owned by Thomas Chaseling who, by chance, had two lovely daughters, both of whom proved a great attraction for the Everingham brothers. Matthew Jnr and William frequently took their small boat across the river, a perilous undertaking at times, to visit the girls whom they would later marry – Matthew Jnr would marry Ann Chaseling in February 1817 and William would marry Jane Chaseling three years later.

In 1816, the governor finally approved the land grant of 180 acres in the Kurrajong district known as Richmond Hill. Though it had been long awaited, the timing of the grant posed some indecision for Matthew and Elizabeth.

"If we move there now," Matthew told his wife, "we'll lose the government provisions for the District Constable position. I wouldn't be able to carry out my duties from there."

Elizabeth considered the option for some time and Matthew knew she was thinking about the financial implications of losing those provisions.

"'nd, there's no 'ouse at Kurrajong," she finally said. "We'd 'ave t' build a 'ouse, and there'd be other costs too if we move there. I'm not sure we ken afford it at the moment."

Matthew realised they were both thinking the same thing – it would be better for them to stay at Portland Head, at least for a time. They decided to lease out the new land grant at Kurrajong and talked about building a stone house there, perhaps in 1817 or 1818. It was a sound financial decision, for the rent money from Kurrajong would be very welcome but, as subsequent events would prove, it was a decision which would ultimately cost Matthew his life.

Yet, for the time being, the Everingham family seemed to be enjoying halcyon days at Portland Head and, much to Elizabeth's delight, the extended family was growing rapidly. Sally and Richard Woodbury had produced yet another grandson for Elizabeth and Matthew – Jeremiah Woodbury, born 8th August 1816. Matthew Jnr married Ann Chaseling on 17th February 1817, and within four months, Ann was pregnant with the couple's first child and Elizabeth looked forward to yet another grandchild in March 1818.

Thus it was a very happy gathering on 25th December 1817 when the entire Everingham and Woodbury families, seventeen persons in all, gathered at the small fifteen-acre farm at Portland Head to celebrate a family

Christmas. All the Everingham children were present, including Matthew Jnr and his pregnant wife, Ann. Sally and Richard Woodbury came from Windsor with their four children and a sumptuous Christmas lunch was prepared – roast chickens, roast pork, fresh damper, sweet corn on the cob and potatoes baked in their skins. To help with the celebrations, Richard had brought with him a large amount of Kable and Woodbury ale – perhaps too much.

They ate on a grassy knoll in front of the house, shaded from the hot Australian summer sun by a stand of eucalyptus and sheoak trees. Before eating, the family bowed their heads and Sally hushed the children as Elizabeth gave thanks for the meal.

"We thank y', God, f' this food 'nd f' all o' yer blessin's 'nd provisions t' us. Most o' all, on this special day, we thank y' f' our family. Amen."

As they neared the end of the meal, the children tired of their games and running around and gravitated towards their grandparents. The two boys, Richard Jnr and William, sat by their grandfather, while five-year-old Elizabeth lay down with her head in her grandmother's lap. Sitting there in the shade of the trees and stroking her granddaughter's hair, Elizabeth could not remember feeling more contented.

"Y' know, Matthew," she said, "I'm 'appy livin' 'ere on this little farm. I think I'd be quite 'appy t' live out the rest of our days 'ere."

"You don't miss the Red House in Windsor?"

Elizabeth pursed her lips and screwed her nose a little, a habit of hers which Matthew recognised as a sign of ambivalence.

"I liked living in big Red 'ouse, o' course. It were a lovely 'ouse. Who wouldn't enjoy living in a 'ouse like that? 'nd it were nice 'avin' Sally close by too. But, y' know, Matthew, we's not the kinda people t' be livin' in a 'ouse like that. It were a grand 'ouse, made f' grand people, not f' the likes of us."

Matthew gazed at his wife lovingly. He had never loved her more than at that moment. It would be the last time he would see her in that light.

Samuel Bannister, who regularly accompanied Matthew on his duties as District Constable, arrived on horseback while the family was still seated in the shade of the trees. Matthew was almost dozing, while he sat with his back resting against a large eucalypt tree and the front of his hat pulled down to shade his eyes.

"Sorry to interrupt your Christmas Day," Bannister said. "Word from Windsor is there's a group of smugglers using a boat to sell grog up and down the river. Seems they're cashing in on Christmas by selling sly grog to help people celebrate. Windsor wants us to go check it out."

"Let them enjoy Christmas Day with their sly grog," Matthew said. "Every man's entitled to a drink today."

"Windsor won't be pleased, Matthew. They want us to catch the smugglers in the act."

Matthew groaned audibly.

Christmas Day of all days, he thought. *I should tell him I'll investigate it tomorrow. If the sloop's still around tomorrow, we can deal with it then. If they've moved on, then damn the consequences.*

Yet he knew his duty as District Constable required him to act on instructions from Windsor, no matter how daft or how inconvenient they might be. As he stood, preparing to go and saddle his horse, Elizabeth pleaded with him not to go. She thought he had indulged in too much ale and she was probably right.

"I'll be all right," he assured her. "I'm not going to make a great effort to apprehend these fellows on Christmas Day, but I need to make a token effort to satisfy the authorities in Windsor. I doubt we'll even find the sloop."

It was six o'clock in the early evening when Samuel Bannister returned to the small farm with a sad message for the Everingham family – Matthew had fallen overboard from the sloop and had been drowned in the strong tide and the treacherous eddies of the Hawkesbury.

Words cannot tell the measure of grief felt by the entire family, none more so, of course, than by Elizabeth, who literally collapsed when she heard the awful news. The love of her life and her partner in marriage since the age of sixteen had been taken from her so suddenly, so unexpectedly and on a such a day of joy and celebration for the whole extended family. It was largely Sally, who, in the midst of her own grief, lifted her mother and carried her through her grief. George too was a great support to his mother and to the rest of the family for he was a devout man who in recent years had become the spiritual head of the family.

Elizabeth had lost her life's partner, her nine children had lost their father, Richard Woodbury and Ann Everingham had lost their father-in-law, Sally's four children had lost their grandfather and the Hawkesbury community had lost a much-respected pioneer settler.

Following an inquest into his death, Matthew's body was laid to rest two days later, on 27th December 1817, in St John's Cemetery, Wilberforce, NSW. He was forty-eight years of age.

In 1818, Elizabeth with the assistance of her son, Matthew Jnr, applied to Governor Lachlan Macquarie for a land grant on the small fifteen-acre farm. Macquarie refused her application and it was not until 1838 that Governor George Gipps approved it and granted the farm to her. Thereafter, the farm was known as "The Elizabeth Everingham Farm".

Elizabeth did spend the rest of her days on the small farm, outliving Matthew by twenty-four years. Ten years after his death, on 20th August 1827, Elizabeth remarried in St John's Church Wilberforce. Her new husband was Patrick McGahy, an Irish convict with his Ticket of Leave, twenty-eight years her junior. They remained married and lived on the small farm at Portland Head until Elizabeth's death. They had no children together.

Elizabeth passed away peacefully, surrounded by her family, on 12th December 1841. She was sixty-seven years of age and was buried in a family burial plot on the farm known as "Knight's Retreat", then owned by her son, Matthew Jnr.

1. Gray, Nancy. *Australian Dictionary of Biography, Volume 1, 1966.* https://adb.anu.edu.au/biography/howe-john-2205 (Accessed August 2022)

APPENDIX
The Native "Problem"

Something, I feel, must be said here about the cataclysmic impact that white settlement of this country has had on the indigenous population. I preface this by declaring I am not an indigenous Australian. I am a descendant of white colonialists – those whom indigenous Australians might rightly define as "invaders". I openly acknowledge here, too, that I am not an historian and certainly am no authority on the extent to which white colonisation of this land impacted the indigenous people. Yet, I still feel something should be said here on the issue.

The headstone on Lachlan Macquarie's grave in Scotland carries the inscription, "The Father of Australia". His statue in Sydney's Hyde Park bears a plaque which includes the words, "He was a perfect gentleman, a Christian and supreme legislator of the human heart". Yet, every year, on 26th January, Aboriginal activists and their supporters throw red paint, representing Aboriginal blood, on the Hyde Park statue and frequently write slogans declaring Macquarie to have been a mass murderer. I don't approve of their actions, but they have a point.

Governor Lachlan Macquarie, fifth Governor of the Colony of New South Wales, like Governor Arthur Phillip, first Governor of the Colony, hoped and expected to have friendly and peaceful relations with the indigenous population. Such could probably be said of all the early governors of the colony but let us focus our attention on Phillip and Macquarie, for both hold prominent positions in the nation's history – Phillip as the founder of the Colony of New South Wales, and Macquarie as the one who largely transformed a penal colony into a so-called free colony – free for whites, that is.

Both, initially, demonstrated relatively humane and progressive policies in their dealings with the indigenous people. Their policies and objectives, however, were predicated upon British control, and ownership, of the land they had invaded. Effectively, the British had come ashore, planted a flagpole, raised the English flag and declared that the continent and the indigenous people were now ruled by a king who lived on the other side of the world. It was staggering in its audacity, it displayed an arrogant right-to-rule posture, and they should not have been surprised, though they were, when the indigenous people resisted. Faced with the forced dispossession of their land, desecration of their sacred sites, denial of access to their food sources and the genocidal intent of many settlers, the indigenous people had no option but to resist with force.

Both Phillip and Macquarie became frustrated at the rejection of what they saw as their generous, humanitarian policies towards the indigenous peoples, so ordered military actions to drive them further and further away from white settlements. Both ordered the killing and decapitation of Aboriginals who refused to submit to British rule. They both ordered, too, the hanging of Aboriginal bodies from trees in prominent places, an action designed to strike terror into those who survived.

So, were Phillip and Macquarie mass murderers, as Aboriginal activists claim, or were they engaged in legitimate warfare? It is not a valid question for, even if it is argued that they were engaged in warfare, actions such as decapitations, and the hanging of bodies for public display, are clearly war crimes. Both showed themselves unafraid to use military might to enforce their will on Aboriginal people who refused to submit to colonial rule.

On Wednesday, 10th April 1816, Macquarie wrote in his journal:

> *I have this Day ordered three Separate Military Detachments to march into the Interior and remote parts of the Colony, for the purpose of Punishing the Hostile Natives, by clearing the Country of them entirely, and driving them across the mountains …*
>
> *In the event of the Natives making the smallest show of resistance – or refusing to surrender when called upon so to do – the officers Commanding the Military Parties have been authorized to fire on them to compel them to surrender; hanging up on Trees the Bodies of such Natives as may be killed on such occasions, in order to strike the greater terror into the Survivors.*[1]

Seven days after Macquarie wrote those words in his journal, at least fourteen Aboriginal men, women and children were massacred when soldiers of the 46th Regiment shot at and drove a group of Aboriginal people over the cliff and into the gorge of the Cataract River on the Cumberland Plain near Appin. Notwithstanding Macquarie's words in his journal, indicating that the Aboriginals would be fired upon only if they refused to surrender, it is believed the soldiers attacked the Aboriginal camp in the pre-dawn darkness, without warning and without calling on the Aboriginals to surrender.[2]

More than two hundred years later, the war, effectively, goes on – not with open killing, decapitations and hangings, but with a real, enduring sense of divide between the indigenous peoples and many sectors of the white Australian community. Tentative steps towards reconciliation have been made and are ongoing, but it seems, to this writer at least, that real reconciliation will only come when white Australia fully and openly acknowledges the injustices which white settlement of this country inflicted on the Aboriginal people.

1. Macquarie, Lachlan. *Diary 10 April 1816 - 1 July 1818.*.
   Original held in the Mitchell Library, Sydney.
   ML Ref: A773 pp.1-8. [Microfilm Reel CY301 Frames #237-245].
2. Karskens, Grace, Appin massacre, Dictionary of Sydney, 2015, http://dictionaryofsydney.org/entry/appin_massacre, accessed Sep 2022

AUTHOR'S CLOSING COMMENTS

As with the other books in this Everingham trilogy, I feel a need to give my readers some indication as to which parts of this book are factual and which are supposition. The book is based primarily upon the known facts of Matthew's life but, of course, conversations and day-to-day activities were not recorded for us and have been added to Matthew's story in an attempt to produce a readable and interesting narrative. Those conversations, however, should not be totally discounted as fiction because, in many cases, although created by this author, they are used as the vehicle to convey factual information about Matthew and his family.

Matthew's trial in the Old Bailey

The in-court dialogue described in Chapter 2, is taken almost verbatim from the official trial transcripts of the Old Bailey. We know for a fact that, after Matthew's conviction, Samuel Shepherd, who had brought the charge against Matthew, did approach the judge in an attempt to mitigate the severity of Matthew's sentence. Indeed, Shepherd became a life-long supporter of Matthew and corresponded with him regularly after his transportation to New South Wales. The discussion between Samuel Shepherd and Judge Rose, when Shepherd appealed for leniency, did occur, though the words used in my representation of the discussion are, of course, supposition.

Matthew's parentage

Details of Matthew's parentage and genealogy remain a matter of debate amongst some Everingham descendants and historians. Some contend that

Matthew was raised in a London orphanage, whilst others, particularly descendants still bearing the Everingham name, believe he was born into the noble de Everingham family of York. What we do know is that Matthew had been given a very sound education which, in 18th century London, meant a moneyed family. It therefore seems, to this author at least, more likely that he was born into a noble family. Thus, in this book, I have chosen to portray Matthew as being descended from the de Everingham family of York. I believe that to be the case, but I acknowledge I may be wrong.

Convict names

Numerous convicts who were either transported together with Matthew Everingham as part of the First Fleet or whom he encountered in New South Wales are mentioned by name – James Bellett, William Blunt, Lawrence Byrne, Francis Carthy, Philip Farrell, Thomas Griffiths, Thomas Hylids, Nathaniel Lucas, Samuel Mobbs, Charlie Peet, John Ramsey, James Ruse and Cornelius Teague. All of those convicts did exist, and most arrived with the First Fleet. Details given of their crimes and sentences are accurate, though the conversations and the actions attributed to some of them are, of course, fictitious.

Special mention should be made of John Ramsey and William Reid who joined Matthew on the failed attempt to cross the Blue Mountains in 1795. Ramsey had arrived as a convict with the First Fleet. William Reid had also arrived with the First Fleet but not as a convict. William Reid was an able seaman on *HMS Sirius*.

James Ruse was a convict who arrived, with Matthew Everingham, on board *Scarborough* as part of the First Fleet and was the first emancipated convict to be given a land grant in New South Wales.

Some other convicts assigned as labourers on the Everingham farms did exist, but their names are unknown. Thus, the names Charlie Harrison, Owen Maguire, Thomas Moran and Charles Weston are fictitious, though the persons are not.

John Anderson and Curtis Brown were factual persons – ex-convicts who held land grants bordering on the Everinghams' fifty-acre land grant at The Ponds.

Noah Wright, portrayed as a prisoner in Newgate Prison and later on the hulk *Censor*, did not exist. Noah was created as a fictitious character merely to provide one with whom Matthew could engage in conversation – a means of conveying an accurate portrayal of Matthew's life of incarceration at that time.

Names of official persons
Government officials listed by name, those in England and those involved in the Colonial Government in New South Wales, Norfolk Island or Van Diemen's Land, were factual persons of official rank who were, in various ways, instrumental in the establishment and continuance of the penal colony at Sydney Cove.

Special mention should be made of John Macarthur and the manner in which I have described him in this book. John Macarthur and his wife Elizabeth Macarthur née Veale were factual and historic persons who arrived at

Sydney Cove with the Second Fleet on 28th June 1790. Generations of Australian school children, this author being one of them, were taught to revere John Macarthur as an Australian icon – the father of the Australian Merino wool industry. This book, and my earlier book *Elizabeth Rymes – A Remarkable Life*, present John Macarthur in a very different and less favourable light. He was a man despised by the early governors of NSW and by many of the early settlers. Furthermore, the genetic strain of the Australian Merino, with their fine wool, was largely developed by Elizabeth Macarthur during the years her husband was exiled in England. John Macarthur's rightful place in Australian history, I believe, is very much as described in this book, unflattering though it is.

Zachariah Clarke, Henry Dodd, Lieutenant William Dawes and Lieutenant Watkin Trench were factual persons who played important roles in the early days of the penal colony in New South Wales. Their roles and the actions attributed to them are, as far as I have been able to portray them, factual, though their conversations are, of course, fictitious.

Dates

Most dates given are accurate. The one exception would be Arthur Phillip's journal entry which, on p72 of this book, purports to have been written on 24th January 1788, but was actually written several months later, on 15th May 1788. I have unashamedly taken the liberty of massaging that date to facilitate the storyline. I believe it likely, however, that the words would already have been in Phillip's mind when he first sighted Port Jackson on 24th January of that year.

Relationships with the indigenous people

This book depicts Matthew Everingham and his wife Elizabeth as having a respectful and, for the times, an enlightened attitude towards the indigenous peoples of the New South Wales. I may be accused of presenting Matthew and Elizabeth in a more favourable light than that which they deserve, for sound evidence of their attitudes in respect to this issue is difficult or impossible to uncover. I acknowledge that the stories of Matthew being invited to visit an Aboriginal camp at The Ponds and of the family's discovery of ancient Aboriginal rock-art at Portland Head are fictional. There are, however, other facts and family lore which point to a progressive and an evolving relationship with the First Peoples of this land.

For example, Matthew and Elizabeth's youngest son, John, married an Aboriginal woman. The union was not a de facto relationship, reasonably common at the time between white men and Aboriginal women, but a marriage solemnised according to Aboriginal law. John's wife was of the Darug Aboriginal people and the offspring of a union between a convict, Lampett Saunders, and an unknown Darug woman. She had been named Mildred Saunders but had also retained her Aboriginal kinship and totem name of Burtha Emu. Through this union, a long and strong line of indigenous descendants became part of the Everingham family.

Furthermore, John's sister, Elizabeth (b 1805), according to her descendants, spoke Darug, an Aboriginal language, and was in the practice of frequently going to live for three or four days at a time with the local Darug people. It seems reasonable to assume, to this author at least, that such close links with Aboriginal Peoples would only have developed through an attitude of accord and respect for indigenous people within the broader Everingham family during Matthew's lifetime. Thus, I feel reasonably comfortable portraying Matthew's family as being at least sympathetic and respectful to the indigenous people of New South Wales, notwithstanding the fact that later generations of the family may or may not have different attitudes. Again, I acknowledge, I may be wrong.

Matthew's death

Some current-day descendants of Matthew James Everingham have claimed that he was murdered by the grog smugglers when he boarded their sloop on the Hawkesbury on Christmas Day 1817. Such claims appear in oral histories passed down through the generations. However, Matthew's two eldest sons, Matthew James Everingham Jnr and William Everingham, were present at the inquest into Matthew's death and one would assume that, had there been any evidence of trauma on Matthew's body, they would have raised the issue then. They did not, and the inquest returned a finding of "Accidental Death". It remains a possibility that the smugglers may have simply pushed Matthew overboard in an altercation, though, had that been the case, it is likely Samuel Bannister would have witnessed such an altercation and reported it at the inquest. It seems, therefore, that Matthew may have simply fallen overboard, having been unsteady on his feet, perhaps because of intoxication, perhaps simply because the boat was rocking in the Hawkesbury waters.

Matthew's legacy

Matthew James Everingham was a prominent pioneer of colonial New South Wales. He is probably the most documented convict ever to have been transported to these shores, in no small part because of the extensive research and writing of Ms Valerie Ross.[1] He was witness to the founding of the Colony of New South Wales, he endured floods, fires and exploitation, he lived through the times of the first five governors of NSW and the military backed coup which deposed Governor William Bligh in January 1808 – the only political coup in Australian history.

Perhaps his greatest legacy, though, is that he and his wife Elizabeth left a family of nine children and eighty-five grandchildren to establish the Everingham dynasty, a dynasty which endures today, and which has been prominent in many aspects of modern Australian life – political, scientific, professional, entrepreneurial, industrial, sporting and cultural.

Ian J White
2022

1. Ross, Valerie
   - *Cornstalks: a genealogy*, Library of Australian History 1980
   - *Matthew Everingham – A First Fleeter and His Times*, Library of Australian History 1980
   - *The Everingham Letterbook*, VALROS, Sydney, 1985
   - *A Hawkesbury Story*, Library of Australian History, 1989

OTHER BOOKS BY THIS AUTHOR

Brand New Every Morning
A daily guide to reading the Bible in one year.

The Mustard Seed
God's plan for New Creation

Glass Half Full
An uplifting book of encouragement for Christians and for non-Christians alike as we attempt to deal with the rollercoaster ride of life.

Elizabeth Rymes – A Remarkable Life
The life and times of Elizabeth Rymes, a truly remarkable woman pioneer in the early colonial days of Australia. The second book in the trilogy about the Everingham Dynasty.

The Woodbury Line – An Australian Convict Family
The third book in the trilogy about the Everingham Dynasty. The saga of one branch of the Woodbury family, descended from the eldest daughter of Matthew and Elizabeth Everingham, Sarah (aka Sally), who married ex-convict Richard Woodbury and commenced the Woodbury line of descendants.

Details of all books can be found at
www.themustardseed.net.au/books

www.ingramcontent.com/pod-product-compliance
Ingram Content Group UK Ltd.
Pitfield, Milton Keynes, MK11 3LW, UK
UKHW022229230426
12048UKWH00016BA/1142